CASE IS SOFTWARE AUTOMATION

A Carma McClure BOOK

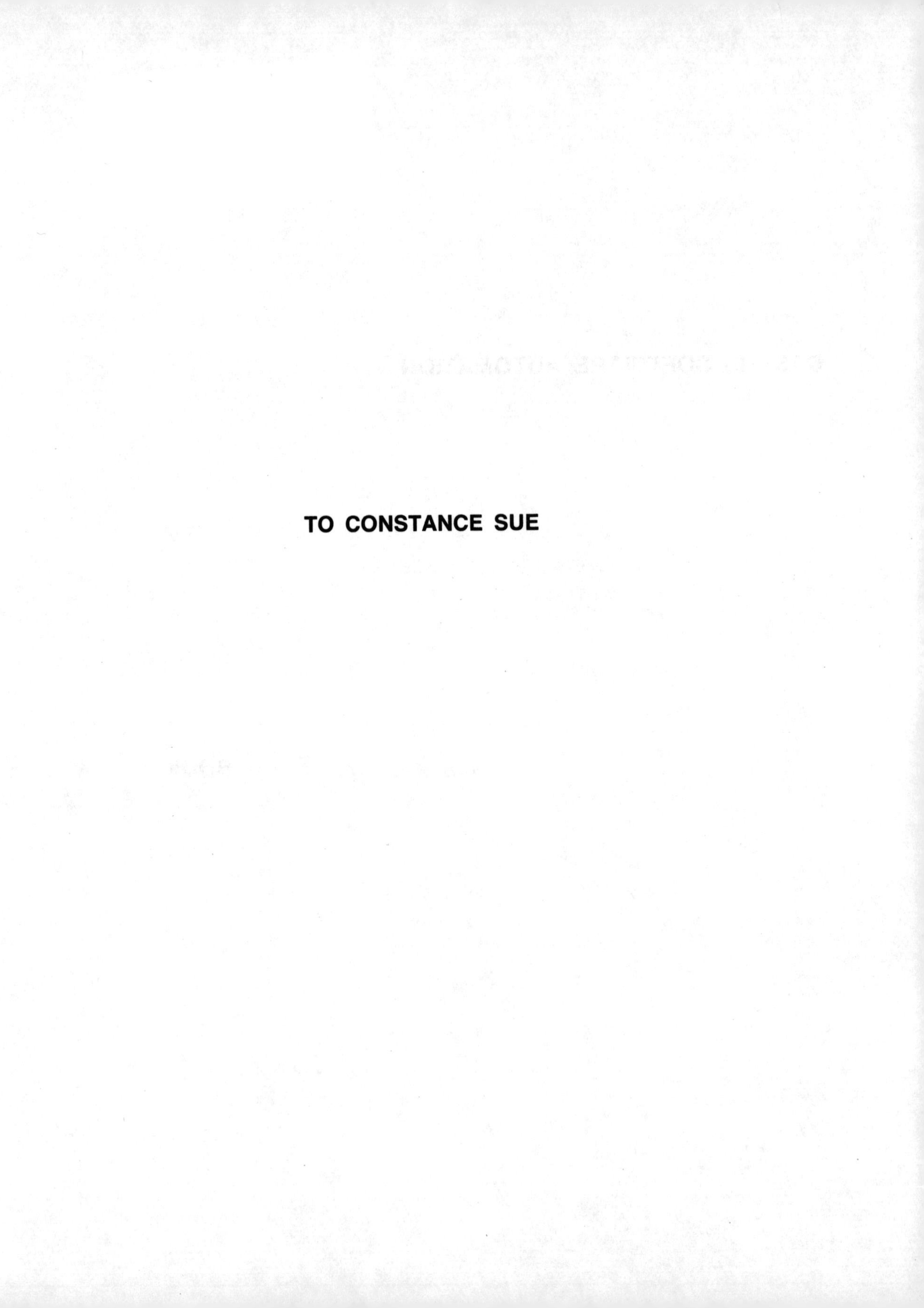

TO CONSTANCE SUE

CASE IS SOFTWARE AUTOMATION

CARMA MCCLURE

PRENTICE HALL, Englewood Cliffs, New Jersey 07632

Library of Congress Cataloging-in-Publication Data

McClure, Carma L.
CASE is software automation / by Carma McClure.
p. cm.
Bibliography: p.
Includes index.
ISBN 0-13-119330-9
1. Computer-aided software engineering. I. Title. II. Title:
Computer-aided software engineering is software automation.
QA76.758.M33 1989
005.1—dc19

Editorial/production supervision: Kathryn Gollin Marshak
Cover design: Bruce Kenselaar
Manufacturing buyer: Mary Ann Gloriande
Cover photograph: Reginald Wickham

Printed in the United States of America

10 9 8 7 6 5 4 3 2 1

ISBN 0-13-119330-9

PRENTICE-HALL INTERNATIONAL (UK) LIMITED, *London*
PRENTICE-HALL OF AUSTRALIA PTY. LIMITED, *Sydney*
PRENTICE-HALL CANADA INC., *Toronto*
PRENTICE-HALL HISPANOAMERICANA, S.A., *Mexico*
PRENTICE-HALL OF INDIA PRIVATE LIMITED, *New Delhi*
PRENTICE-HALL OF JAPAN, INC., *Tokyo*
SIMON & SCHUSTER ASIA PTE. LTD., *Singapore*
EDITORA PRENTICE-HALL DO BRASIL, LTDA., *Rio de Janeiro*

CONTENTS

LIST OF BOXES

PREFACE

Revolution. Revolution. REVOLUTION! No. The subject of this book is not yet another technology revolution. Rather, it is about a change that is taking place in software development tools. As it is a change that makes so much sense and that seems to be the natural next step in advancing software technology, it has captivated the interest of the software industry practically overnight. At the beginning of 1987, this change could be described as a new infatuation for MIS. As often happens with infatuations, it caused the MIS world to set aside other technologies, including fourth- and fifth-generation technologies. By the end of 1987, the infatuation spread to developers of real-time/embedded systems as well as to commercial data processing systems.

This change in software tools is part of a new technology called *computer-aided software engineering* or *CASE*. It is the technology for automating the software development and maintenance, and is a very practical answer to the 25-year-old software crisis. Actually, the CASE technology is not really all that new since it builds on structured techniques that were developed in the 1970s. This is part of the reason for its rapid, widespread acceptance.

This book is intended for the software practitioner involved in the development and maintenance of software systems. It is also intended for software managers and students of software/information engineering.

The purpose of the book is to introduce the CASE technology by exploring what it is, how it is being used to improve software productivity, and how it relates to other software technologies. Although much of the early focus on the CASE technology has centered on software tools, CASE is much broader than this. There are software, hardware, methodology, and management aspects to the CASE technology. Each of these CASE aspects is discussed in this book to give the reader a complete state-of-the-art understanding of CASE.

The ultimate goal of the book is to present practical tools, methods, and management techniques to help meet the ever-growing needs for more and better quality software: CASE can help us achieve this goal.

Sometimes a change can be more exciting than a full-blown revolution, which can also bring about disruption and waste. CASE is this type of exciting change. It has injected the software industry with a high level of hope and enthusiasm for conquering software problems. CASE may very well be the most profound change ever to hit the industry. At the very least, it is the next major step toward higher levels of software automation.

A special thank you to all the CASE vendors who contributed the CASE product examples that appear throughout the book. Also, a sincere thank you to Debbie Jackson for typing and editing the book manuscript.

Carma McClure

PART I INTRODUCTION TO COMPUTER-AIDED SOFTWARE ENGINEERING

1 COMPUTER-AIDED SOFTWARE ENGINEERING: STATE OF THE ART

JUST IMAGINE . . . Imagine developing software at your own dedicated workstation (see Figure 1.1). It is probably a powerful personal computer with a color graphics screen and printer attached. A local-area network connects you to project teammates and the rest of your department. Also, your workstation is connected to a host computer where corporate dictionaries and databases link you to the rest of your organization. Each step of your work is computer assisted, with the use of a great variety of powerful workstation tools—from tools that help you keep track of your work to tools that help you rapidly develop prototype models of the system you are building. You communicate with your workstation by using the keyboard or clicking the mouse buttons. You use your workstation to check your work as you go, to access a library of reusable "software chips," and to perform many routine tasks that are part of every software development project.

There are many powerful standalone software tools in widespread use, but the key difference is that the workstation provides an *assembly of integrated tools*—tools that are accessible from one place and in a form where they can easily call, feed, and use one another. The difference among the individual tools is hidden from the user's view by one common user interface. In other words, the workstation provides a complete environment of hardware and software working in unison to support software development. This enormously simplifies the use of software tools, reduces the learning curve, and speeds up the production of the software.

Is this fact or fantasy? Is it a picture of the present or the future software development environment? Fortunately, this picture of software development is already more fact than fantasy.

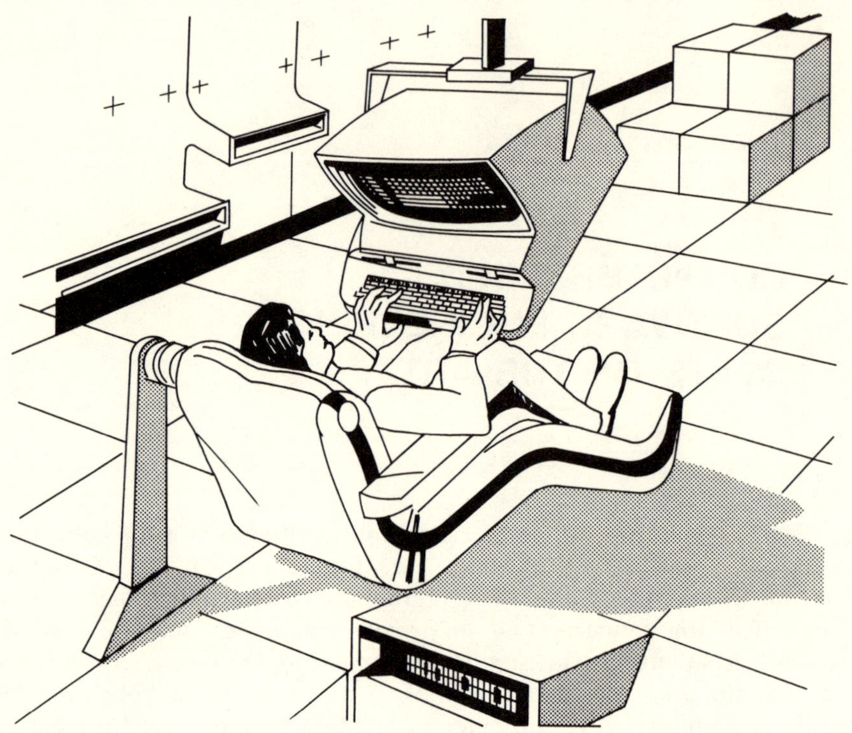

Figure 1.1 Imagine developing software at your own dedicated workstation.

COMPUTER-AIDED SOFTWARE ENGINEERING

There is a dramatic change taking place in software tools today. Tools designed to automate various life cycle tasks are being created for use on micros. Many of these tools focus on software analysis and design tasks. With the assistance of these tools, software developers can create software systems interactively at personal computers and workstations.

Both MIS departments and developers of real-time/embedded systems are welcoming this change with open arms. They are more than ready for a new software technology that can solve 25-year-old software productivity problems. This new technology is called *computer-aided software engineering*.

Simply defined, computer-aided software engineering is the *automation of software development*. Commonly referred to as the *CASE technology,* computer-aided software engineering is the most advanced software technology yet. There is more excitement and hope associated with CASE than with any previous software technology. CASE is making software developers forget about third-, fourth-, and even fifth-generation technologies as CASE replaces fourth-generation languages as the most powerful software development technique.

What is CASE?

SOFTWARE AUTOMATION

CASE proposes a new approach to the software life cycle concept, that is based on automation. The basic idea behind CASE is to provide a set of well-integrated, laborsaving tools linking and automating all phases of the software life cycle (see Figure 1.2).

Traditional software technologies are of two types: tools and methodologies. The tools category includes a variety of third-, fourth-, and most recently, fifth-generation tools. Most software tools are stand-alone, mainframe-based, and concentrate on the implementation part of the software life cycle.

The software methodology category includes manual software development methodologies such as structured analysis, structured design, and structured programming. These methodologies define a step-by-step disciplined process for developing software.

The CASE technology is a *combination* of software tools and methodologies. Furthermore, CASE is different from earlier software technologies because it focuses on the entire software productivity problem, not just on implementation solutions. Spanning all phases of the software life cycle, CASE is the most complete software technology yet. CASE attacks software productivity problems at both ends of the life cycle by automating many analysis and design tasks, as well as program implementation and maintenance tasks.

Because manual structured methodologies are too tedious and labor intensive, in practice they are seldom followed to the most detailed level. CASE

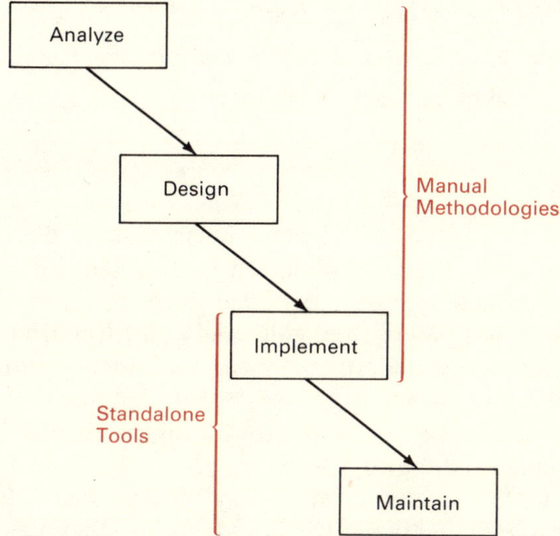

Figure 1.2 Traditional software technologies are of two types: manual methodologies and stand-alone tools. The CASE technology is a combination of well-integrated tools and methodologies, with the emphasis on automation of the software life cycle.

makes manual structured methodologies practical to use by automating the drawing of structured diagrams and the generation of system documentation.

BENEFITS OF CASE

Box 1.1 lists the benefits that CASE offers the software developer. This list suggests that CASE is not an entirely new technology but rather, built on techniques and tools that have been proven to work in practice. In this sense CASE can be defined as *a repackaging of structured concepts and methodologies* with a new twist. That new twist is automation.

BOX 1.1 CASE benefits

- Makes structured techniques practical
- Enforces software/information engineering
- Improves software quality through automated checking
- Makes prototyping practical
- Simplifies program maintenance
- Speeds up development process
- Frees developer to focus on creative part of software development
- Encourages evolutional and incremental development
- Enables reuse of software components

CASE TOOLS

The backbone of the CASE technology is a new breed of software tools. Many of these tools are micro-based, use powerful graphics to enhance the user interface, and are incorporated into workbenches where they can easily call, feed, and use each other. CASE tools focus on the productivity of the individual, professional software developer. With the use of workstations, local-area networks, and PC-based tools, the software developer can work from a highly responsive, dedicated development environment for the first time.

Since CASE tools are used primarily by professional software developers, not end users, the CASE technology should not be thought of as just an enhancement of fourth-generation tools. Also, CASE tools differ from fourth-generation tools in two other respects. First, many CASE tools are workstation-based, whereas most fourth-generation tools are mainframe-based. Second, CASE is a general-purpose software technology to be used in the development of all types of systems (i.e., large and small, commercial and scientific, on-line and real-time), whereas fourth-generation tools are used mainly to develop small-to-medium-sized commercial applications.

In general, CASE tools are different from earlier software tools in some important ways. Namely, they are designed to:

1. Support a dedicated, personal computing environment.
2. Use graphics to specify and document software systems.
3. Link together all phases of the software life cycle.
4. Capture and link together on the computer all information about an evolving software system from initial requirements through ongoing maintenance activities.
5. Use artificial intelligence to perform many routine software development and maintenance tasks automatically.

EXAMPLE OF CASE TOOLS

Furthermore, CASE tools perform many more types of tasks than do third- and fourth-generation tools. They support the automation of a wide variety of software development and maintenance tasks, including project management. As shown in Figure 1.3, examples of CASE tools include:

- Diagramming tools for drawing structured diagrams and creating pictorial system specifications
- Screen and report painters for creating system specifications and a form of simple prototyping
- Dictionaries, data base management systems and reporting facilities for storing, reporting, and querying technical and project management system information
- Specification checking tools to detect, automatically, incomplete, syntactically incorrect, and inconsistent system specifications
- Code generators to generate executable code automatically from pictorial system specifications
- Documentation generators to produce technical and user system documentation required by structured techniques

Although tools are an important part of CASE, the CASE technology consists of more than software tools. CASE is a *redefinition of the entire software environment*.

A key way in which CASE changes the software development environment is that many CASE tools operate in a workstation environment. This changes software development into a highly interactive process in which error checking can begin from the early steps of system requirements definition.

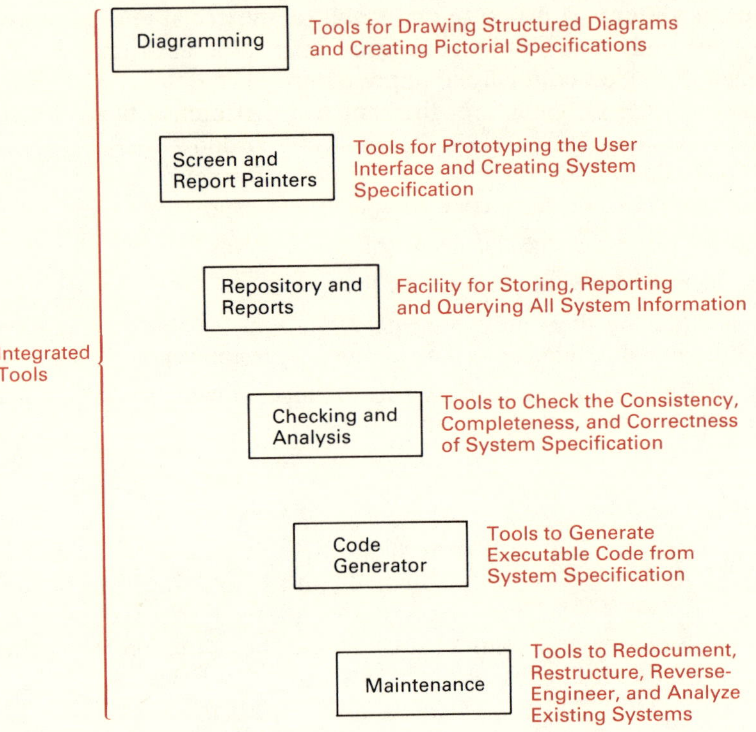

Figure 1.3 CASE tools cover many types of software development and maintenance tasks.

CASE HISTORY

As shown in Figure 1.4, the history of the CASE technology began in the early 1980s with the introduction of computer-aided documentation and diagramming tools. These tools represent some of the first PC-based software development tools and some of the first attempts to automate analysis and design tasks. These tools are simple,

CASE technology evolution

Early 1980s	Mid-1980s	Late 1980s	Early 1990s
Computer-aided documentation Computer-aided diagramming Analysis and design tools	Automatic design analysis and checking Automated system information repository	Automatic code generation from design spec Linking design automation and program automation	Intelligent methodology driver Habitable user interface Reusability as a development methodology

Figure 1.4 CASE is a new technology with a brief history of only a few years.

stand-alone drawing tools. They are used to create structured diagrams, such as data flow diagrams, structure charts, and entity relationship diagrams. Their purpose is to produce automatically the structured documentation required by various structured development methodologies. Different CASE tools support different development methodologies, such as Yourdon structured analysis and design, or Jackson structured design, or Martin information engineering.

Figure 1.5 is a hand-drawn structure chart representing the design of a temperature monitoring program. It uses the Yourdon notation. Figure 1.6 is a structure chart, again using the Yourdon notion, and drawn automatically with a CASE tool. Figure 1.7 is a data flow diagram using the Gane and Sarson

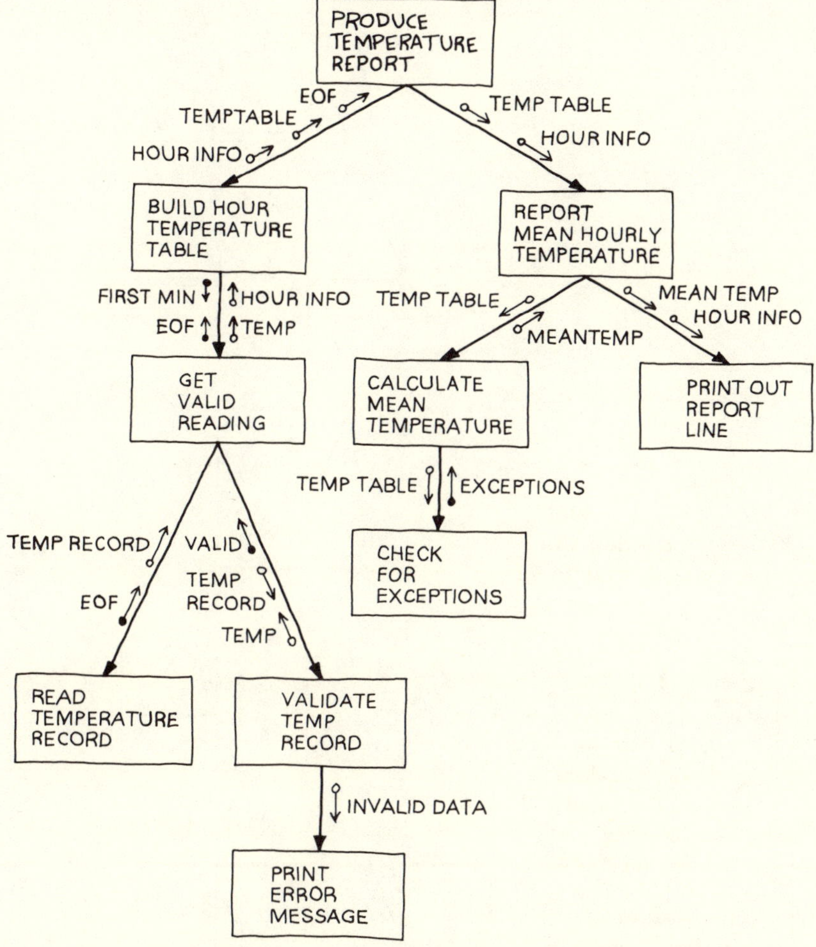

Figure 1.5 Hand-drawn structure chart using the Yourdon notation. It is tedious and very time consuming when drawn by hand.

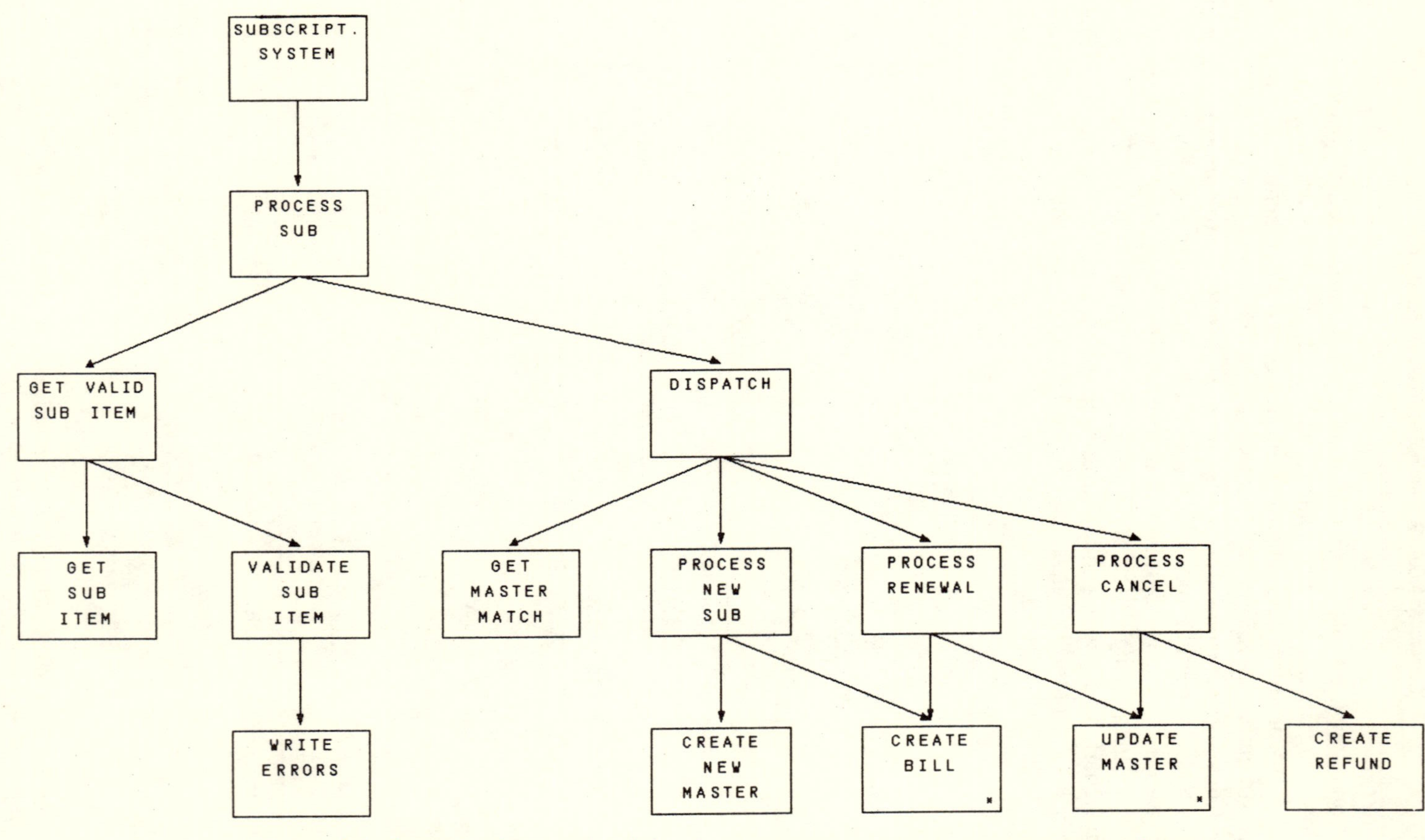

Figure 1.6 Structure chart produced by the INFORMATION ENGINEERING WORKBENCH from KnowledgeWare.

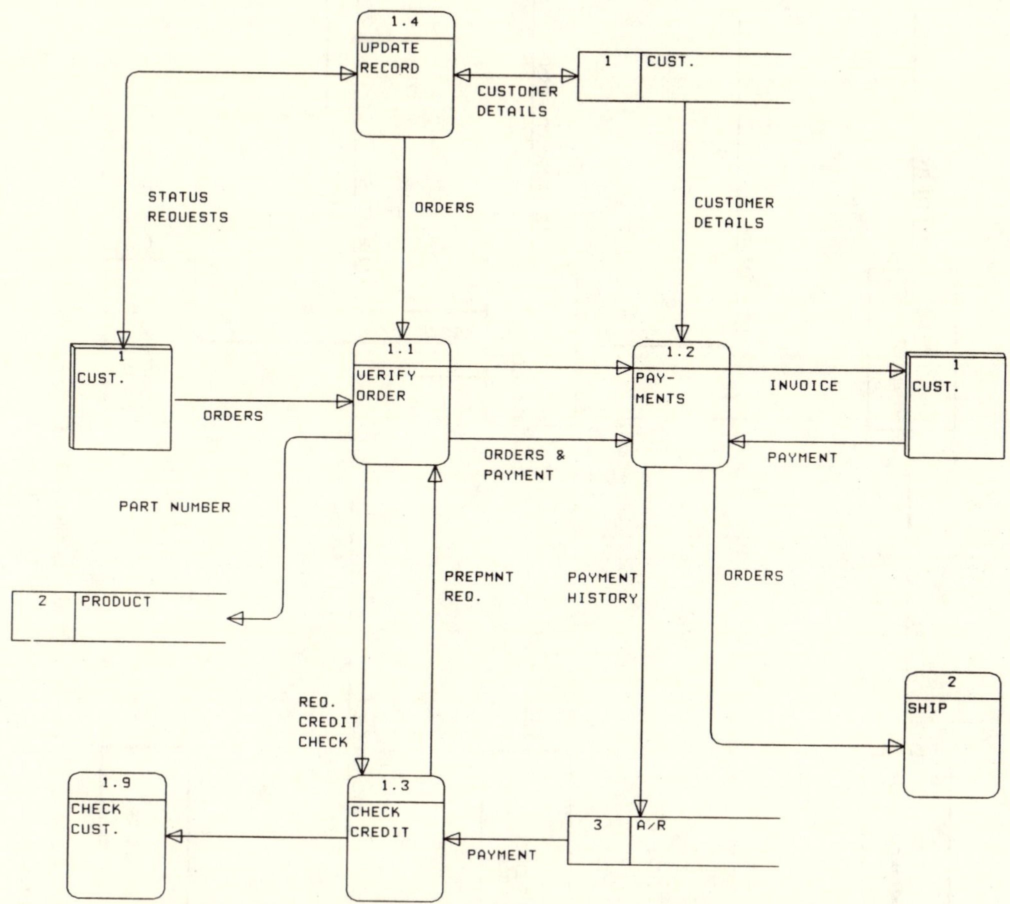

Figure 1.7 Data flow diagram, a popular system analysis structured diagram, automatically drawn by EXCELERATOR from the Index Technology Corporation.

notation drawn with another CASE tool, and Figure 1.8 is an entity relationship diagram drawn automatically using the information engineering notation of Martin.

Early CASE tools addressed mainly the automation of documentation and communication as the key to software productivity improvements. In the mid-1980s, CASE tools were enhanced to provide two very important functions:

1. Automatic checking of structured diagrams
2. Storage of structured diagrams in automated design libraries called dictionaries, repositories, or encyclopedias

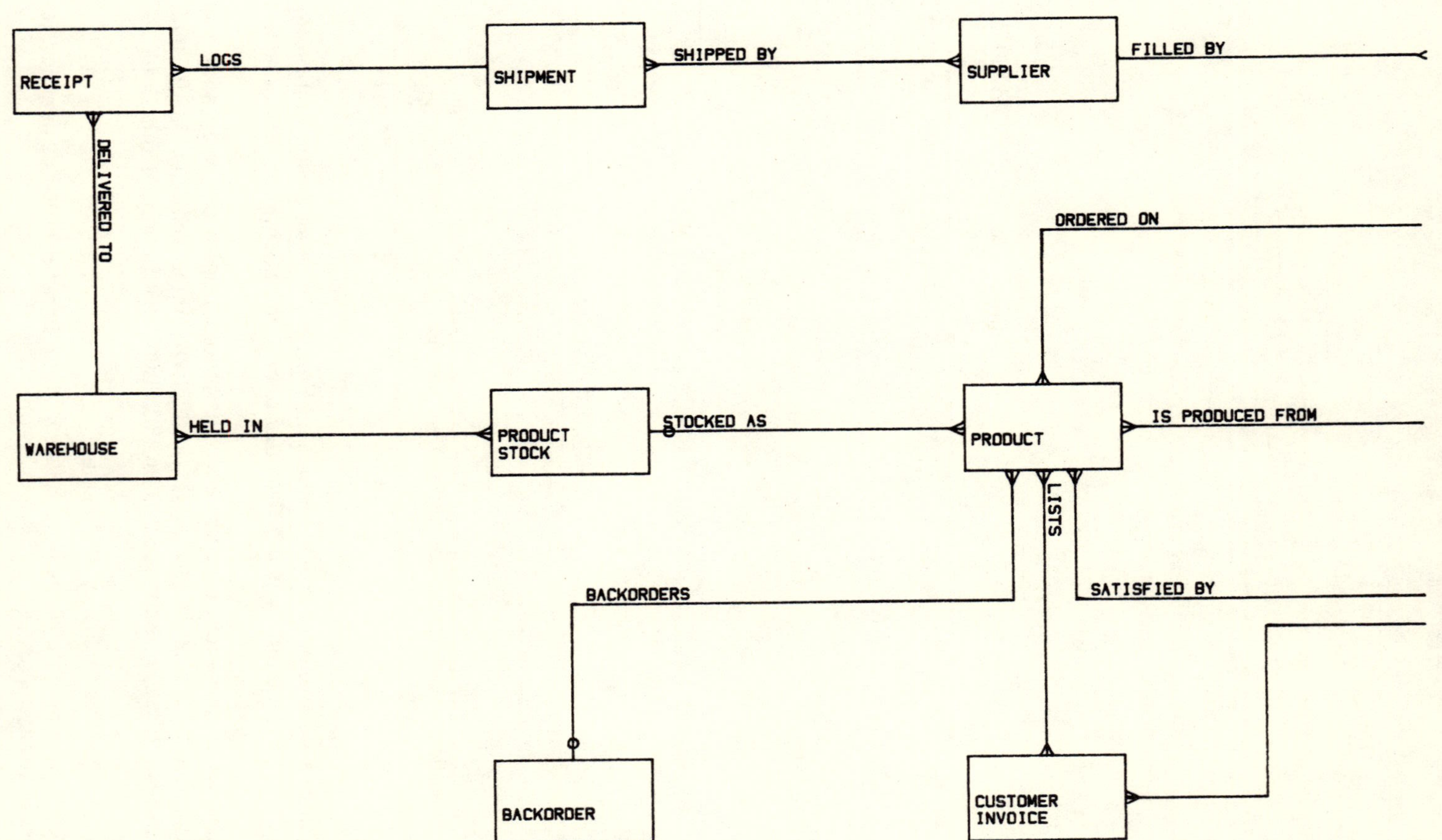

Figure 1.8 Entity relationship diagram produced by the INFORMATION ENGINEERING FACILITY™ from Texas Instruments Incorporated.

The diagrams are checked to ensure their completeness and correctness before using them as the design specifications for program implementation. The checks are based on the rules of the structured methodology supported. In addition, cross-reference information is recorded and redundancies are eliminated.

After the diagrams are checked, they are stored in automated dictionaries or data bases called the CASE repository. Once stored, the diagrams can be easily updated, shared among project teammates, and later reused in other software development projects.

At this stage, the CASE focus was on design automation because analysis and design are viewed as the most critical software life cycle phases. Doing a better job up front in the early life cycle phases can greatly affect system quality and costs. With automated assistance from CASE tools, design time can be reduced substantially while still producing high-quality, error-free design specifications.

The next step in the evolution of the CASE technology is to link design automation and program automation. Whereas design automation is concerned with computerized assistance for analysis and design tasks, program automation means automatic code generators. Linking the two will mean that 80 to 90 percent of a complete software system can be generated from structured design diagrams (see Figure 1.9).

Design automation is supported by the PC-based CASE tools developed in the early and mid-1980s. Program automation is provided by fourth-generation application generators and code generators, most of which are mainframe-based. To join together design automation and program automation will require bridging two hardware environments—PC and mainframe—and two software tech-

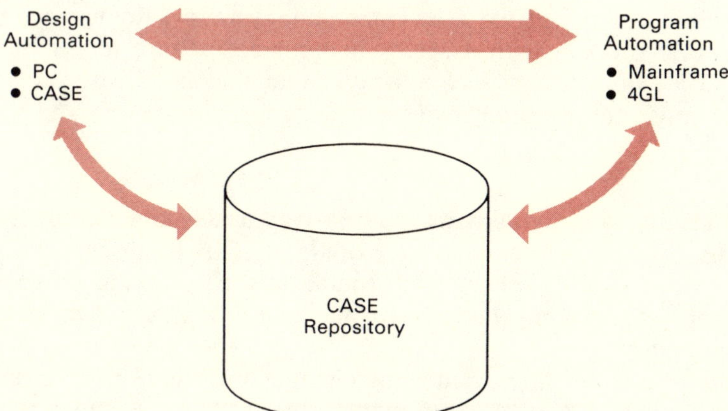

Figure 1.9 Linking design automation and program automation means that a complete software system can be automatically generated from a high-level pictorial system specification. An important part of this link is the CASE repository.

nologies—CASE and fourth generation. An important part of this bridge will be the addition of a repository to the CASE environment.

The CASE repository is a mechanism for storing and organizing all information about a software system. Some of this information is needed for project management and some for automatic code generation. It includes information on the problem to be solved, problem domain, software process being used, data models, process models, prototypes, project resources and history, and organizational context.

Besides linking design automation and program automation, the CASE repository makes software reusability a practical concept for the first time. Reusing software components is the key to dramatic software productivity increases. Instead of building each new software or enhancement from scratch, software developers can reuse software components stored in CASE repositories. Not only will software developers reuse source code modules, they will also reuse project plans, prototype models, data models, and design specifications.

GOAL OF CASE

To summarize, CASE dramatically changes the way we build software systems by providing three key advancements:

1. An interactive development environment with rapid response time, dedicated resources, and early error checking
2. Automation of many software development and maintenance tasks
3. Visual programming provided by a powerful graphics interface

The ultimate goal of the CASE technology is to automate the entire software life cycle process with a set of integrated software tools. However, the state of the art of software technology is that this is still a goal that we are striving towards, not a present reality.

A CHANGE IN ATTITUDE

Perhaps the best way to describe CASE today is as a change in attitude. CASE represents a fundamental change in attitude toward software development that is a necessary step paving the way for the revolutionary advancement of software technologies.

CASE is not the first significant change in attitude toward the software process. In the late 1960s, the introduction of structured techniques represented a change in attitude. Reacting to the emergence of the software crisis, the viewpoint then was that software development was a complicated, tedious, and error-prone process. It should not be treated as a private art left to the whim of each individual programmer, but rather, as an engineering-like, disciplined process.

The structured emphasis was on programming standards and procedures and management control. The attitude was that software quality and productivity could best be controlled through discipline, formality, and standardization.

Then in the late 1970s, another change in attitude toward the software process occurred. This time the viewpoint was that software productivity could be increased through the use of tools that simplified the development of software. The software crisis could be alleviated if more people (and less technically skilled people) could develop certain types of software application systems. This change in attitude was marked by the introduction of fourth-generation tools and end-user computing.

Now in the late 1980s, we see another change in attitude toward the software process. In a sense, this change represents a step backward toward an earlier, more conservative view of software development. Once again, the viewpoint is that software development is a difficult task that requires an engineering-like disciplined approach and for complex systems should be performed by highly trained, professional software developers. Although end-user computing and fourth-generation tools have made a valuable contribution, experience has shown that they have a limited place in software development. For the most part they are useful in building small-to-medium-sized commercial applications. They are not general-purpose, software-building tools.

This most recent change in attitude is a rediscovery of the fundamental software engineering principles that have been defined over the last 25 years. Structured techniques are a recurring theme, but this time with an emphasis on automation of the software process. At this stage, CASE is a revival of structured techniques.

The CASE attitude is that software development and maintenance should be viewed as a formal, disciplined activity to enable more extensive correctness checking and automation of the process. The only realistic way to increase software quality and productivity significantly is through automation.

THE DIRECTION OF AUTOMATION

The subject of this book is software automation. The CASE technology, which is the vehicle for moving the software process in the direction of automation is discussed. We explore what CASE is, what CASE is not, and what CASE is likely to become in the future. Box 1.2 presents the basic definitions for the CASE technology.

In Part I we have introduced the subjects of software automation and computer-aided software engineering. In Part II we define the components of a CASE system in Chapters 2 and 3 and categorize the basic types of CASE tools in Chapter 5. In Chapter 4 the hardware platforms for a CASE system are discussed. In Part III we explore the impact of CASE on the software process. User experiences with CASE tools are presented in Chapter 6. In Chapter 7 methods for introducing CASE into an organization are suggested. In Chapter 8

BOX 1.2 Definitions

CASE: computer-aided software engineering

CASE technology: a software technology that provides an automated, engineering discipline for software development, maintenance, and project management; includes automated structured methodologies and automated tools

CASE tool: a software tool that automates (at least in part) a particular software life cycle task

CASE system: a set of integrated CASE tools that share a common user interface and run in a common computer environment

CASE toolkit: a set of integrated CASE tools that have been designed to work together and to automate (or partially automate) a phase of the software life cycle or a particular software job class

CASE workbench: a set of integrated CASE tools that have been designed to work together and to automate (or provide automated assistance for) the entire software life cycle, including analysis, design, coding, and testing

CASE methodology: an ''automatable'' structured methodology that defines a disciplined, engineering-like approach for all or some aspects of the development and maintenance of software

CASE methodology companion: a set of CASE tools that automate tasks in a particular CASE methodology and/or automate the production of documentation and other deliverables required by the methodology

CASE workstation: a 32-bit technical/engineering workstation or personal computer equipped with CASE tools that automate various life-cycle functions

CASE hardware platform: a one-, two-, or three-tiered hardware system architecture that provides an operating platform for CASE tools

we discuss how the CASE technology changes the traditional software life cycle. The relationship of the CASE technology to third-, fourth-, and fifth-generation technologies is clarified in Chapter 9.

In Part IV we explore what software development will look like as we near the end of this decade. The software development environment of the 1990s is introduced in Chapter 10. In Chapter 11 we describe the habitable environment, which is an intelligent user interface for the 1990s software development environment. The methodology driver, an expert system that provides methodology guidance through the 1990s software life cycle, is described in Chapter 12. In Chapter 13 we explain how and why software reusability will become the foremost software development strategy in the 1990s. The book closes with a short epilogue in Chapter 14, Part V.

PART II COMPONENTS OF A CASE SYSTEM

2 THE CASE SOFTWARE DEVELOPMENT ENVIRONMENT

THE NEW SOFTWARE DEVELOPMENT ENVIRONMENT

As new advances in hardware and software technologies have occurred, the software development environment has changed from a stand-alone mode in the 1950s and early 1960s to a batch mode in the late 1960s and early 1970s, and then to a time-sharing mode in the late 1970s and early 1980s [1]. In the late 1980s, a new mode based on *personal workstations* is becoming the preferred environment for developing software. Workstations have potentially far-reaching implications for changing and improving software development. The introduction of powerful workstation tools and accompanying engineering-like structured methodologies transforms and automates the software development process.

The CASE *workstation* is a complete environment, including hardware and software, whose function is to provide computerized assistance for the production, maintenance, and project management of software systems.

In addition, the workstation provides word processing, information storage and retrieval, electronic mail, and calendar functions. It is a personal machine dedicated to providing the maximum possible support for the individual software developer.

The primary objective for using CASE workstations is to increase software productivity. Running a close second is the objective of improving software quality. Other objections frequently cited are listed in Box 2.1.

CASE WORKBENCH

An extensive set of intelligent, integrated software tools called the *CASE workbench* make up the ''soft part'' of the workstation environment. They are tailorable to each individual developer's preferences; assist specialized tasks such as project management, design, and maintenance, and replace traditional tools

BOX 2.1 Objectives of software workstations

- Maximize productivity of software developer
- Improve software quality and reduce errors
- Simplify the software development process
- Speed up software development process
- Enable more efficient use of machine resources
- Reduce software costs
- Improve reliability of development environment
- Provide a development environment having better human interface with the system
- Revolutionize the software development process
- Automate generation of software documentation
- Automate generation of executable code
- Support rapid prototyping
- Automate error checking throughout the development process
- Automate project management
- Formalize and standardize software development process
- Standardize software documentation
- Integrate development steps and tools
- Promote software reusability
- Promote greater overall control of software development and maintenance
- Improve software portability across environments

that are bound to batch processing and third-generation languages of the 1960s and 1970s.

CASE workbenches differ from early programming environments such as Unix and Interlisp in their breadth of coverage of the software life cycle. Unix is a time-shared operating system in which a uniform file format is the primary means of integrating a rich array of programming tools [2]. Unix is a general-purpose programming environment in that it does not support a particular programming language or software development methodology. Interlisp, on the other hand, is a programming environment that supports only the programming language Lisp. This gives Interlisp the advantage of tailoring and optimizing its tools for a single programming language [3]. All Interlisp tools are written in

Lisp and provide tightly integrated operating system, utility functions, editors, and debuggers.

Whereas programming environments of the 1970s and 1980s have concentrated on tools for the coding and implementation phases, CASE workbenches provide powerful tools for specification, design, implementation, testing, and documentation. They are a general-purpose software support environment attempting to support the full range of the software job as well as its management.

To meet the objectives of enhancing productivity and simplifying the process of software development, the CASE workbench cannot simply consist of a collection of even the best tools of the 1970s and 1980s. These tools were not designed to be used in a dedicated, personal computing environment allowing customization for each individual workstation owner. They were not designed to use powerful graphics capabilities to enhance the human interface. They were not designed to be used in cooperation with one another linking together all aspects of the development process. They were not designed to capture information about an ongoing development process and evolution of a software product. Finally, they were not designed as intelligent tools capable of performing many development tasks on their own.

Instead, the CASE workbench assembles tools that can provide full functional support for the software process:

- Creating graphical system requirements and design specifications
- Checking, analyzing, and cross-referencing system information
- Storing, managing, and reporting system information and project management information
- Building system prototypes and simulating systems
- Generating system code and accompanying documentation
- Enforcing standards and procedures
- Testing, validating, and analyzing programs
- Interfacing to outside dictionaries and data bases

To provide full software support, a complete CASE workbench must have the following capabilities:

- Graphics capability
- Error checking
- Information repository
- Tightly integrated toolset
- Full life cycle coverage

- Prototyping support
- Automatic code generation
- Structured methodology support

In this chapter we discuss the first four capabilities, and in the next chapter we discuss the remaining four capabilities of a CASE workbench.

GRAPHICS CAPABILITY

When using a CASE workstation, one is first impressed by the graphics editor. The ease with which objects are made to appear, disappear, and move around the workstation screen with a mere click of a mouse button is amazing. However, behind the graphics is a very important capability. The better the graphics interface, the more productive the user can be.

Figure 2.1 is a narrative description of the specifications for a subscription system. Figure 2.2 also describes the specifications for the subscription system, but in graphical form (i.e., a data flow diagram). Most people prefer the graphical form because the human mind is pictorially oriented. While narrative text is one-dimensional, pictures are multidimensional, borrowing properties such as size, shape, and color from the physical world. Since the language of pictures is richer than the language of text, more information can be represented in a picture than in text, and the reader can grasp the meaning more quickly [4].

Subscription System Program Definition

The subscription system processes subscription transactions against a subscription file. There are three types of transactions: new subscriptions, renewals, and cancellations. Each transaction is first validated and then processed against the master file. For new subscriptions, a customer record is built and a bill is generated for the balance due. For renewals, the expiration date is updated and a bill is generated for the balance due. For cancellations, the record is flagged for deletion and a refund is issued.

Figure 2.1 Narrative description of the specifications for a subscription system.

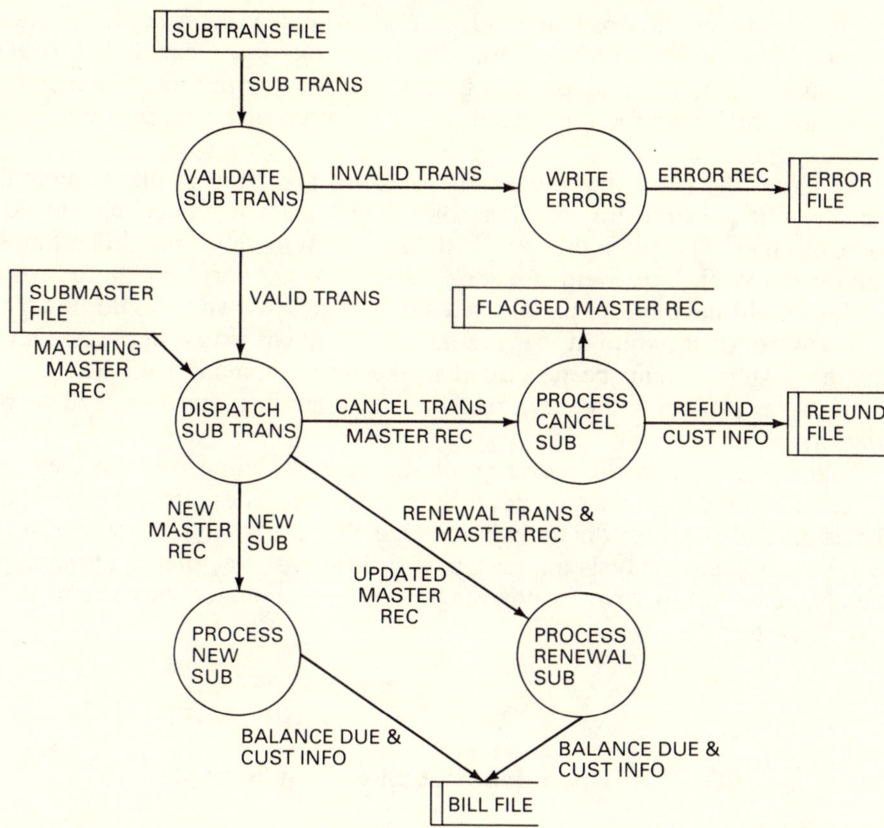

Figure 2.2 Data flow diagram used to explain graphically the specification for the subscription system.

THE NEED FOR DIAGRAMS

Graphical representations (or diagrams) have always played an important role in software development. Diagrams are used to define program specifications and to represent program designs. They provide the blueprint for implementing the design into code, and are an important form of software documentation.

Clear diagrams play an essential part in designing complex systems and developing programs. If only one person is developing a system design or program, the diagrams are an aid to clear thinking. A poor choice of diagramming technique can inhibit thinking, but a good choice can speed up the work and improve the quality of the results.

When a number of people work on a system or program, diagrams are an essential communication tool. A formal diagramming technique is needed to enable developers to exchange ideas and to make their separate system components fit together with precision. When debugging, clear diagrams are a highly valuable tool for understanding how another programmer intended the programs to work, and for tracking down the source of errors and the impact of change.

The larger the team, the greater the need for precision in diagramming. It is difficult or impossible for members of a larger team to understand in detail the work of others. To solve this problem, each team member should be familiar with an overview of the system and see where his or her part fits into the whole. He or she should have clear, precisely defined interfaces, and should be able to view the system or program at varying degrees of detail. Most important, every part of the system should be described in the same, standardized way to ease communication problems and to avoid misunderstanding that can lead to program errors.

Diagrams are really the language of software modeling because they offer a concise, unambiguous way of describing software. They are fundamental to good system and program documentation (see Box 2.2). Also, they are so fundamental to software analysis and design that different structured methodologies can be characterized in terms of the diagramming techniques they use to model a software system.

BOX 2.2 Good documentation requirements

Good system and program documentation is a fundamental component of the structured philosophy. Good documentation meets the following requirements:

- Enhances the understandability of software systems
- Is easy and inexpensive to produce and update, and can be produced automatically
- Gives a high-level view of the system (program), explaining its purpose and the relationship of the various data and procedural components
- Describes in detail the components of each data structure and procedural component
- Provides a blueprint for representing problem requirements in a system (program) design and then for translating the design into program code

ADVANTAGES OF STRUCTURED DIAGRAMMING TECHNIQUES

Structured diagramming techniques such as data flow diagramming and entity relationship diagramming apply the basic structuring principles to program documentation. Structured diagramming techniques offer many advantages. First, they combine graphic and narrative notations to increase understandability. Graphics are especially useful because they tend to be less ambiguous than a narrative description. Also, because they tend to be more concise, graphics can be drawn in much less time than it would take to write a narrative document containing the same amount of information.

Second, structured diagramming techniques are top-down hierarchical. This means that they support a top-down, structured development approach. They can describe a system, program, or data structure at varying degrees of detail during each step of the decomposition process. Also, they clarify the steps and the results of the decomposition process by providing a standardized way of describing procedural logic and data structures.

Finally, structured diagramming techniques help developers deal with the large volume of detail generated during the program development process. They give a logical rather than a programming-oriented representation which is more meaningful to users and nontechnical managers.

USES OF STRUCTURED DIAGRAMS

Diagramming techniques have evolved along with programming methodologies. In the 1950s and 1960s, flowcharts were used to plan out detailed and complicated program logic. They fell out of favor because they can give neither a high-level nor a structured view of a program. In the 1970s, structured techniques became widespread, and structured diagramming techniques such as data flow diagrams and structure charts were introduced along with them.

Some diagramming techniques are used as analysis tools, others as program design tools, and still others as data base/file design tools. Box 2.3 lists examples of structured diagramming techniques according to these categories.

The data flow diagram, decomposition diagram, and control flow diagram are examples of analysis tools (see Figures 2.3 through 2.5). For example, the data flow diagram is used to describe the transformation that data undergo as they flow through a system. The control flow diagram adds control information needed to describe real-time systems. The decomposition diagram is used to identify an organization's structure and its basic business functions.

The structure chart (see Figure 2.6) is used as a program design tool to define the hierarchical organization of a program, including its procedural

BOX 2.3 Structured diagramming techniques

	Documentation Type	
	Procedural	Data
Analysis tools		
Data flow diagram	×	
Control flow diagram	×	
Decision table, trees	×	
Matrix	×	×
Dependency diagram	×	
Decomposition diagram	×	
Design tools		
Structure chart	×	
Action diagram	×	
Warnier–Orr diagram	×	×
State transition diagram	×	
Decision tables, trees	×	
Pseudocode	×	
Flowcharts	×	
Screen layouts		×
Dialogue flow		×
Database/file design		
Data model		×
Entity relationship diagram		×
Data structure		×
Logical records		×
Physical database and files		×

components and the data interfaces connecting them. The action diagram and the Warnier–Orr diagram (see Figures 2.7 and 2.8) can be used to show the program hierarchical organization as well as detailed procedural logic.

Entity relationship diagrams and data model diagrams are used to describe data structures (see Figures 2.9 and 2.10). Each data entity, its attributes, and its relationships to other data entities can be defined in these diagrams. In addition, cardinality can be indicated to distinguish optional and mandatory relationships when capturing business rules.

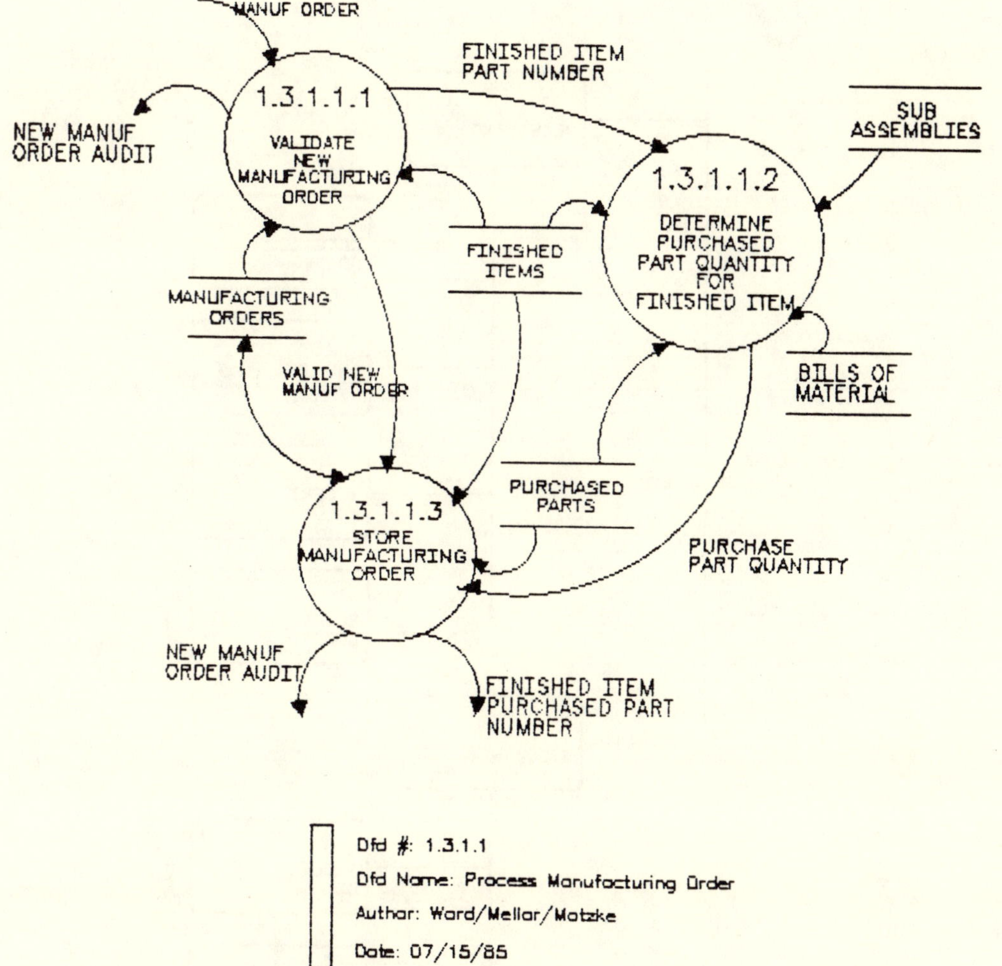

Figure 2.3 Data flow diagram drawn with the ANALYST DESIGNER TOOLKIT from Yourdon Software Engineering Company.

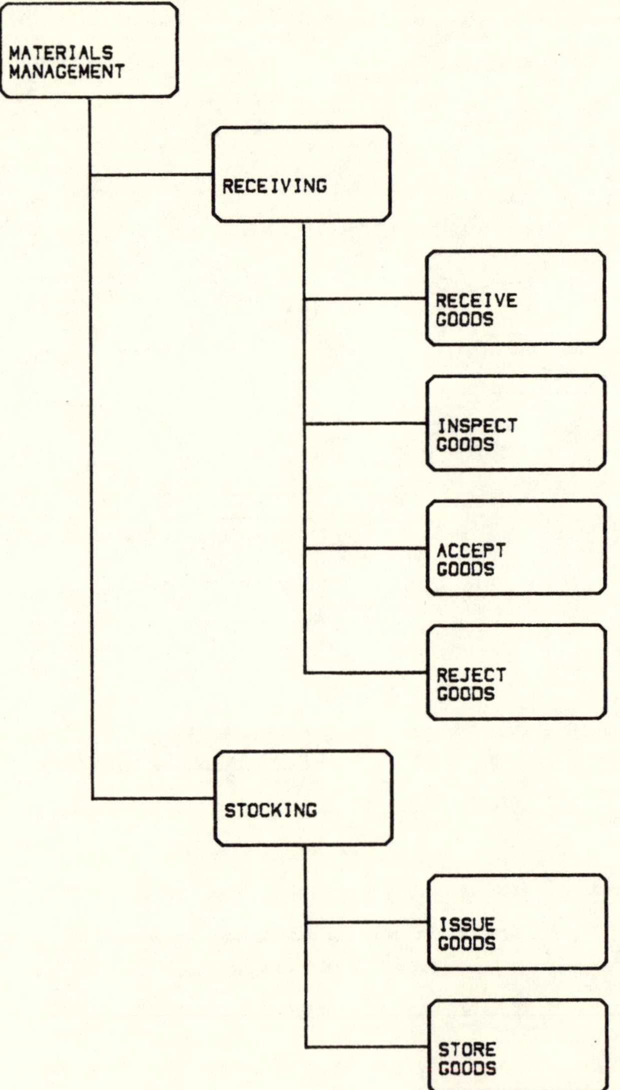

Figure 2.4 Decomposition diagram drawn using the INFORMATION ENGINEERING FACILITY™ from Texas Instruments Incorporated.

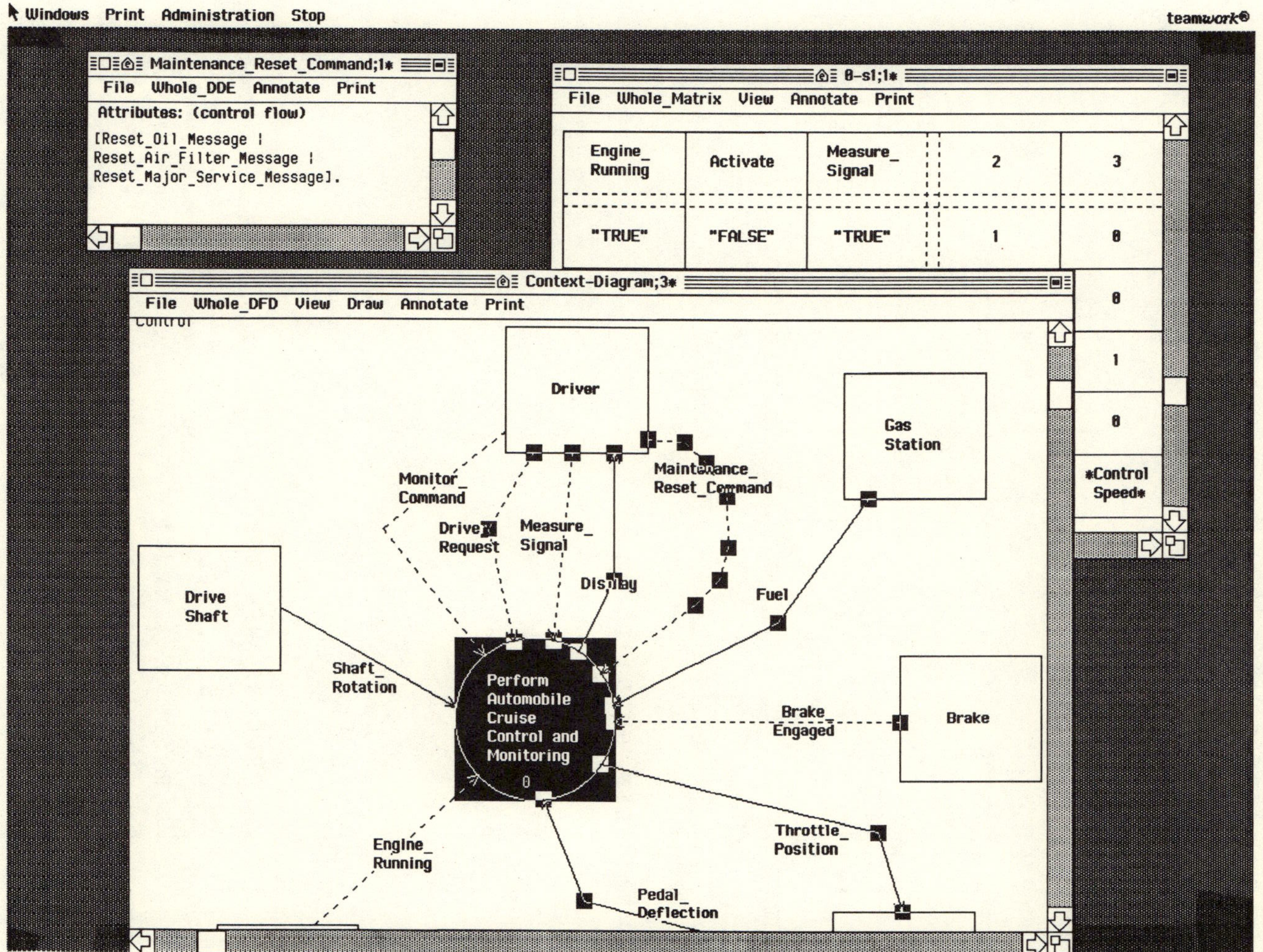

Figure 2.5 Example of the multiple-window screen of TEAMWORK from Cadre Technologies. It shows a context diagram which is a type of control flow diagram used in designing real-time systems.

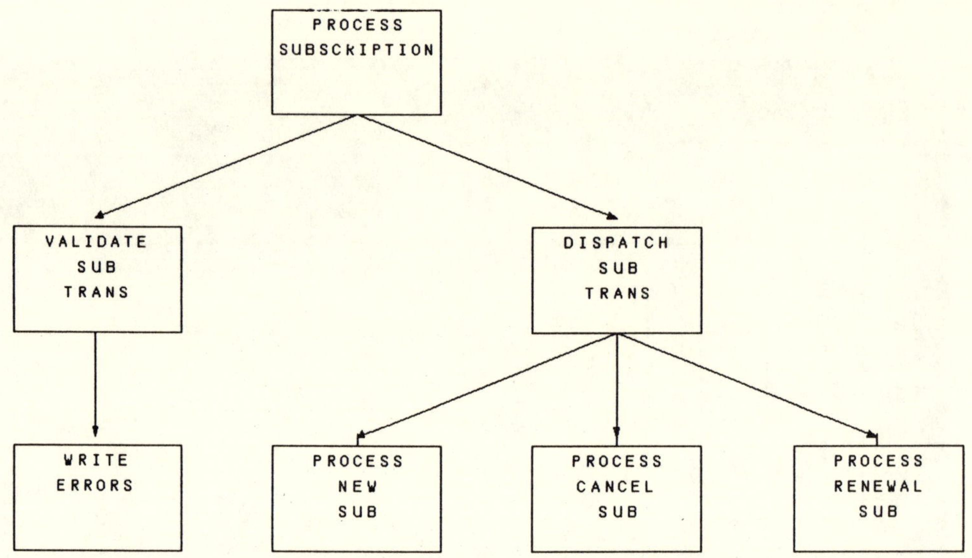

Figure 2.6 Structure chart of subscription system, produced with the INFORMATION ENGINEERING WORKBENCH from KnowledgeWare.

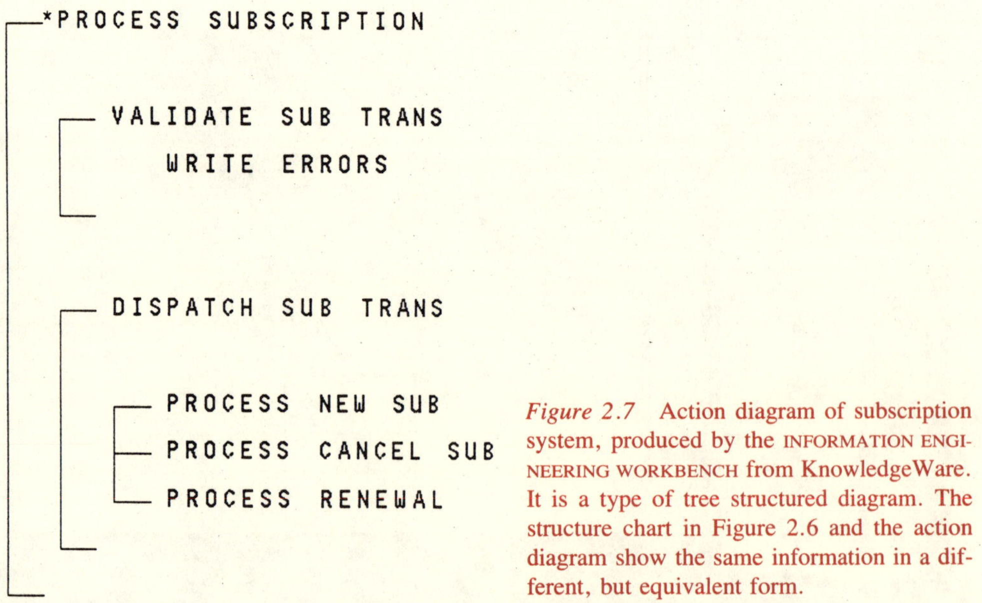

Figure 2.7 Action diagram of subscription system, produced by the INFORMATION ENGINEERING WORKBENCH from KnowledgeWare. It is a type of tree structured diagram. The structure chart in Figure 2.6 and the action diagram show the same information in a different, but equivalent form.

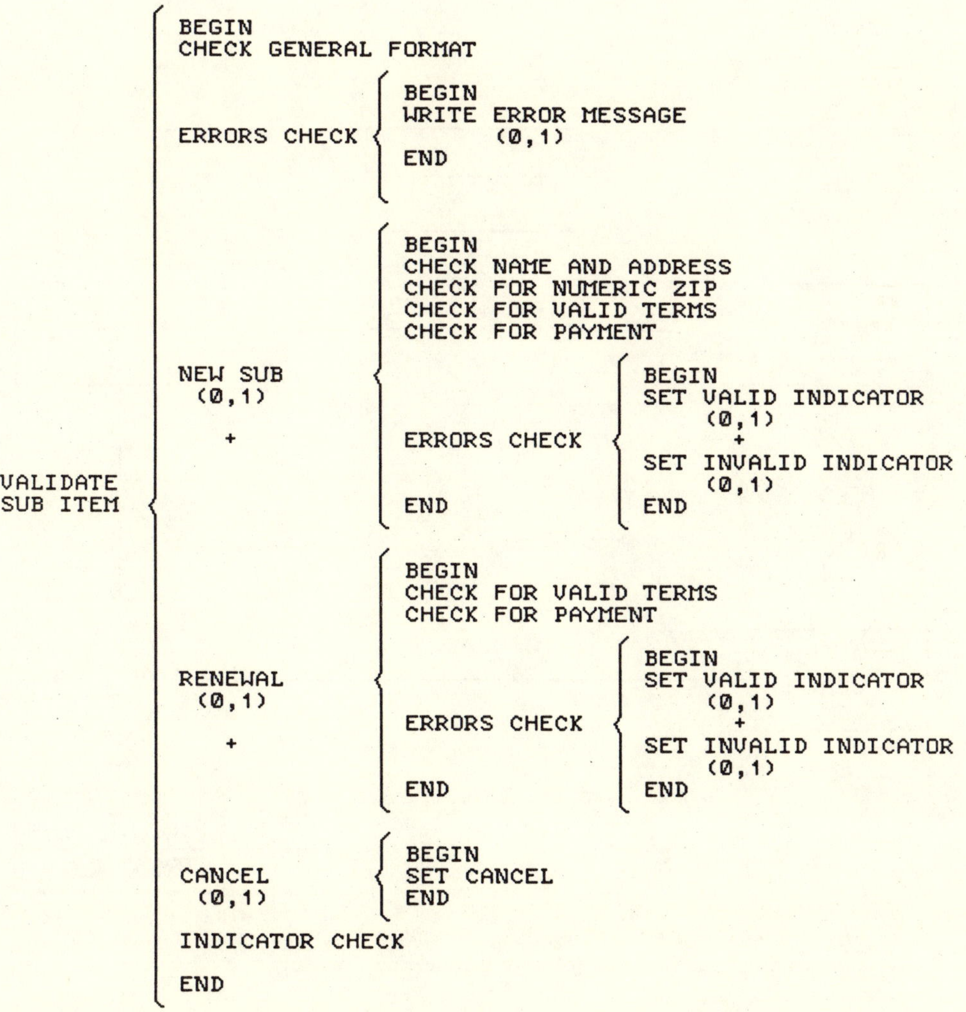

Figure 2.8 Warnier–Orr diagram produced by DESIGNAID from the Nastec Corporation.

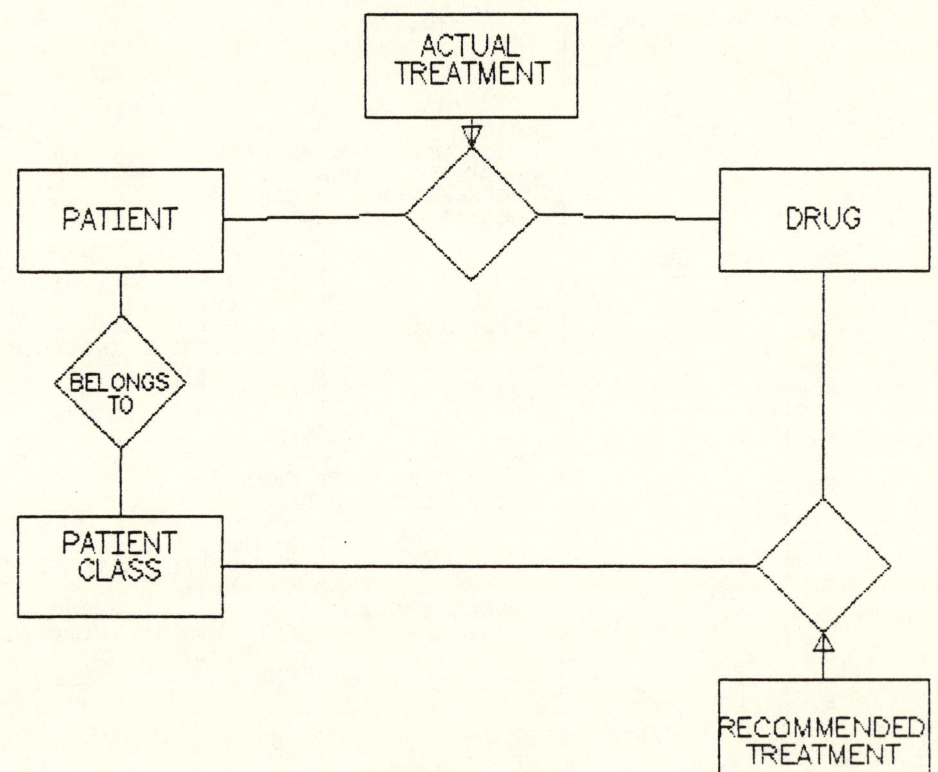

Figure 2.9 Entity relationship diagram produced by the ANALYST/DESIGNER TOOLKIT from the Yourdon Software Engineering Company.

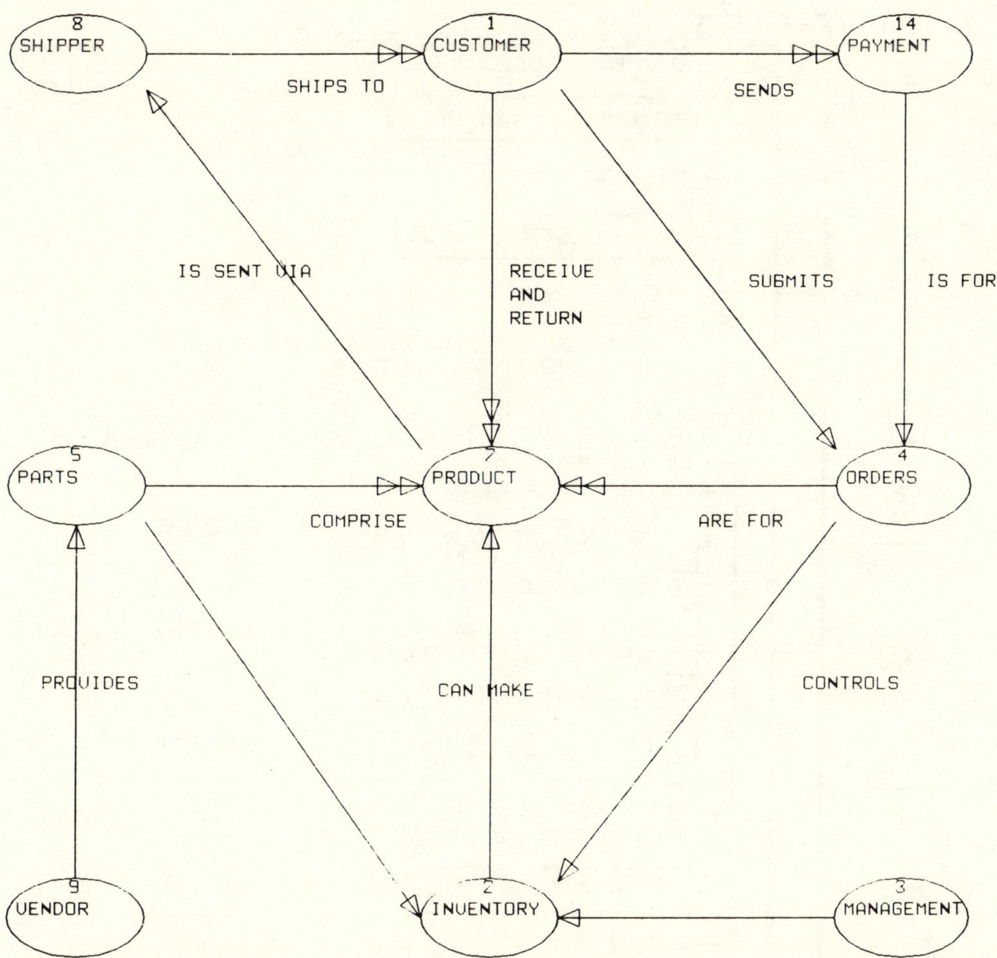

Figure 2.10 Data model diagram produced by EXCELERATOR from Index Technology Corporation.

MULTIPLE SYSTEM VIEWS

Diagramming techniques are used to give both a high-level and detailed view of a system (program). For example, structure charts give a high-level overview of a program. They can be used to explain in general terms what major functions the program performs and what data and procedural components make up the program. On the other hand, pseudocode and action diagrams can give an instruction-level view of a program (see Figure 2.11). They show where each program variable is initialized, tested or referenced in the program code.

A high-level and/or a detailed view of a program are important depending on the reader's purpose. If the reader is searching for a bug, detailed documen-

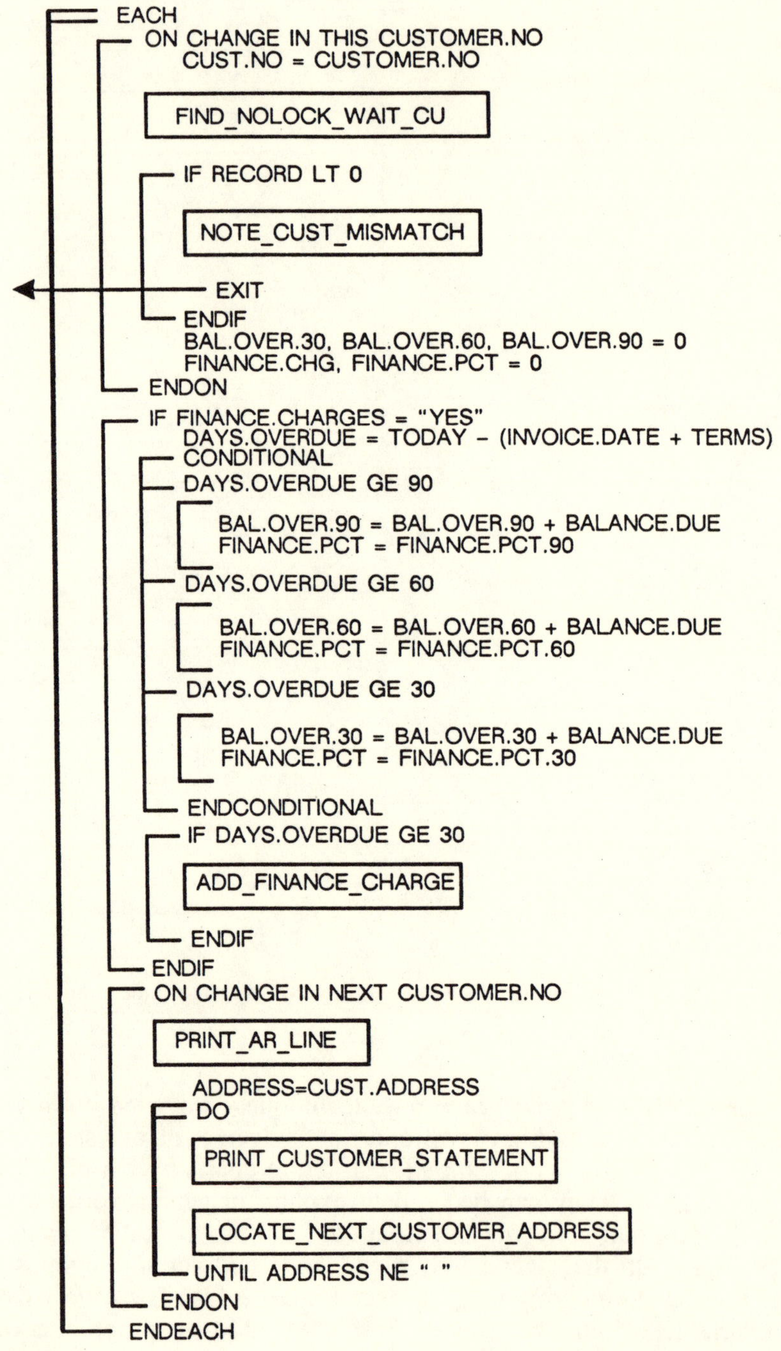

Figure 2.11 Action diagram using the BUILDER LANGUAGE from the Cortex Corporation.

tation may guide him or her to the exact location of the error. If the person wants to determine in which of several programs a certain function is performed, a high-level view may be the most helpful.

Different diagrams are better suited for high-level or detailed representation. For example, structure charts are well suited for high-level representation that introduces the program to its reader. But at a detailed level, structure charts can become too cluttered with boxes and errors to present program details clearly.

To represent a system fully with diagrams both a high-level and detailed process structure view and a high-level and detailed data structure view are necessary. The process (or system) structure view identifies the system process components and the relationships between them by showing data flow, control flow, and timing and sequence information. The data structure view describes data entities and their attributes and relationships among data entities. With the aid of both views, the developer can see how data are derived or used by the system processes and in the case of real-time systems, how external events (signals) cause the system to change states.

ESSENTIAL TRIO OF DIAGRAM TYPES

Although there are many different structured diagramming techniques in use, there is an essential trio of diagramming types that is needed to represent a software system [5, pp. 1–22]:

1. Data flow diagram: a friendly and familiar diagram used during analysis to define the problem components and to sketch a first, rough cut of program components and the data that pass among them
2. Data model diagram: a diagram used during the data modeling processing to represent the data records/entities and the logical associations among them
3. Tree structure diagram: a hierarchical diagram created during system/program design to define the overall architecture of a system/program by showing the program/modules and their relationship to one another

At minimum, a CASE workbench should provide the capability of automatically drawing and updating one version of each of these three types of diagrams. When representing real-time/embedded systems, other types of diagrams, such as control flow diagrams, decision trees, and finite-state diagrams, are needed to show control, timing, and sequence requirements.

AUTOMATED DIAGRAMMING

The problem with graphical representation is the time it takes to draw them and the time it takes to change them manually. Automation eliminates this problem. The less time spent drawing, the more productive the system developer can be.

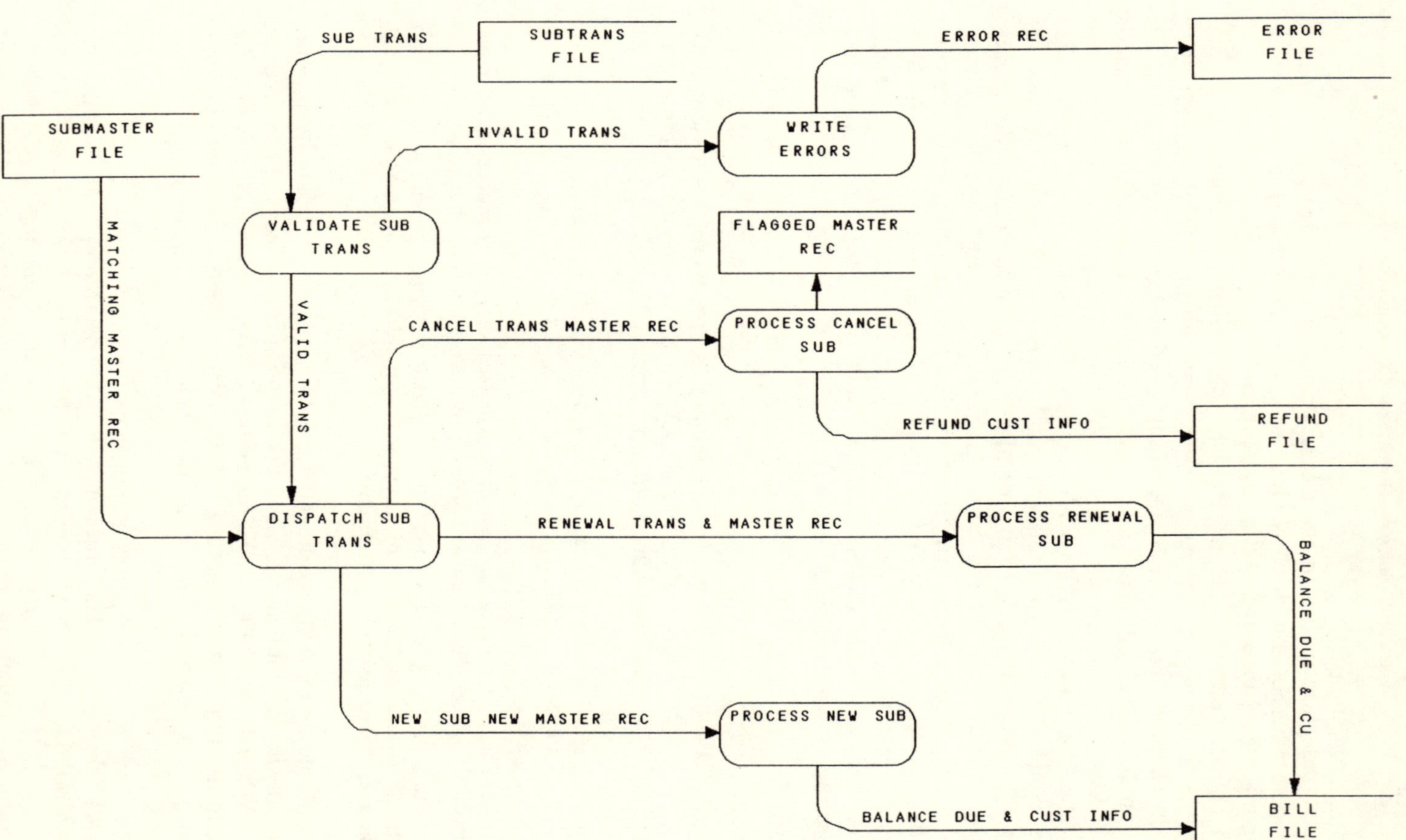

Figure 2.12 Data flow diagram drawn by the INFORMATION ENGINEERING WORKBENCH from KnowledgeWare. It is equivalent to the manually drawn data flow diagram shown in Figure 2.2.

Figure 2.12 shows the manually drawn data diagram in Figure 2.2 drawn automatically with a CASE workbench.

Interactive diagramming on a computer screen has several major advantages: It speeds up the process greatly; it enforces standards; it can automate the documentation process. Box 2.4 summarizes the advantages of automated structured diagramming tools.

BOX 2.4 Structured diagramming tool functions

Automatic structured diagramming tools provide the following important functions:

- An aid to clear thinking and problem solving
- Precise and recorded communication between members of the development team, users, and management
- Standardized representation of program architectural structure and data structure
- An aid to finding program bugs
- An aid to analyzing and understanding existing programs
- An aid to changing systems and programs (as they are being built and during maintenance)
- Fast development with computer-aided diagramming
- A mechanism enabling users to review program requirements and design specifications
- A mechanism for automatic program documentation production

When an analyst or programmer is creating procedures, he or she makes modifications to the design continually as ideas form. The analyst repeatedly refines the control structures, data structures, and logic; inserts new structures into existing ones; adds new condition tests; moves or duplicates processing logic; saves procedures for later use; and so on. To do this quickly and correctly, a computer is needed, as shown in Figure 2.13. The computer can guide each step of the design process and apply many types of checks. For example, is each variable defined in the repository? If so, is it being used properly? Some important questions to ask about the automatic drawing capability of a CASE workbench are listed in Box 2.5.

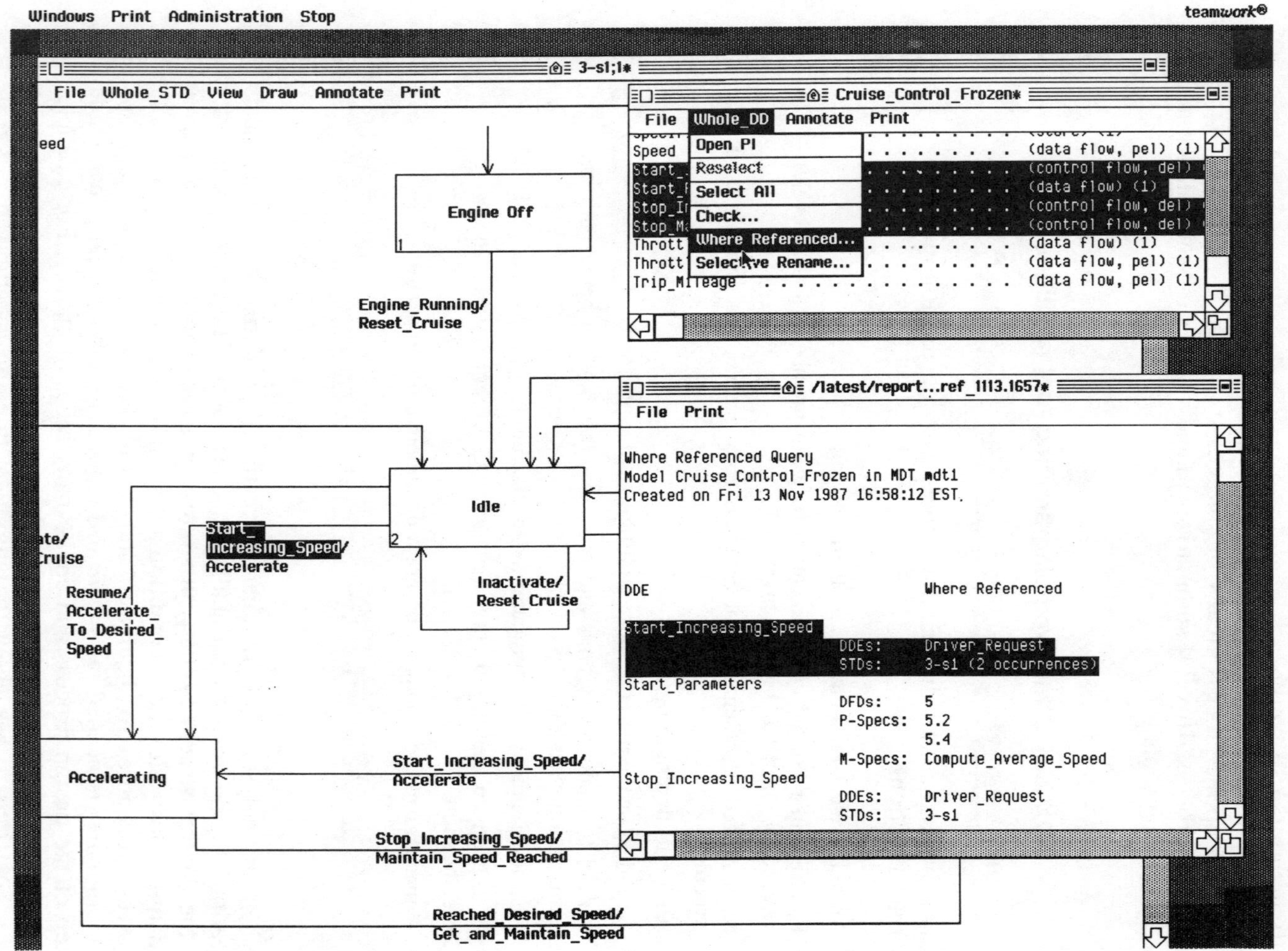

Figure 2.13 The multiple window capability provided by TEAMWORK from Cadre Technologies gives the user an opportunity to view many types of system information at the same time.

BOX 2.5 Automatic diagramming capabilities

- What types of diagrams can be drawn?
- Is it possible to create user-defined symbols?
- What are the limitations on diagram size and number of diagrams?
- How can the diagrams be manipulated on the workstation screen (MOVE, DELETE, COPY, CUT AND PASTE, ZOOM OUT, SUPPRESS DETAIL, LABEL OBJECT, CONNECT OBJECTS, etc.)?
- Is there color, what information does it add to the diagram, and can the user change the use of color?
- How easily can a diagram be saved and retrieved for later use?
- How quickly can a diagram be changed and redrawn?
- Can an object in a diagram be linked to another diagram that describes it in more detail? How many levels can be linked together?
- Each time a change is made to a diagram, are all related affected diagrams automatically changed?
- Can the user define new diagram types, their notation, and their syntax rules?
- Is there automatic conversion of one version of a diagram type to another?
- Can the user select one version of a diagram type to be the organization's standard?
- Are character graphics or bit-mapped graphics supported?
- Are windows and pop-down menus provided?
- How easily can textual information such as object labels and free-format commentary be added to the diagrams?
- Is the text editor loosely interfaced or fully integrated with the graphics editor?

BEYOND AUTOMATIC DRAFTING

For the most part, the questions listed in Box 2.5 are concerned with the graphics editing and text editing capabilities of a CASE workbench. Although this is an important element in increasing productivity, it is just the beginning. It is the first level of diagramming support. To increase productivity significantly the CASE workbench must go beyond automatic diagramming functions to the next level of diagramming support. At this level,

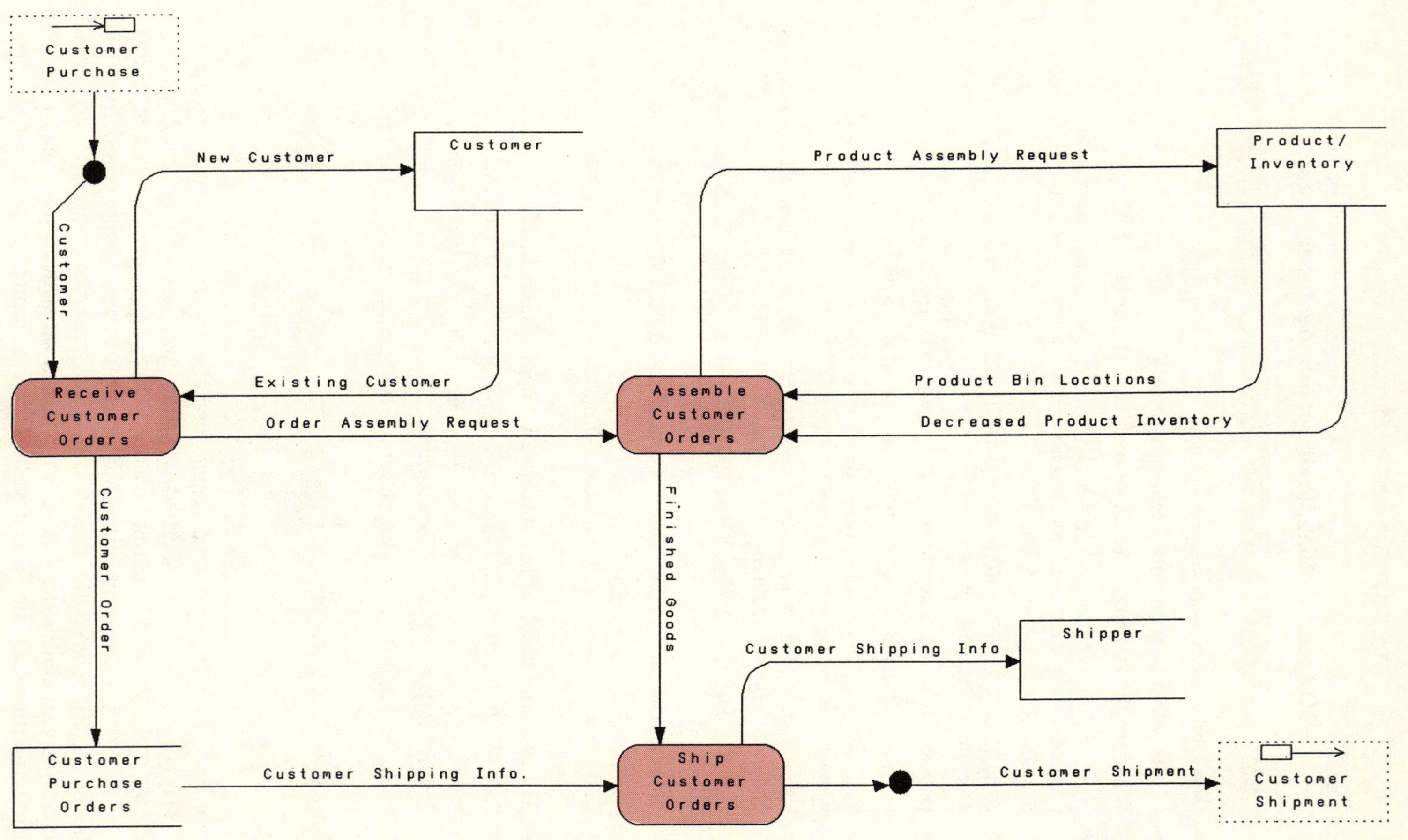

Figure 2.14 Data flow diagram for the Process Customer Orders program produced by the INFORMATION ENGINEERING WORKBENCH from KnowledgeWare.

diagrams are stored in an on-line repository and analyzed to detect errors, omissions, and inconsistencies.

To discover how much beyond simple automatic diagramming a particular CASE workbench goes, the first question to ask is: What, if anything, is represented by an object drawn on the computer screen? In other words, is there an underlying computational meaning associated with the graphics object that is understood and captured by the workbench? This is an important question for three reasons. First, when the meaning associated with the graphics is captured, the correctness and completeness of the diagrams can be checked more thoroughly. Some examples are included in the section entitled "Error Checking." Second, when the meaning of the graphics symbols is captured, the same information can be represented in different, but equivalent forms. For example, a data flow diagram can be *converted automatically* into a tree structure diagram (e.g., decomposition diagram) after the root is identified (see Figures 2.14 and 2.15). Or a tree structure diagram (e.g., structure chart) can be converted automatically to an action diagram [6] (see Figures 2.6 and 2.7). In both diagrams it is the same information; only the form in which the information is represented has been changed. In this way, the workbench can accommodate the preferences of different developers and can conform to the diagramming standards of different organizations. Third, when the meaning of the symbols is stored, information necessary for *automatically generating code* from the diagram is captured.

The second question to ask is: What, if anything, is stored when a diagram is drawn? Most workbench tools store the information that the diagram represents in some sort of CASE dictionary or repository. Each symbol, all its related information, its logical relationship to other symbols, and its meaning are stored in the CASE repository. This is essential to providing the capability of quickly changing and redrawing a diagram as well as automatically changing all the associated diagrams that are affected by the change. This powerful capability enables all associated diagrams to be updated automatically and kept in "sync" with each other. We know from past experience that this is a tedious, almost impossible task if done manually. It also gives the developer the ability to manage better all system-related information. The storage capability of a CASE workbench is discussed later in this chapter in the section entitled "CASE Information Repository."

The third question to ask is: What error checking of the diagrams is performed automatically? The diagrams must be complete and rigorous enough to be used as the primary source of information for code and database generation.

ERROR CHECKING

Error checking is one of the most important capabilities of CASE workbenches. Getting the errors out early is an excellent way of reducing software costs. Automating error checking helps developers find more errors earlier in the software life cycle. The quality of a software system depends on its specification, and the quality of a system

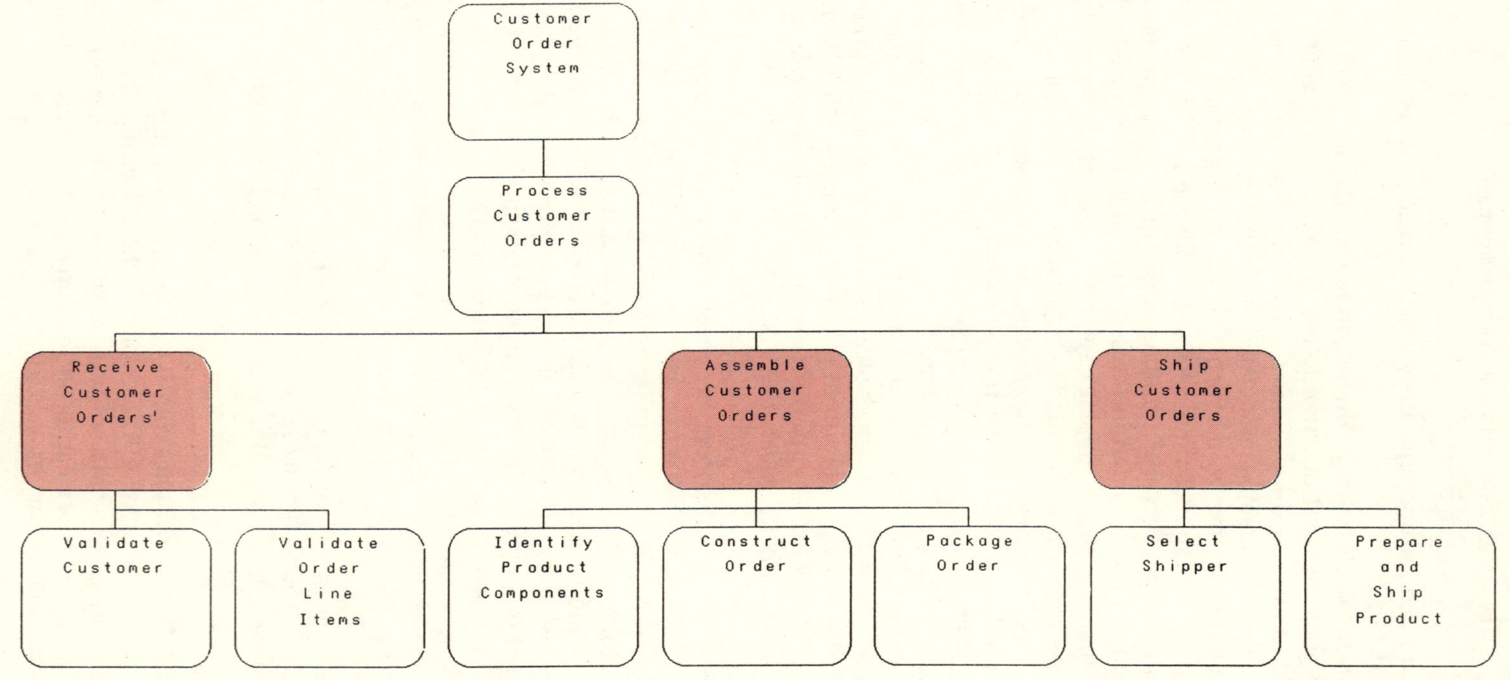

Figure 2.15 Decomposition diagram for the Process Customer Orders program produced by the INFORMATION ENGINEERING WORKBENCH from KnowledgeWare. The decomposition diagram was derived from the data flow diagram shown in Figure 2.14. Notice the three processes shown in red on the structure chart were derived from the three corresponding processes shown on the data flow diagram.

specification depends on its completeness and consistency. Box 2.6 lists five basic types of error checking for diagrammatic system specifications. Automatic error checking begins as soon as the developer starts drawing a structured diagram on the CASE workstation screen.

BOX 2.6 Types of error checking for structured diagrams

- Syntax and type checks
- Completeness and consistency checks
- Functional decomposition checks
- Cross-checking—consistency across all levels and views
- Requirements traceability checks

Syntax and Type Checking

The first type of checking is for *syntax and type errors*. As an example, consider the data flow diagram in Figure 2.16. One syntax rule for a data flow diagram is that each process bubble must have at least one data flow entering it and at least one data flow leaving it. Notice that ORDER ACCEPTANCE PROCEDURE in Figure 2.16 is incorrect because there is no data flow arrow entering it. Another example of a data flow diagram syntax rule is that two data stores cannot be directly connected. Notice that the data flow arrow connecting the INVENTORY FILE and the CUSTOMER FILE is incorrect.

Other types of structured diagrams, such as structure charts, entity relationship diagrams, and control flow diagrams, have syntax rules that also can be checked.

Type rules also govern the construction of structured diagrams. For example, in a data flow diagram, a process symbol must always be used to represent a procedural component (e.g., business function, a process task, a program module). Similarly, a data flow in a data flow diagram must represent a data component (e.g., a variable, a data record). Type rules are enforced to eliminate ambiguities that cause confusion when trying to understand a specification or to implement it into code.

Syntax and type checking are usually performed interactively when the diagram is being created at a CASE workstation. The purpose of interactive checking is to prevent the developer from entering incorrect, nonsensical information into the specification.

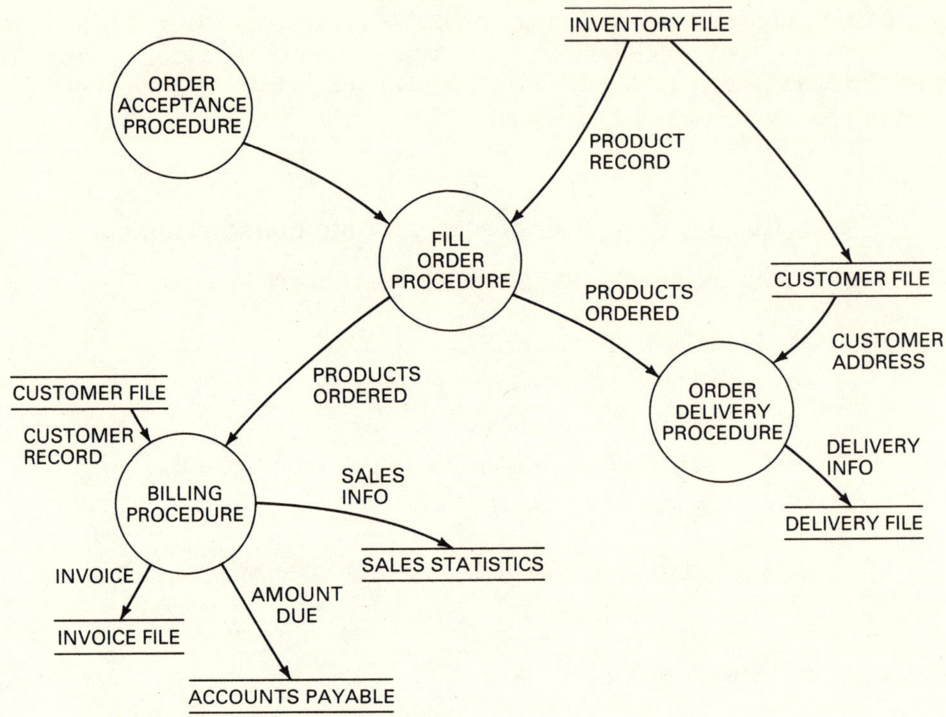

Figure 2.16 Data flow diagram showing the four subprocedures in the sales distribution system.

Completeness and Consistency Checking

The second type of checking is *completeness and consistency checking* for a diagram. As its name suggests, the purpose of completeness and consistency checking is to assure that a diagram has been completed and contains all the necessary information. This type of checking is user controlled and is normally activated when the user has completed drawing a diagram and requests that automatic completeness and consistency checks be applied against the diagram before it becomes part of the system specification.

Again, consider the data flow diagram in Figure 2.16. In a completed data flow diagram all the data flow arrows between processes are labeled with the data that are passed between processes. Notice that this data flow diagram is not complete because the data flow arrow between ORDER ACCEPTANCE PROCEDURE and FILL ORDER PROCEDURE is not labeled. Another rule for a completed data flow diagram is that there must be at least one data flow into and one data flow out of each process bubble. This data flow diagram is not complete because there is no data flow into the ORDER ACCEPTANCE PROCEDURE.

Completeness checking should go beyond simply checking that the entire diagram has been labeled properly. It should also check that a completed definition for each object in the diagram exists in the CASE repository, and that this definition is consistent with any previous information stored about that object.

As an example of completeness checking for a hierarchical tree structure diagram, consider the structure chart shown in Figure 2.17. This structure chart is not complete because the data couple arrow between REMOVE PATIENT and UPDATE PATIENT CAUSE OF REMOVAL has not been labeled.

Completeness and consistency checking can be applied against any type of diagram (e.g., control flow diagrams, entity relationship diagrams) that the developer creates with the CASE workbench.

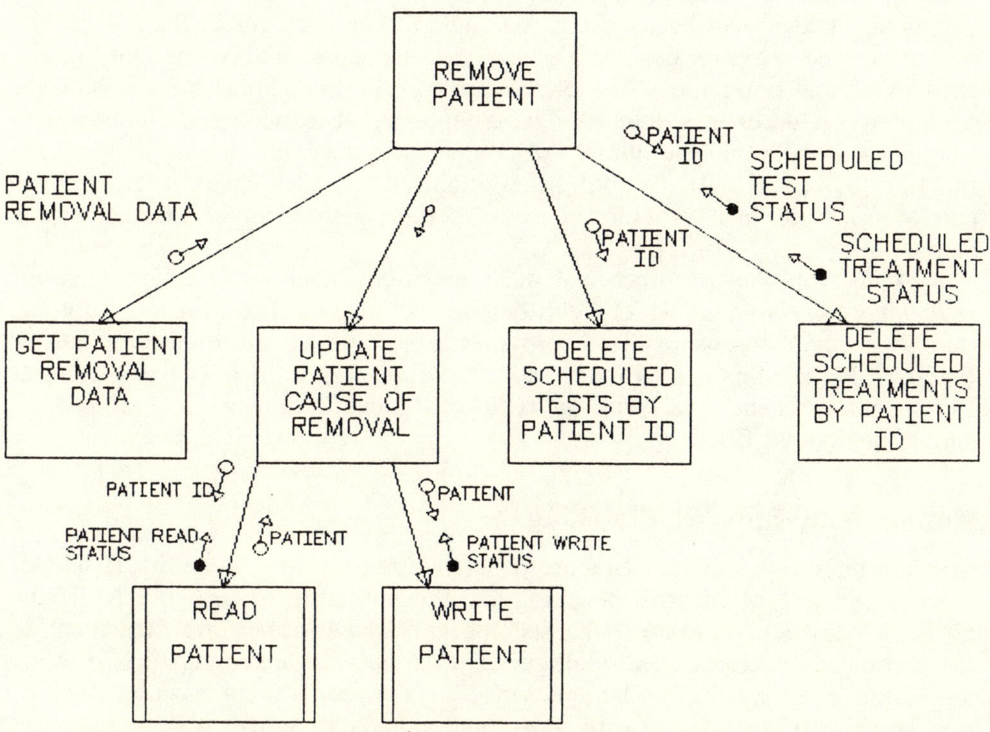

Figure 2.17 Structure chart produced by the ANALYST/DESIGNER TOOLKIT from the Yourdon Software Engineering Company.

Functional Decomposition Checking

The next type of diagram checking is concerned with *hierarchical tree structure diagrams,* which are a form of functional decomposition. The tree structure diagram consists of a set of hierarchically ordered functional components. Components performing high-level functions are placed at the upper levels of the hierarchy, while components performing lower-level, more detailed functions appear at the lower levels. Looking down the hierarchy, the components at each successive level contain functions that further define (refine) functions residing at the preceding level.

Structured methodologies contain rules for functional decomposition. For example, the Yourdon structured design methodology allows a functional component to be decomposed (i.e., to fan out) into at most seven subfunctions [7, pp. 148–170]. Also, strict structured programming does not allow a function to invoke itself [8, pp. 45–65].

Functional decomposition checks are a form of quality control checking that can be performed on tree structure diagrams. Complexity analysis is another example of quality control checking for tree structure diagrams. The McCabe complexity metric can be used for quantitative measurement of the complexity of a structured program design. To lie within the acceptable complexity range, each functional component in the tree structure diagram must have a McCabe complexity value of less than 10. The complexity of a functional component is calculated by counting the number of compares in the logic that implements the function [8, pp. 67–82]. Counting the number of couples passed between each pair of functions in a structure chart is another method for calculating design complexity [8, pp. 67–82].

A special kind of functional decomposition checking is called *semantic refinement checking,* in which each decomposition of a function into subfunctions is checked to ensure that it provides more detailed information about the function. For example, if at one level a function is described as performing an I/O operation, at the next level, the type of I/O operation (e.g., a read or write) should be defined [9].

Methodology-Specific Checking

The first three types of checking are concerned with errors in one diagram. This is the simplest type of error checking and the minimum to be expected from a CASE workbench. However, the specific checks performed are dependent on the particular structured methodology(ies) that the workbench supports. For example, different checks can be performed on Yourdon structure charts, Jackson tree structure diagrams, Warnier–Orr diagrams, and Martin action diagrams. Although they are all types of hierarchical tree structure diagrams, they belong to different structured methodologies, have different syntax rules, and have different quality assurance checks. Similarly, DeMarco data flow diagrams, Gane–Sarson data flow diagrams, Martin dependency diagrams, and Ward–Mellor control flow diagrams have different syntax rules, although they are all forms of the basic data flow diagram.

Checking Across a Family of Diagrams

Structured methodologies support a top-down development approach in which a design is created by beginning with a general overview of the system and progressing to finer and finer levels of detail. Each level is represented by a diagram (or set of diagrams), and all levels are linked to support these "explosions" of detail. For example, when the developer wants to see a more detailed view of a process in a data flow diagram, he can "explode" it into the next level of detail, which may be represented by a data flow diagram, structure chart, action diagram, pseudocode (minispec), or source code (see Figures 2.18 through 2.20). A data store, a data flow, or a data couple can be exploded into a data model diagram, a record layout, or a dictionary entry.

The fourth type of diagram checking is concerned not with just one diagram but with a *family* of diagrams related by explosions. One example of a family of diagrams is a set of leveled or layered data flow diagrams in which successive levels describe processes in greater and greater detail. Figure 2.16 identifies the ORDER ACCEPTANCE PROCEDURE as a process in the SALES DISTRIBUTION SYSTEM. Figure 2.21 shows in detail what happens inside the ORDER ACCEPTANCE PROCEDURE, and Figure 2.22 shows in detail VALIDATE CUSTOMER, which is one of five processes inside the ORDER ACCEPTANCE PROCEDURE.

Consistency checking across a family of diagrams checks that information is consistent from layer to layer. Consistency checking is also called *balancing* or *conservation analysis*.

For example, if at the first layer (Figure 2.16) the CUSTOMER ORDER FILE is required input into the ORDER ACCEPTANCE PROCEDURE, for the two views to be consistent, the file must also appear as required input at the next layer (Figure 2.21). As another example of consistency, if CUSTOMER RECORD is a data flow in Figures 2.21 and 2.22, it cannot also be used as the name of a procedure in the data flow diagram in Figure 2.22.

Consistency and completeness checking can deal with all related diagrams for a system or program or some subset as designated by the developer. Consistency and completeness checking is done at the request of the workbench user, who specifies the scope of checking to be done.

Checking consistency and completeness across a family of diagrams eliminates ambiguities that make it possible to use this information as the primary source for automatic code generation or for project team communication purposes. This type of checking can be the most helpful in finding the more subtle and also the more expensive specification errors.

Requirements Traceability Checking

Requirements traceability is a method of demonstrating that the software system produced satisfies user requirements. Usually, this is demonstrated in steps by

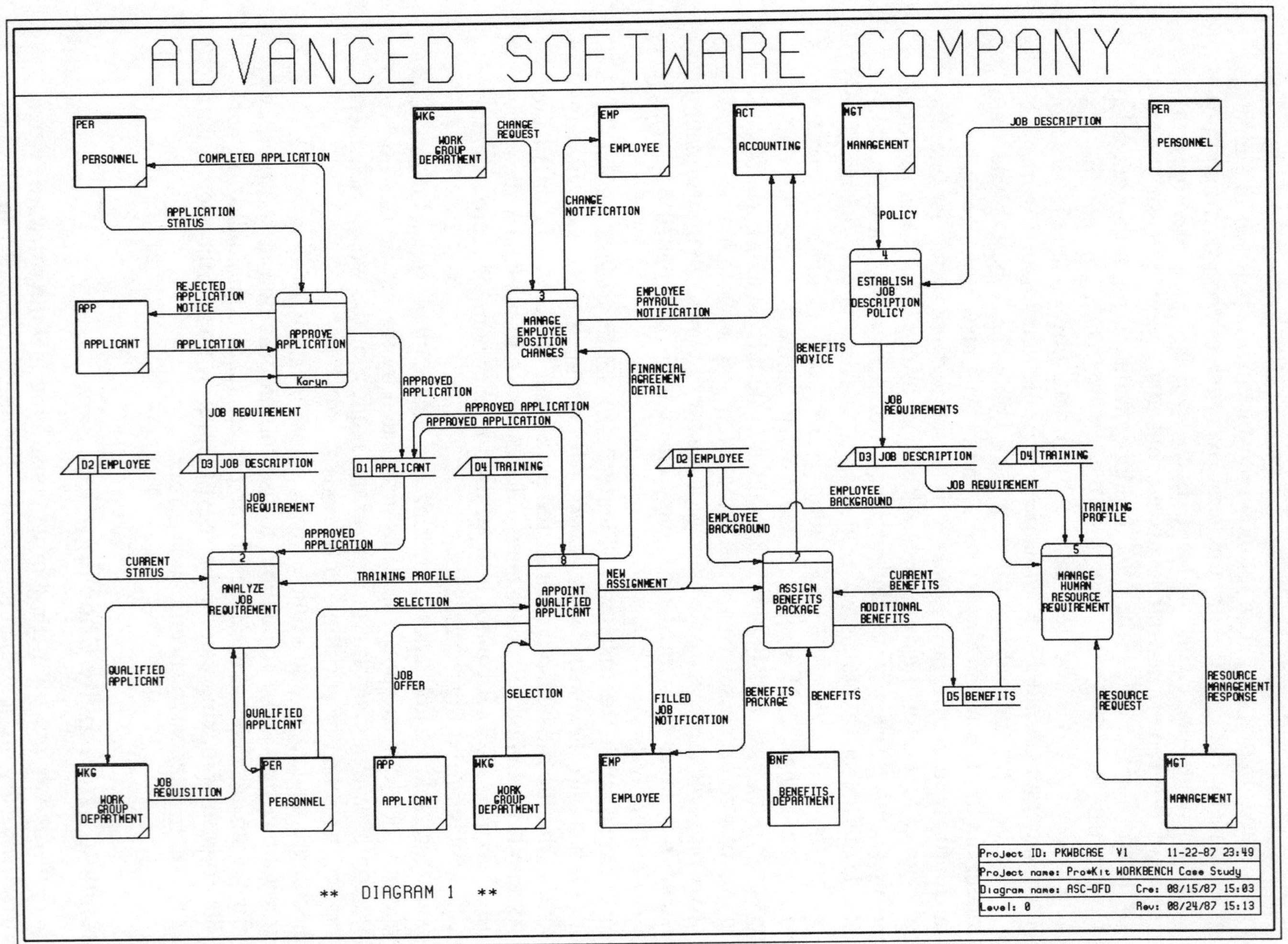

Figure 2.18 Data flow diagram for the Advanced Software Company System produced by PROKIT*WORKBENCH from the McDonnell-Douglas Company.

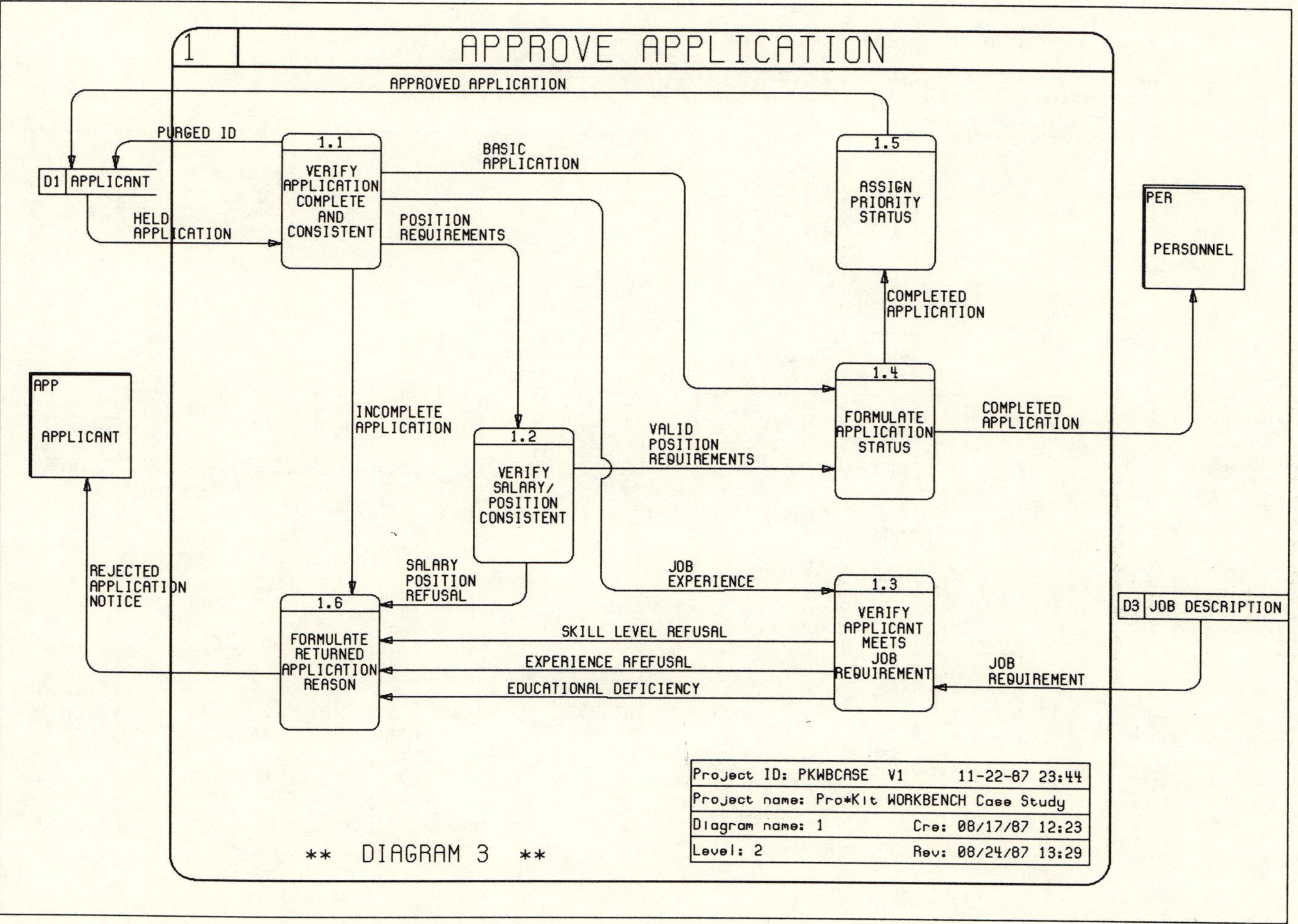

Figure 2.19 Data flow diagram of the exploded process Approve Application defined in the data flow diagram in Figure 2.18. It is produced by PROKIT*WORKBENCH from the McDonnell-Douglas Corporation.

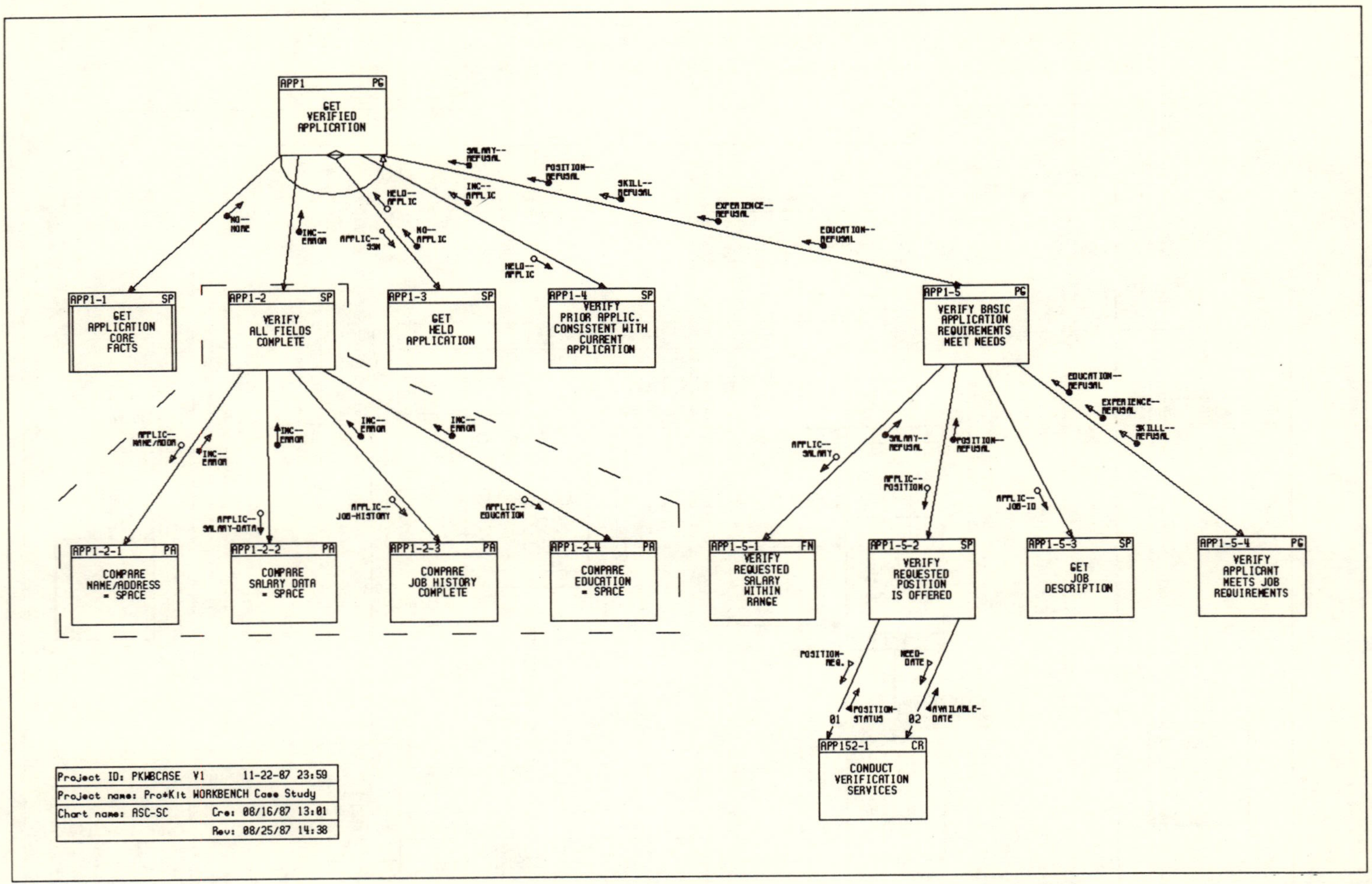

Figure 2.20 Structure chart for the Approve Application process shown in Figure 2.19 produced by PROKIT*WORKBENCH from the McDonnell-Douglas Corporation. The three diagrams shown in Figures 2.18 through 2.20 are members of a family of related diagrams for the Advanced Software Company System.

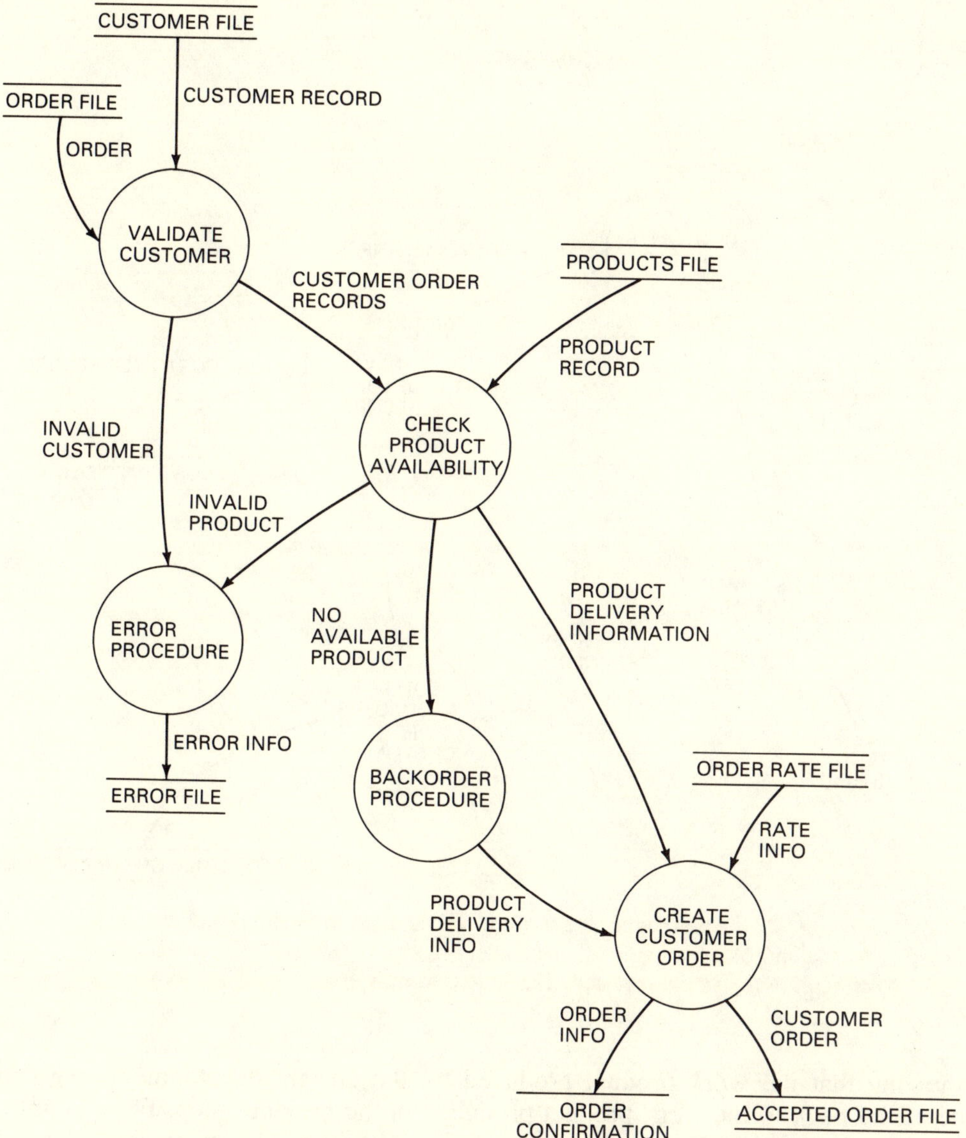

Figure 2.21 A data flow diagram for the ORDER ACCEPTANCE PROCEDURE shows the data flow and processes performed to handle customer orders.

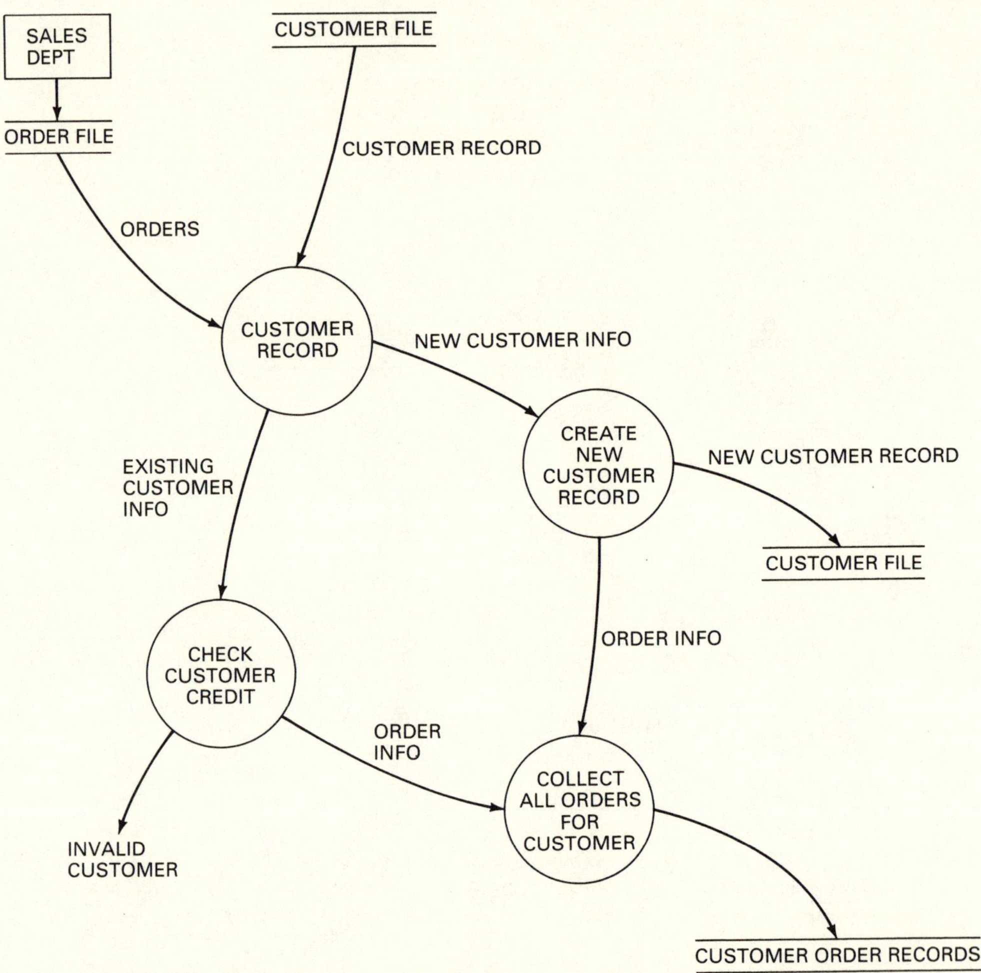

Figure 2.22 An expanded view of the VALIDATE CUSTOMER procedure shows four subprocedures: GET CUSTOMER RECORD, CREATE NEW CUSTOMER RECORD, CHECK CUSTOMER CREDIT, and COLLECT ALL ORDERS FOR CUSTOMER.

showing that the work product produced by the current development step can be traced back to the work product produced in the previous step. For example, from the design specification we can trace back to the requirements specification or from the source code to the design specification. One type of requirements traceability at the code-back-to-design level is shown by automatically creating a structure chart from the source code and comparing it to the structure chart created during the design phase. Any differences between the two structure charts will be noted and must be reconciled to show why the source codes does not match the design. This technique can help identify missing requirements, unimplemented requirements, unused input and code.

In this way we can validate that the code produced from a set of design specifications, which in turn were derived from the requirements specifications, satisfies a particular requirement. Then, when testing a system or changing a requirement, the developer can easily pinpoint exactly which portions of the system should be studied.

In its DOD Standard 2167, the Department of Defense has mandated that requirements traceability documentation is a critical and required component when developing mission critical defense systems. However, it should be considered a critical component in any system development project since the ability to trace the correspondence between requirements and the derived code and data structures is necessary and invaluable to a thorough system validation effort. Requirements traceability is a method to ensure that not only is a software system correct, but it is also complete. It gives a path from requirements to code that the developer can trace in either direction.

Error Reporting

Diagram checking includes a reporting function. The developer can request either on-line or off-line reports listing all five types of errors. Cross-reference reports and requirements traceability documentation are also available to show in which diagrams each procedural component and data component is included. Figures 2.23 through 2.26 show examples of error checking reports.

CASE INFORMATION REPOSITORY

Although not as visually impressive as the graphics capabilities, the information repository is the real heart of a CASE workbench. It is a basis for:

- CASE tools integration
- System specification consistency and integrity controls
- System information sharing
- Documentation standardization
- System documentation generation
- Code generation
- Software reusability
- Project management and control

The CASE repository is a mechanism for storing and organizing all information concerning a software system, including planning, analysis, design, implementation, and project management information. A key to high productivity

IEW® Case Study Connectivity Analysis
(excerpted from longer report)

```
Information Engineering Workbench Report
Connectivity Analysis Report
April 29, 1986   2:19:26


Data Flow Assembled Order

    Location
        Activity Assemble Customer Orders

    Immediate Source
        Activity Prod. Construct. & Order Assemb.
        in context of Activity Assemble Customer Orders

    Immediate Destination
        Activity Package Order
        in context of Activity Assemble Customer Orders


    The data flow has no unconnected ends

Data Flow BO Order Assembly Request

    Location
        Activity Assemble Customer Orders
        in context of Activity Process Customer Orders

    Immediate Source
        Activity Process Backorders
        in context of Activity Process Customer Orders

    Immediate Destination
        Activity Assemble Customer Orders


    The data flow has no unconnected ends

Data Flow BO Order Assembly Request

    Location
        Activity Assemble Customer Orders

    Immediate Source
        Internal Junction in
            Activity Assemble Customer Orders

    Immediate Destination
        Activity Prod. Construct. & Order Assemb.
        in context of Activity Assemble Customer Orders


    The data flow has no unconnected ends
```


Figure 2.23 The Connectivity Analysis Report produced by the INFORMATION ENGINEERING WORKBENCH from KnowledgeWare lists syntax errors in data flow diagrams.

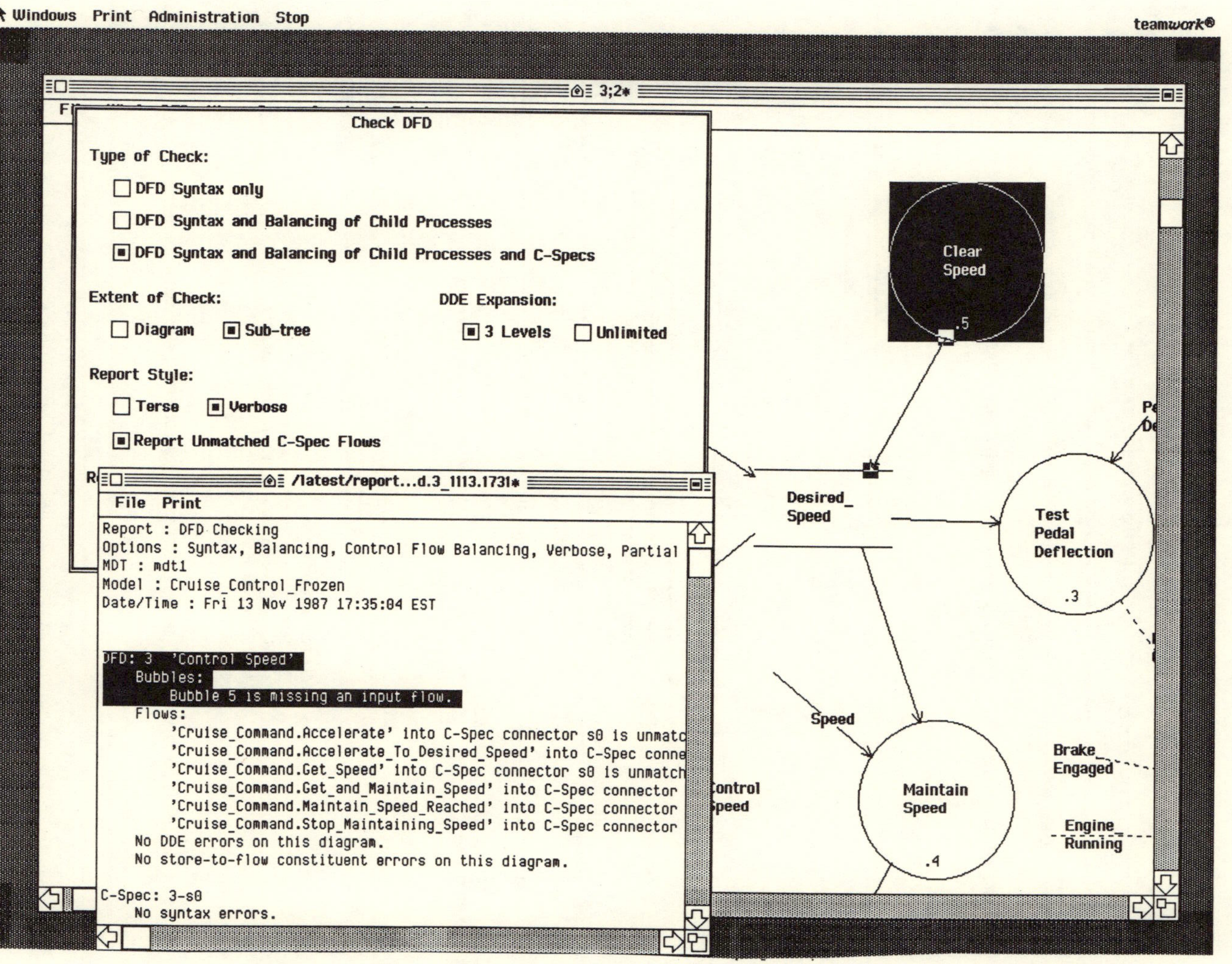

Figure 2.24 TEAMWORK from Cadre Technologies reports syntax, balancing, and missing information errors in data flow and control flow diagrams.

```
                                          ANALYST Case Study                          ANAR2I01, PAGE    1
ID:          VERSION: 6                                                              06/03/86,  13:30:37
                                   DATA ELEMENT INCOMPLETE DEFINITIONS

=========================================================================================================

------DATA ELEMENT NAME-------    ----------------------DATA ELEMENT DESCRIPTION----------------------

                                                                                    DATA ELEMENT TYPE: C
CUSTOMER ADDRESS                  This includes the customer street address, city, state and     SIZE: 0090
                                  zip code.                                                  DECIMALS: 0
                                                                                                CLASS: _
                                                                                               UNIQUE: _

                                  ----------------------DATA ELEMENT EDIT RULES------------------------  ---DATA ELEMENT OWNER----

                                  No editing required.                                  William H. Threlkeld

                                                                                        (222) 222-2222


                                  -------------------DATA ELEMENT DERIVATION RULES--------------------

                                  ---------------------------------------------------------------------
                                  ---------------------------------------------------------------------
                                  ---------------------------------------------------------------------
                                  ---------------------------------------------------------------------
=========================================================================================================

------DATA ELEMENT NAME-------    ----------------------DATA ELEMENT DESCRIPTION----------------------

                                                                                    DATA ELEMENT TYPE: N
PART NO                           The PART NO is used to identify the equipment or service       SIZE: 0007
                                  requested by the customer.                                 DECIMALS: 0
                                                                                                CLASS: _
                                                                                               UNIQUE: Y

                                  ----------------------DATA ELEMENT EDIT RULES------------------------  ---DATA ELEMENT OWNER----

                                  The PART NO consists of a base number and a check digit.     -----------------------
                                  The check digit will occupy the units position of the
                                  number.  The check digit will be calculated using the        (___) ___-____
                                  modulus 10 remainder method.

*** NOT CONTAINED IN ANY DATA STRUCTURE, DATA FLOW, DATA STORE AND NOT DERIVED BY ANY PROCESS.

=========================================================================================================
```

Figure 2.25 PROKIT*WORKBENCH from McDonnell-Douglas reports errors such as incomplete process and data element definitions.

```
-----------------------------------------------------------------

                         FACT SHEET
                 UNDEFINED DICTIONARY ENTRIES
                 ============================
08/06/86                                                13:17:13


ALLOW SETUP
AUTO
BIN
CHANNEL
CLOCK PULSE
CURRENT FORMAT
CURRENT LOGIC STATE
CURSOR POSITION
DESIRED TRIGGER WORD
DISPLAY STATES
DOWNARROW
ENABLE/ DISABLE
ENABLE/DISABLE (LOGIC ACQUISITION PROCESSOR)
HEX
LEFT ARROW
LEVEL
LIST
LOGIC ACQUISITION COMPLETE
LOGIC STATE DISPLAY
LOGIC STATES
MANUAL
MATCH LEVEL
MENU
RIGHT ARROW
SET TIMER
SETUP PARAMETERS
START AUTO
START MANUAL
STOP
TIMER EXPIRED
TRIGGER
TRIGGER STATE
TRIGGER WORD CONTEXT
TRIGGER WORD DISPLAY
TRIGGER WORD FOUND
TRIGGER WORD NOT FOUND
UPARROW
WINDOW
```

Figure 2.26 The ANALYST/DESIGNER TOOLKIT from Yourdon Software Engineering reports undefined repository entries.

is getting information to developers when it is needed and in a form that is directly useful.

Alternatively, the CASE repository is referred to as a design dictionary, database, object-oriented database, knowledge base, or encyclopedia. However, regardless of what it is called, its basic purpose is the same—it serves as a single place in which all system information can be entered once, kept consistent, and be made available to everyone needing it. It is also important to note that the repository is a much broader concept than a mere data dictionary since the repository stores more types of system information, the relationships among the various information components, and the rules for using or processing the components.

The CASE repository performs the functions of storing, accessing, updating, analyzing, and reporting on system information. From the information perspective, the primary function of CASE workbench tools is to manage system information. They capture analysis and design specification information; they control and analyze specification information; and they transform specification information into program code and documentation; they support project management and maintenance functions. In a CASE workbench, it is the repository that is primarily responsible for managing system information (technical and project management). In effect, it holds all information needed to create, modify, evolve, and maintain a software system. This includes information on:

- Problem to be solved
- Problem domain
- Emerging solution system
- Software process (methodology) being followed
- Project resources and history
- Organizational context

Repository Contents

As shown in Figure 2.27, structured diagrams, screen and menu definitions, report layouts, record descriptions, process logic, data models, organization models, process models, source code, business rules, project management

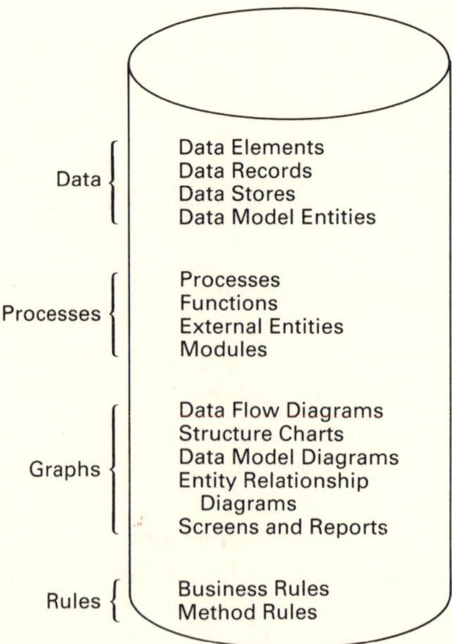

Figure 2.27 The CASE repository is the real heart of the CASE workbench. It contains all system information, including technical information, project management information, and relationships among the various system components.

forms, data elements as well as relationships between system information components are examples of information objects that can be stored in the CASE repository. It is not unusual for a repository to maintain over 100 types of objects and relationships.

Each information object stored in the repository is described in terms of its properties, namely:

- ID
- Alias names
- Type
- Narrative description
- Component parts
- File where stored
- Range values
- Edit and derivation rules

Also, each object's relationship to other system objects and audit information are stored in the repository. For example, relationship information includes all layers of explosions for an object, all objects in which this object is used, and cross-references. Audit information is concerned with ownership identification and change control rules for an object. For example, audit information includes:

- Who created the object
- Project in which the object was created
- When the object was created
- When the object was last updated
- Version number
- Whether the object can be updated

Repository contents grow over time as more system information is stored. As more information is stored, less new information is needed to build new systems since much of the project management information, organization models, data models, data entities, and even some process models may be similar across applications within the same organization or across an application domain.

Repository Reports

The CASE repository automatically tracks and maintains all stored information. A set of standard reports is provided as a quick view of the contents of the repository. Both on-line and off-line reports, as well as preformatted reports, custom reports, and ad hoc queries, are provided. For example, information such as where each data element is used in the system, who created it, and when and how many times its definition has been revised are all at the developers' fingertips in cross-reference reports. The basic types of repository reports include:

- Contents/lists reports
- Cross-reference/where-used reports
- Analysis reports
- Explosion reports

Box 2.7 lists examples of each type of repository report. CASE workbench reports are available at the developers' workstation or at the mainframe host level. Figures 2.28 through 2.30 give examples of repository reports.

BOX 2.7 Examples of types of case information repository reports

Contents/Lists Report Examples

- Description of a data flow, including its component parts
- Description of all couples at an interface in a structure chart
- List of inputs and outputs for each process in a data flow diagram and highlights for data elements derived or updated by a process
- List of all system objects changed after a certain date
- History of all changes made to an object
- Description of a module, including its description, parameters, and database/file access profiles
- Test plan for a particular module, subfunction, or program
- List of all data entities and their attributes, plus relationships and business rules for a given data model

Cross-Reference/Where-Used Examples

- All data flow diagrams in which a process appears
- All modules invoked by a module and all modules that invoke that module

BOX 2.7 *(Continued)*

- All objects in repository for which a certain developer has responsibility
- All diagrams in which a data entity is referenced
- Path tracing the course of data from source to destination in a family of leveled data flow diagrams
- For a given process, all the entities that support it and organizational units that perform it

Analysis Report Examples

- Level-to-level balancing in a family of data flow diagrams
- All undefined information objects in a system
- Incomplete data flow diagrams, decomposition diagrams, entity relationship diagrams, and so on
- Complexity analysis of a structure chart/program design
- Object naming, type, or description inconsistencies across diagrams and repository contents
- Unused objects
- Consistency analysis, noting absence of relationship between two objects whose parents are related
- Impact of deleting an object
- Horizontal balance of process outputs from inputs and derivations

Explosion Report Examples

- Hierarchical table of an object and all its lower-level explosions

Information Management

Automatic management of all system information is the primary reason for storing it on the computer and is one of the primary benefits that the CASE workbench offers to the software developer. It is impossible to maintain the integrity of system information with using informal, manual methods—especially in a project team environment. To enable developers to share system information in a secure and orderly manner, a formal, automated information management facility is needed.

IEW® Data Flow Conservation Analysis (example)

```
Information Engineering Workbench Report
Data Conservation Analysis
April 29, 1986    2:28:21                                    Page 1


Activity Package Order
in context of Activity Assemble Customer Orders

     Incoming data flows
          Data Flow Assembled Order
          Data Flow Packaging Materials

     Outgoing data flows
          Data Flow Finished Goods
          Data Flow Decreased Packing Materials

     Data Conservation Failure
          Outgoing Data Flow Finished Goods involves
          Entity Type Customer PO
          not involved in Composite Sequential Process Package Order

     Data Conservation Failure
          Incoming Data Flow Assembled Order involves
          Entity Type Customer PO
          not involved in Composite Sequential Process Package Order

     Data Conservation Failure
          Outgoing Data Flow Finished Goods involves
          Entity Type Customer PO Line Item
          not involved in Composite Sequential Process Package Order

     Data Conservation Failure
          Incoming Data Flow Assembled Order involves
          Entity Type Customer PO Line Item
          not involved in Composite Sequential Process Package Order

     Data Conservation Failure
          Outgoing Data Flow Finished Goods involves
          Attribute Type Customer PO Expected Delivery Dt of
               Entity Type Customer PO
          not involved in Composite Sequential Process Package Order

     Data Conservation Failure
          Outgoing Data Flow Finished Goods involves
          Attribute Type Customer PO Delivery Address of
               Entity Type Customer PO
          not involved in Composite Sequential Process Package Order

     Data Conservation Failure
          Outgoing Data Flow Finished Goods involves
          Attribute Type Customer PO # of
               Entity Type Customer PO
          not involved in Composite Sequential Process Package Order
```


Figure 2.28 The Data Flow Conservation Analysis Report produced by the INFORMATION ENGINEERING WORKBENCH from KnowledgeWare provides detailed information about data flows in a data flow diagram.

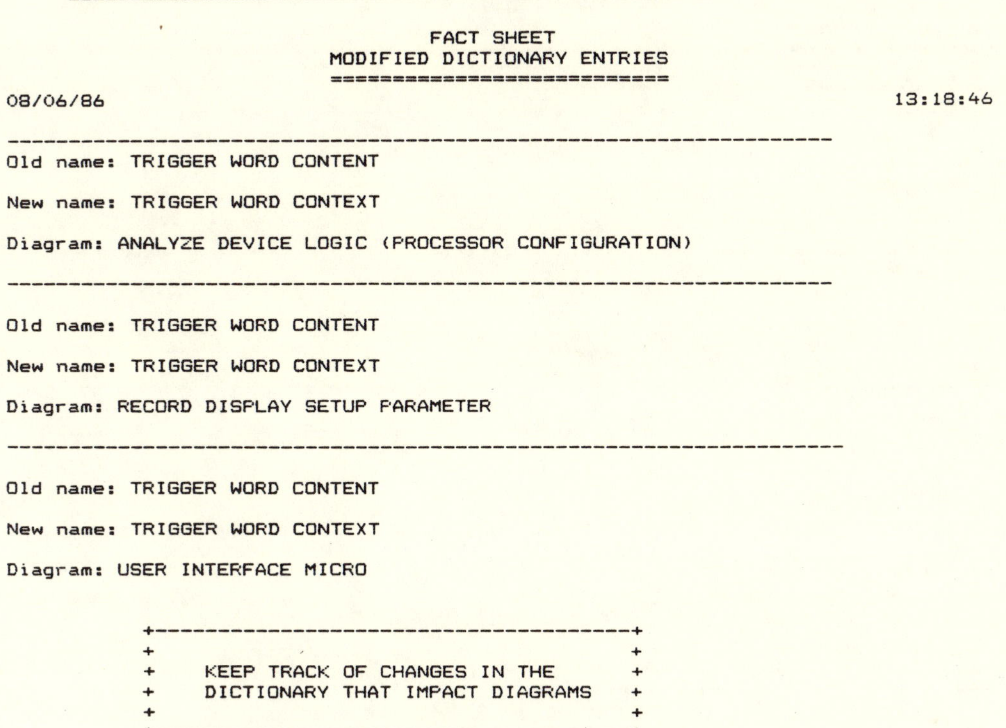

```
Fact Sheet
------------------------------------------------------------------------------

                          FACT SHEET
                  MODIFIED DICTIONARY ENTRIES
                  ===========================
08/06/86                                                              13:18:46

------------------------------------------------------------------------
Old name: TRIGGER WORD CONTENT

New name: TRIGGER WORD CONTEXT

Diagram: ANALYZE DEVICE LOGIC (PROCESSOR CONFIGURATION)

------------------------------------------------------------------------

Old name: TRIGGER WORD CONTENT

New name: TRIGGER WORD CONTEXT

Diagram: RECORD DISPLAY SETUP PARAMETER

------------------------------------------------------------------------

Old name: TRIGGER WORD CONTENT

New name: TRIGGER WORD CONTEXT

Diagram: USER INTERFACE MICRO

          +----------------------------------------+
          +                                        +
          +    KEEP TRACK OF CHANGES IN THE        +
          +    DICTIONARY THAT IMPACT DIAGRAMS     +
          +                                        +
          +----------------------------------------+
```

Figure 2.29 The ANALYST/DESIGNER TOOLKIT from Yourdon Software Engineering reports on modifications made to the contents of its CASE repository.

The information management facility of the CASE repository provides:

- *Security controls* in the form of passwords to limit access to the contents (or selected portions of the contents) of the repository
- *Access privileges* enabling the assignment to individual developers of read-only or full-update privileges
- *Version controls* to track the evolution and history of a system and to allow multiple current versions, such as production, test, and individual developer working sets
- *Multiuser access* to allow multiple developers to access the same repository information concurrently but not to attempt to update the same information concurrently
- *Change control* to track changes automatically and to incorporate changes automatically throughout the repository

```
VERSION        :1                         ProKit*WORKBENCH CASE STUDY                              PAGE        1
USER ID        :SYSTEM                 DATA ELEMENT CROSS-REFERENCE REPORT                         DATE:11/04/87
WORKSTATION ID:MASTER              COMPLETE CROSS-REFERENCE OF ALL DATA ELEMENTS                   TIME:15:11:47
MACRO NAME     :A.EH.DE.XREF
==============================================================================================================
                                    SHORT     DATA     LENGTH/   STORAGE
------DATA ELEMENT NAME-------   --NAME--  --TYPE--  PRECISION  --SIZE-
ADDITIONAL-BENEFIT-CODE                    CHARACTE         3        3

-----------------------------------APPEARS ON STRUCTURE CHARTS (SC)-------------------------------------------

***CONTAINS NO ITEMS***

-----------------------------------ATTRIBUTE OF DATA ENTITIES (DN)--------------------------------------------
----ID----- -------DATA ENTITY NAME-------   ----ID----- -------DATA ENTITY NAME-------   ----ID----- -------DATA ENTITY NAME------
DN5         BENEFITS

TOTAL ITEMS :       1

-----------------------------------BOUNDED BY DOMAIN RANGES---------------------------------------------------

***CONTAINS NO ITEMS***

-----------------------------------BOUNDED BY DOMAIN VALUES---------------------------------------------------
     ---------VALUE---------                             ------------------MEANING------------------
     DEN                                                 DENTAL PLAN
     HLT                                                 HEALTH PLAN
     HOS                                                 HOSPITALIZATION PLAN
     VAC                                                 VACATION PLAN

TOTAL ITEMS :       4

-----------------------------------CONTAINED IN ACCESS PROFILE OF DS/DE (DS,DN)-------------------------------

***CONTAINS NO ITEMS***

-----------------------------------CONTAINED IN DATA STRUCTURES (DX)------------------------------------------
------DATA STRUCTURE NAME-----   ------DATA STRUCTURE NAME-----   ------DATA STRUCTURE NAME-----   ------DATA STRUCTURE NAME-----
EMPLOYEE-INFORMATION             JOB-HISTORY-INFORMATION

TOTAL ITEMS :       2

-----------------------------------CONTAINED IN DATA FLOWS (DF)-----------------------------------------------
------------DATA FLOW NAME------------      ------------DATA FLOW NAME------------      ------------DATA FLOW NAME------------
ADDITIONAL BENEFITS                         BENEFITS                                    BENEFITS ADVICE
BENEFITS PACKAGE

TOTAL ITEMS :       4

-----------------------------------CONTAINED IN DATA STORES (DS)----------------------------------------------
----ID----- -------DATA STORE NAME-------   ----ID----- -------DATA STORE NAME-------   ----ID----- -------DATA STORE NAME-------
D5          BENEFITS

TOTAL ITEMS :       1
****CONTINUED****
```

Figure 2.30 PROKIT*WORKBENCH from McDonnell-Douglas provides a cross-reference report of all data elements stored in its CASE repository.

Case Repository Implementation Considerations

As mentioned earlier, the CASE repository is more than a simple data dictionary because of the need to store many types of information objects and relationships between objects and because of the need for a powerful information management facility. Usually, the repository is a relational database supported by a full database management system (e.g., DB2, VSAM, DL1, dBASE III architectures).

This architecture enables automatic population of the CASE repository from outside dictionaries and databases. Because there is a need for two-way information flow between the repository and outside dictionaries and databases, the CASE workbench must provide mechanisms for importing and exporting system information to and from the repository.

Repository Capabilities

In summary, the CASE repository is a central concept of the CASE technology. Specification information stored in the CASE repository is used to generate system code, to maintain systems, and to be reused in the development of future systems. By storing system information on the computer, it will be easier to adapt to higher levels of software automation as they become available in the future. Box 2.8 lists some important questions to ask about the capabilities of a CASE workbench repository.

INTEGRATION

Specification language, diagramming tools, prototyping tools, dictionaries, database management systems, compilers, various types of generators, and so on are the high-productivity tools of the early 1980s. However, a major obstacle to their ease of use is that they tend to be standalone tools capable of supporting only part of the software process. Usually, they do not have standard interfaces to one another and they are highly dependent on a particular computer, operating system, and programming language. As a result, software developers must learn to use a different set of tools for each environment in which they work. Even within a single environment, they cannot apply their knowledge of one tool to another because each tool has its own command format, specialized file structure, and range of available options.

Despite their power, many potentially powerful tools have failed to improve software productivity and quality substantially because they do not provide integrated, continuous support to software developers in their actual day-to-day work [10]. The lack of integration decreases productivity.

Integration of tools lies at the very foundation of the software development workbench concept. It is the key to making the use of powerful software tools practical. The CASE workbench tools should interact with each other in a consistent, intuitive way and should conform to a set of well-understood standards. They should appear to the user to be cooperating with each other and aware enough of each other not to duplicate functions or messages. This reduces the opportunity for user errors and avoids redundant data entry when the same information is needed for different tools.

BOX 2.8 CASE information repository capabilities

- Is the information repository fully integrated or only loosely connected to the CASE workbench? (An integrated repository is superior because it enables fast storage of information via the diagrams or directly into the repository and one-step updates when either the repository contents or the diagram is changed.)
- Is the information repository architecture a dictionary or a database? (A database with a powerful information management system is needed to manage all system information.)
- What types of system information can be stored in the information repository, and how much? (All types of system information (both technical and project management), as well as relationships among information objects, must be stored in the repository.)
- How is the information repository shared among developers? (To support project teams and the development and maintenance of large systems, the repository must provide multiuser access and controls.)
- What types of reports about the information repository are provided? (Preformatted reports and ad hoc queries must be provided to the developer to enable easy viewing and evaluation of the repository contents.)
- Is there an import/export capability to and from outside dictionaries and databases to the information repository? (Links to outside dictionaries and databases are needed to access standard system information that has already been defined for an organization.)
- When a change is made to some information in the information repository, can the impact of that change on the system be analyzed and reported and all affected objects changed appropriately? (Automatic change analysis and control are two of the most important capabilities that the repository provides.)

Box 2.9 lists five levels of integration. The first level, *common user interface,* is the minimum expected in a CASE workbench. It reduces the learning curve associated with the workbench since experience acquired using one part of the workbench can then be applied to learning other parts. For example, HELP and other major functions are accessed in the same way throughout the workbench. A common user interface is the bridge connecting various workbench tools. When third-party tools are added, individual tool differences are covered under the umbrella of a common menu system.

BOX 2.9 Levels of integration

- Common user interface
- Transferability of data between tools
- Integration of development phases through one system representation stored in the CASE information repository
- Transferability of data and tools between hardware environments
- Everything available at workstation level

The second level of integration, *transferability of data between tools,* is another kind of bridge connecting workbench tools. When necessary, data selection routines, conversion routines, and file transfer routines are supplied to convert data automatically into an appropriate input format for a particular tool or software package. In a smoothly running workbench it is easy for the user to pass data from tool to tool. It is expected that the output of each tool will become the input to another [10].

The first two levels of integration are concerned with integrating across tools—a way of linking tools together for ease of use and ease of learning. The third level of integration is concerned with linking the phases of the software life cycle—integrating across the process steps of developing and maintaining software systems. In this case the bridge between the various life cycle phases is one common representation of the system (but allowing multiple user perspectives or views) stored in a CASE information repository and shared among project teammates. A structured methodology is another type of bridge tying together the steps of software development into a meaningful, manageable process. This level of integration unites teammates, users, and management and reduces communication problems by providing one, easily updated source for all information about a system and a common development procedure to follow.

The last two levels of integration are concerned with integrating across hardware environments—linking mainframe and micro levels, and in some cases a "middle" minicomputer level as well. The objective is to be able to perform development activities in whichever environment is most expedient. This is possible only if text, code, data, and graphics can easily be transferred between software packages and between hardware environments. In addition, CASE workbenches offer integration across functions—graphics, word processing, data processing, and office automation—by providing all these functions at workstation level.

SUMMARY

In this chapter we discussed the CASE workbench, a full-function environment supporting the software process. The basic functional capabilities of the CASE workbench are summarized in Box 2.10. We discussed the first four capabilities in this chapter; the remaining capabilities are discussed in Chapter 3.

BOX 2.10 CASE workbench: the new software development environment

CASE workbenches provide computerized assistance for the development, maintenance, and management of software systems. They differ from earlier programming environments in their breadth of coverage of the software life cycle. A complete CASE workbench must have these characteristics:

- Graphics interface for drawing structured diagrams
- Information repository for storing and managing all software system information
- Highly integrated toolset sharing a common user interface
- Tools to assist every phase of the life cycle
- Prototyping tools
- Automatic code generation from design specifications
- Software life cycle methodology support with extensive checking built into tools

REFERENCES

1. S. Gutz, A. Wasserman, and M. Spier, "Personal Development Systems for the Professional Programmer," *Computer,* Vol. 14, No. 4, April 1981, pp. 45–53.
2. B. Kernighan and J. Mashey, "The Unix Programming Environment," *Computer,* Vol. 14, No. 4, April 1981, pp. 12–24.
3. W. Teitelman and L. Masinter, "The Interlisp Programming Environment," *Computer,* Vol. 14, No. 4, April 1981, pp. 25–34.
4. G. Raeder, "A Survey of Current Graphical Programming Techniques," *Computer,* Vol. 18, No. 8, August 1985, pp. 11–25.

5. James Martin and Carma McClure, *Diagramming Techniques for Analysts and Programmers*. Englewood Cliffs, N.J.: Prentice-Hall, 1985.

6. James Martin and Carma McClure, *Action Diagrams*. Englewood Cliffs, N.J.: Prentice-Hall, 1985.

7. Edward Yourdon and Larry Constantine, *Structured Design*. Englewood Cliffs, N.J.: Yourdon Press, 1978.

8. James Martin and Carma McClure, *Structured Techniques: The Basis for CASE*. Englewood Cliffs, N.J.: Prentice-Hall, 1988.

9. M. Mariconi and D. F. Hare, ''PegaSys: A System for Graphical Explanation of Program Designs, *SIGPLAN Notices,* Vol. 20, No. 7, July 1985, pp. 148–160.

10. L. Osterweil, ''Software Environment Research: Directions for the Next Five Years,'' *Computer,* Vol. 14, No. 4, April 1981, pp. 35–44.

3 CASE SOFTWARE PROCESS SUPPORT

SOFTWARE PROCESS AND METHODOLOGY SUPPORT

The function of a CASE workbench is to support every phase of the software development and maintenance process with a set of integrated tools. CASE tools automate the tasks performed by and the production of the documentation required by each development and maintenance phase.

For example, in the early phases of the software life cycle, CASE tools such as screen painters and executable specification languages are used to build prototype models and simulations to discover system requirements and test system behavior. In the implementation phase of the software life cycle, CASE tools such as code and database generators are used to write documented program code automatically from high-level design specifications.

An important part of supporting the software life cycle is supporting the methodologies that structure the process steps within the life cycle. A CASE workbench supports the use of structured methodologies by automating the production of the documentation required by the methodology and guiding the user in the correct use of the methodology.

In this chapter we take a closer look at how the CASE workbench supports both the software life cycle process and structured methodologies by discussing the following four workbench capabilities:

- Software life cycle coverage
- Prototyping support
- Automatic code generation
- Structured methodology support

FRONT-END LOADING OF THE LIFE CYCLE

An important part of the CASE technology is an emphasis on the early software life cycle phases. This front-end emphasis, or "front-end loading," of the life cycle comes from recognizing analysis and design as the most critical life cycle phases.

Specification errors can be very expensive if they are not detected and corrected in the early phases. Correcting a specification error during the maintenance phase may be 100 times more expensive than if it had been corrected during the analysis phase [1]. The completeness and correctness of the system specification affect the success of the entire software development effort. The specification is the basis for project schedules and assignments, test plans, user documentation, and program design. Poorly understood system requirements cause software failures.

Design errors often dominate software projects in terms of their number and their cost to correct, especially when not detected early. In large projects, design errors often exceed coding errors. In a TRW study of errors detected during or after acceptance testing, design errors outweigh coding errors 64 percent to 32 percent [2]. Not only did more design errors occur, but they also were more costly than coding errors to correct.

More care given to design means lower-cost, more reliable systems. A system design is the blueprint for system implementation. If the blueprint does not exist or if it is incorrect, the system produced is probably poorly organized, poorly documented, and a nightmare to maintain.

PROTOTYPING

Prototyping tools play an important part in automating the early life cycle phases. They are used to determine system requirements and answer questions about the behavior of the emerging system. Box 3.1 lists some CASE tools that are used to prototype various aspects of a software system.

BOX 3.1 CASE prototyping tools

- Screen painters
- Report generators
- Menu builders
- Fourth-generation languages
- Executable specification languages

Screen generators, report generators, and menu builders are used mainly to prototype the user interface as a quick, friendly way of clarifying the user requirements (see Figures 3.1 through 3.3). The prototype provides the user with a concrete model of how the system will look from the user's perspective. At this level of prototyping, screen dialogue and navigation with data entry and edits can be simulated with or without compiles. Also, source code for record, file, screen, and report descriptions can be generated automatically. This is an effective method for identifying and correcting misunderstandings about user expectations for the system.

Fourth-generation languages can be used to develop a more complete model of the system. In this case the prototype includes the major functions of the system but does not check for exceptions or invalid input data and does not worry about execution performance. The purpose is to give the user experience with the system by using a fairly complete model. Sometimes the model is found to be adequate enough to serve as the actual system.

```
PANEL DEFINITION MENU *************** *************** END PROCESSING PERFORMED
COMMAND ==> ____________________________________________________________

FUNCTION: UP   CR-CREATE   UP-UPDATE   PU-PURGE   SH-SHOW   LI-LIST

ITEM      PI   PI-IMAGE    PD-DEFIN
                                FD-FIELD    CE-CONSIS    SL-SEGLOOP
                                  (UP)       (CR,UP)      (CR,UP,PU)
MEMBER NAME:
      HEADER  TR
      ID      XXAD_ PRE-CLASS ASSIGN, STUDENT NAME
      DESC    ________________________________

ENTER VALUE FOR SPECIFIC ITEM TO BE PROCESSED:
     1. IMAGE        < > + | \  (INPUT OUTPUT OUTIN SELECT LIT-BREAK CHARACTERS)
                     24  080    (LINE-COLUMN IMAGE SIZE)
                     U          (UPPER/LOWER CASE LITERALS)
     2. DEFIN        Y Y Y Y N  (INPUT OUTPUT OUTIN SELECT LITERAL FIELDS LISTED)
     3. FIELD                   (NAME OR LINE,COLUMN OR "*PANEL")
     4. CONSIS       _______    (TYPE - "XFEDIT", "SEGEDIT", OR BLANK FOR LIST)
                     _______    (NAME - IF TYPE SPECIFIED)
     5. SEGLOOP      _______    (TYPE - "FILE" OR "TABLE")
                     _______    (FROM NAME OR LINE,COLUMN)
                     _____        (TO NAME OR LINE,COLUMN)
                     _____
```

Figure 3.1 Example of a screen produced using the screen painter in TELON from Pansophic.

```
TRANCODE                  EXECUTIVE FILING SYSTEM                 MM-DD-YY HH:MM:SS

                         UPDATE APPOINTMENT DETAILS
 DATE: MM-DD-YY  TIME: XXXXXXX          LOCATION: XXXXXXXXXXXXXXX
 OBJECTIVE: XXXXXXXXXXXXXXXXXXXXXXXXX   CONFIRMATION INDICATOR: X

REMARKS:
XXXXXXXXXXXXXXXXXXXXXXXXXXXXXXXXXXXXXXXXXXXXXXXXXXXXXXXXXXXXXXXXXXXXXXXXXXXXXXXX
XXXXXXXXXXXXXXXXXXXXXXXXXXXXXXXXXXXXXXXXXXXXXXXXXXXXXXXXXXXXXXXXXXXXXXXXXXXXXXXX

                   A T T E N D E E   I N F O R M A T I O N
SEL   LAST NAME       FIRST      MI    PHONE NUMBER   COMPANY NAME
 X    XXXXXXXXXXXXXXX XXXXXXXXXX X    ( 999 ) 9999999  XXXXXXXXXXXXXXXXXXXXXXXXX
 X    XXXXXXXXXXXXXXX XXXXXXXXXX X    ( 999 ) 9999999  XXXXXXXXXXXXXXXXXXXXXXXXX
 X    XXXXXXXXXXXXXXX XXXXXXXXXX X    ( 999 ) 9999999  XXXXXXXXXXXXXXXXXXXXXXXXX
 X    XXXXXXXXXXXXXXX XXXXXXXXXX X    ( 999 ) 9999999  XXXXXXXXXXXXXXXXXXXXXXXXX
 X    XXXXXXXXXXXXXXX XXXXXXXXXX X    ( 999 ) 9999999  XXXXXXXXXXXXXXXXXXXXXXXXX
 X    XXXXXXXXXXXXXXX XXXXXXXXXX X    ( 999 ) 9999999  XXXXXXXXXXXXXXXXXXXXXXXXX
 X    XXXXXXXXXXXXXXX XXXXXXXXXX X    ( 999 ) 9999999  XXXXXXXXXXXXXXXXXXXXXXXXX
 X    XXXXXXXXXXXXXXX XXXXXXXXXX X    ( 999 ) 9999999  XXXXXXXXXXXXXXXXXXXXXXXXX
 X    XXXXXXXXXXXXXXX XXXXXXXXXX X    ( 999 ) 9999999  XXXXXXXXXXXXXXXXXXXXXXXXX
 X    XXXXXXXXXXXXXXX XXXXXXXXXX X    ( 999 ) 9999999  XXXXXXXXXXXXXXXXXXXXXXXXX
 <<< PFK <<< PFK <<< PFK <<< PFK <<< PFK >>> PFK >>> PFK >>> PFK >>> PFK >>> PF
 <<< ERR <<< ERR <<< ERR <<< ERR <<< ERR >>> ERR >>> ERR >>> ERR >>> ERR >>> ER
```

Figure 3.2 Screen design example produced with the INFORMATION ENGINEERING FACILITY™ screen generator from Texas Instruments Incorporated.

Executable specification languages are the most sophisticated prototyping tools. They change system development into an iterative process where the system is specified and the specifications are executed to determine if the system is complete and correct. Then based on the experience of using this prototype,

```
                              REPORT LAYOUT CHART
|  1-10   |  11-20   |  21-30   |  31-40   |  41-50   |  51-60   |  61-70   |  71-80  |
|123456789012345678901234567890123456789012345678901234567890123456789012345678 9|

                                     ABC

                                 CORPORATION

                              PARTS MOVE REPORT
                            ---------------------

         PART-ID    MGR   APPR      LOCATION      QTY-STOCK    QTY-REQUEST    STATUS
        ---------  -----  -------  -------------  -----------  -------------  -------

    1)   999999    XXX     XX       9,999.99      9,999.99      99/99/99       XXX

    2)   999999    XXX     XX       9,999.99      9,999.99      99/99/99       XXX

    3)   999999    XXX     XX       9,999.99      9,999.99      99/99/99       XXX

    4)   999999    XXX     XX       9,999.99      9,999.99      99/99/99       XXX
```

Figure 3.3 Example of report painting done with DESIGNAID from the Nastec Corporation.

the specifications are refined and then reexecuted. The iterative process continues until the system is able to perform in a manner that meets all the user requirements.

SIMULATION

Certain types of software systems are embedded within other systems. These systems, called *real-time/embedded systems,* must interact with their outside environment through signals and controls.

For real-time/embedded systems it is valuable to simulate as well as prototype the system at the analysis/design stage of development. Whereas a prototype is a model of the software system, the simulation is a model of the environment to which the software system must respond and control. The simulation enables a preview of how the software system will behave in its actual real-world environment [3]. Realistic real-world inputs from the environment must be provided to verify the correctness and completeness of the system design model. With the aid of CASE simulation tools, the designer can find design errors before even beginning the coding phase of development. Real-time/embedded systems are discussed later in this chapter in the section entitled "Real-Time Systems."

CODE GENERATION

At the other end of the software life cycle from prototyping is code generation. A CASE workbench automates the program implementation step by generating code from the program design specification. Either a skeleton or a full program is generated.

In the case of skeleton generation, code for the database, file, screen, and report descriptions, plus a commented outline of the procedural logic, is generated automatically. Additional program logic must be hand-coded to complete the program.

In the case of full program generation, the complete program plus its documentation are generated automatically from the design specification. This includes:

- Executable code
- JCL
- Database/file access (screens, maps, database/file descriptions)
- Help screens
- Error messages
- User and program documentation
- Test cases

```
        (GROUP-OUTPUT-POS)
     COMPUTE LAST-STATEMENT-NUM = 0000000064
*
     MOVE 192 TO LAST-NAME-DYN1 OF LAST-NAME-ATTR OF ATTENDEE OF
         OUTPUT-Z OF GROUP-OUTPUT  (GROUP-OUTPUT-POS)
     ADD 32 TO LAST-NAME-DYN1 OF LAST-NAME-ATTR OF ATTENDEE OF
         OUTPUT-Z OF GROUP-OUTPUT  (GROUP-OUTPUT-POS)
     MOVE 'B7' TO LAST-NAME-DYN2 OF LAST-NAME-ATTR OF ATTENDEE OF
         OUTPUT-Z OF GROUP-OUTPUT  (GROUP-OUTPUT-POS)
     COMPUTE LAST-STATEMENT-NUM = 0000000065
*
     MOVE 192 TO FIRST-NAME-DYN1 OF FIRST-NAME-ATTR OF ATTENDEE OF
          OUTPUT-Z OF GROUP-OUTPUT  (GROUP-OUTPUT-POS)
     ADD 32 TO FIRST-NAME-DYN1 OF FIRST-NAME-ATTR OF ATTENDEE OF
         OUTPUT-Z OF GROUP-OUTPUT  (GROUP-OUTPUT-POS)
     MOVE 'B7' TO FIRST-NAME-DYN2 OF FIRST-NAME-ATTR OF ATTENDEE
         OF OUTPUT-Z OF GROUP-OUTPUT  (GROUP-OUTPUT-POS)

 PARA-0008651125-EXIT.
     EXIT.
*
*
*
 PARA-0008651138.
*
     COMPUTE LAST-STATEMENT-NUM = 0000000070
     MOVE GROUP-REFD TO GROUP-OUTPUT-REF
     MOVE FUNCTION-CODE OF WORK-AREA OF INPUT-Z OF INPUT-GROUP
         (INPUT-GROUP-POS)
       TO FUNCTION-CODE OF WORK-AREA OF OUTPUT-Z OF GROUP-OUTPUT
         (GROUP-OUTPUT-POS)
     COMPUTE LAST-STATEMENT-NUM = 0000000071
     MOVE GROUP-REFD TO GROUP-OUTPUT-REF
     MOVE LAST-NAME OF ATTENDEE OF INPUT-Z OF INPUT-GROUP
         (INPUT-GROUP-POS)
       TO LAST-NAME OF ATTENDEE OF OUTPUT-Z OF GROUP-OUTPUT
         (GROUP-OUTPUT-POS)
     MOVE FIRST-NAME OF ATTENDEE OF INPUT-Z OF INPUT-GROUP
         (INPUT-GROUP-POS)
       TO FIRST-NAME OF ATTENDEE OF OUTPUT-Z OF GROUP-OUTPUT
         (GROUP-OUTPUT-POS)
     MOVE MIDDLE-INITIAL OF ATTENDEE OF INPUT-Z OF INPUT-GROUP
         (INPUT-GROUP-POS)
       TO MIDDLE-INITIAL OF ATTENDEE OF OUTPUT-Z OF GROUP-OUTPUT
         (GROUP-OUTPUT-POS)
     MOVE AREA-CODE OF ATTENDEE OF INPUT-Z OF INPUT-GROUP
         (INPUT-GROUP-POS)
       TO AREA-CODE OF ATTENDEE OF OUTPUT-Z OF GROUP-OUTPUT
         (GROUP-OUTPUT-POS)
     MOVE PHONE-NUMBER OF ATTENDEE OF INPUT-Z OF INPUT-GROUP
         (INPUT-GROUP-POS)
       TO PHONE-NUMBER OF ATTENDEE OF OUTPUT-Z OF GROUP-OUTPUT
         (GROUP-OUTPUT-POS)
     MOVE CORPORATION OF ATTENDEE OF INPUT-Z OF INPUT-GROUP
         (INPUT-GROUP-POS)
       TO CORPORATION OF ATTENDEE OF OUTPUT-Z OF GROUP-OUTPUT
         (GROUP-OUTPUT-POS)
     COMPUTE LAST-STATEMENT-NUM = 0000000072
*
     MOVE 192 TO LAST-NAME-DYN1 OF LAST-NAME-ATTR OF ATTENDEE OF
```

Figure 3.4 Example of COBOL code generated automatically by the INFORMATION ENGINEERING FACILITY™ from Texas Instruments Incorporated.

All of these components of the completed program are linked together and stored in the CASE repository for easy access, synchronized updating, and maintenance.

Generated code is either object code or source code. Many developers prefer source code because if necessary, it can be understood and supported by human programmers. Also, it is more portable and may be more compatible with existing software systems. Widely used languages such as COBOL, PL/1, C, Ada, Fortran, or proprietary-vendor-supplied languages are generated by CASE workbench generators. Figures 3.4 and 3.5 are examples of automatically generated COBOL source code. Figure 3.6 is an example of automatically generated PL/1 code. Figure 3.7 is an example of proprietary-vendor-supplied source code.

The code is generated for operating environments such as MVS, CICS, IMS/DC, DB2, DL1, VSAM, VM/SQL, DS, TSO, IDMS, ADABAS, DBS, and OS/1100. The ability to generate code for various target environments is an important part of the CASE workbench's code generator capability.

Object code offers the advantage of greater efficiency, and probably will become more widely accepted by CASE workbench users in the future as they become more trusting of the reliability and efficiency of automatically generated code. Also, as the CASE workbench's capability to maintain systems at design specification level improves, object code generated will be seen as more practical than source code.

STRUCTURED METHODOLOGY SUPPORT

The CASE workbench supports structured methodologies such as structured analysis, structured design, and structured programming by providing tools to automate the methodologies. There are two levels of automation:

1. Documentation preparation
2. Methodology process steps

Automating documentation preparation means providing graphics support for drawing structured diagrams such as data flow diagrams, entity relationship diagrams, state transition diagrams, and action diagrams. It also means automating the production of textual specifications such as minispecs and pseudocode. The textual specifications are used to provide more detailed information about program procedures and data structures referenced in higher-level structured diagrams.

Since different structured methodologies use different diagrams to model and document a software system, the structured methodologies supported by a particular CASE workbench will be determined by the types of structured dia-

Data Definition

```
         (NAME('AAAC2.DSNDBC.DR.T0000174.I0001.A001') -
         NONINDEXED SHR(3,3) RESUSE -
         CONTROLINTERVALSIZE(4096) RECORDSIZE(4089,4089)) -
      DATA -
         (NAME('AAAC2.DSNDBD.DR.T0000174.I0001.A001') -
         CYLS(1 1) VOL()) -
      CATALOG (AAAC2)

DEFINE CLUSTER -
         (NAME('AAAC2.DSNDBC.DR.T0000141.I0001.A001') -
         NONINDEXED SHR(3,3) RESUSE -
         CONTROLINTERVALSIZE(4096) RECORDSIZE(4089,4089)) -
      DATA -
         (NAME('AAAC2.DSNDBD.DR.T0000141.I0001.A001') -
         CYLS(1 1) VOL()) -
      CATALOG (AAAC2)

CREATE DATABASE "DR"
       BUFFERPOOL BP0
       ;

CREATE TABLESPACE "T0000023" IN "DR"
       BUFFERPOOL BP0
       LOCKSIZE   PAGE
       CLOSE      NO
       USING VCAT AAAC2
       PCTFREE    48
       ;

CREATE TABLE EXECUTIVE
       (
       LAST_NAME                          CHAR(15)     NOT NULL,
       FIRST_NAME                         CHAR(10)     NOT NULL,
       MIDDLE_INITIAL                     CHAR(1)      NOT NULL,
       DEPARTMENT                         CHAR(25)     NOT NULL,
       LOCATION                           CHAR(25)     NOT NULL,
       JOB_TITLE                          CHAR(20)     NOT NULL,
       OPERATOR_ID                        CHAR(3)      NOT NULL,
       PHONE_AREA_CODE                    SMALLINT     NOT NULL,
       PHONE_NUMBER                       INTEGER      NOT NULL,
       )
    IN "DR"."T0000023"
       ;

CREATE TABLESPACE "T0000005" IN "DR"
       BUFFERPOOL BP0
       LOCKSIZE   PAGE
       CLOSE      NO
       USING VCAT AAAC2
       PCTFREE    48
       ;
```

Figure 3.5 Example of DB/2 tables generated automatically from the entity relation diagram and data structure diagram by the INFORMATION ENGINEERING FACILITY™ from Texas Instruments Incorporated.

```
PL/I OPTIMIZING COMPILER          /* TRPPCDA  T E L O N   C I C S   P R O G R A M      *

    STMT

 322      E_100_INPUT_EDITS: PROC;
            /*******************************************************
             *         E _ 1 0 0 _ I N P U T _ E D I T S          *
             *******************************************************
             *  THIS ROUTINE CONTAINS THE INPUT EDIT LOGIC GENERATED*
             *  FROM THE FIELD STATEMENT PARAMETERS.  STANDARD      *
             *  EDITS SUCH AS REQ, CONVERT AND VALUES ARE GENERATED *
             *  IN THIS SECTION.  SPECIAL FLDTYPES ARE LINKED TO    *
             *  WITH CALL STATEMENTS.                               *
             *                                                      *
             *  GENERATED - FIELD EDIT LOGIC                        *
             *  COPY CODE - SEGLOOP/ICUSTOM                         *
             *  COPY CODE - SCREEN/FLDEDIT                          *
             *******************************************************/
 323             SECTION_NAME_TABLE(SEC_INDEX) = TRACE_SECTION_NAME;
 324             SEC_INDEX = SEC_INDEX + 1;
 325             TRACE_SECTION_NAME = 'E_100    ';
 326             TRACE_FIELD_NAME, TRACE_SEGMENT_NAME = ' ';
            /*
             *    CHECK IF HELP FIELD REQUEST HAS BEEN MADE.
             */
 327             CALL M_100_HELP_ANALYZE;
 328             IF CONTROL_INDICATOR ¬= CONTINUE_PROCESS_LIT
                 THEN GO TO E_100_INPUT_EDITS_RETURN;


            /*    ID FIELD                                  */

 329             TRACE_FIELD_NAME = 'ID       ';
 330             IF TPI_ID ¬= ' '
                 THEN DO;
 331                CALL IFORMAT (FIELD_EDIT_ERROR,
                                  TPI_ID_LTH,
                                  TPI_ID,
                                  WORKFLD_ALPHA,
                                  FORMAT_ID,
                                  FORMAT_ID_LTH);
 332                IF FIELD_EDIT_ERROR = '      '
                    THEN
                       EMPL_ID = SUBSTR(WORKFLD_ALPHA,1,FORMAT_ID_LTH);
 333                ELSE DO;
 334                   CONTROL_INDICATOR = DO_WRITE_LIT;
 335                   TPO_ID_ATTR = ERROR_ATTR;
 336                   END;
 337                END;
 338             ELSE
                    EMPL_ID = ' ';
```

Figure 3.6 Example of edits in PL/1 code generated automatically by TELON from Pansophic.

grams and the notation conventions that it offers. For example, the Yourdon structured design methodology uses a structure chart derived from a data flow diagram to represent a program design; the Jackson design methodology uses tree structured diagrams; and the Orr data structured systems development methodology uses Warnier–Orr diagrams.

The second level of methodology support, *automating the methodology's process steps,* means that the CASE workbench guides the user in correct use of a structured methodology. This requires that at least some level of understanding of the methodology is embedded in the CASE workbench tools. This could be as simple as embedded help panels that describe each step in the meth-

```
        *
*     VALIDATE.INC
*     ------------
*
*   WRITTEN:  07/12/83        JGW
*
*   NARRATIVE:        ROUTINES USED TO VALIDATE ENTRIES
*
***************************
*                          *
┌──SECTION CHECK_VALUE
|  *                          *
|  ***************************
|  *
|  *     INPUT:
|  *             STRING:         VALUE TO BE CHECKED ('T:XXX...XXX')
|  *                             T=EXTERNAL.TYPE, XXX...XXX=VALUE STRING
|  *
|     LET ERROR=""
<─┼────IF 1*STRING EQ "C", EXITB
|  *
|  ┌──IF ";" NIN -2*STRING, THEN
|  |     ##STACK=-2*STRING+" ; ; "
|  |
|  ├──ELSE
|  |     ##STACK=""
|  ├──
|  ┌──IF 1*STRING EQ "D", THEN
|  |  *
|  |  *   VALIDATE DATE
|  |  *
|  |     IF ##STACK NE "", INPUT DATE8D
|  |     IF ##STACK EQ "", LET ERROR="INVALID DATE"
|  |
|  ├──ELSE
|  |  *
|  |  *   VALIDATE NUMBER
|  |  *
|  |     IF ##STACK NE "", INPUT NUMERIC.DOLLARS
|  |  ┌──CONDITIONAL
|  |  ├──##STACK EQ "", LET ERROR="INVALID NUMBER"
|  |  |  *
|  |  ├──-2*STRING LL "...<-*.>-...", LET ERROR= ;
|  |  |        "NUMBER MAY NOT CONTAIN EMBEDDED MINUS SIGNS"
|  |  |  *
|  |  ├──(1*STRING EQ "I" AND ;
|  |  |        -2*STRING LL "...%...."), LET ERROR= ;
|  |  |        "INTEGER VALUE MAY NOT CONTAIN A DECIMAL POINT"
|  |  |  *
|  |  ├──-2*STRING LL "...%....%....", LET ERROR= ;
|  |  |        "NUMBER MAY NOT CONTAIN MORE THAN ONE DECIMAL POINT"
|  |  |  *
|  |  ├──(1*STRING EQ "$" AND ;
|  |  |        -2*STRING LL "...%.***..."), LET ERROR= ;
|  |  |        "DOLLAR VALUE MAY NOT HAVE MORE THAN TWO DECIMAL PLACES"
|  |  ├──
|  ├──
|  *
|  *   DISPLAY ANY ERROR MESSAGE
|  *
|  ┌──IF ERROR NE "", THEN
|  |     ┌────────────────────────────────────┐
|  |     |PERFORM DISPLAY ERROR ;*SCRSTUFF.INC|
```

Figure 3.7 Example of a vendor-proprietary language which is documented automatically using an action diagramming format. It was automatically produced by the application generator in CORVISION from Cortex for the DEC VAX environment.

odology, or checklists that include the input required, and the output produced, by each step. It might include a checking mechanism to ensure that each output deliverable required by the methodology is present, correct, and complete before the user is allowed to go to the next step. In this case the user is not simply guided through the methodology but rather forced to perform the steps in a standardized order and way. The purpose is to standardize and systematize the process of developing software.

There are two schools of thought on whether or not the second level of automation of a structured methodology should be embedded into CASE tools. The argument for it is that this introduces control over the development process and standards for the software system imposed by the CASE tools. Also, more extensive quality and completeness checking can be performed since many quality assurance checks are methodology specific. For example, coupling and cohesion measures are quality checks for design that are only part of the Yourdon structured design methodology. In general, the more specifically the process can be defined, the more potential there is for software automation. Automating the methodology process steps is discussed further in Chapter 12.

On the other hand, the argument against is that not embedding the methodology process into the CASE tools gives the user flexibility in choosing the methodology—or that part of a methodology that is appropriate for developing a particular system. This is a rather weak argument because most software developers barely know one methodology well, let alone are well enough acquainted with multiple methodologies to be able to select the most appropriate one for a particular system development project.

Also, embedding methodology steps into the tools does not mean that the developer will not have the option of overriding the tool's suggestion as to the next appropriate step or a quality deficiency warning.

CLASSIFICATIONS OF STRUCTURED METHODOLOGIES

Structured methodologies can be classified as belonging to either the software engineering or the information engineering school; as either a procedure-oriented, data-oriented, or an information-oriented approach; and as for developing either real-time or information systems.

Software Engineering

Software engineering is a top-down, phased-implementation approach for developing software programs [4]. Its basic premises are listed in Box 3.2. *Software engineering* proposes a step-by-step development process that begins with the most general functional view of what the program is to do, decomposes this view into subfunctions, and then repeats the process for each subfunction until all subfunctions are small enough to be implemented into program code. The result is a hierarchically structured modular program. Although functional com-

BOX 3.2 Basic premises of software engineering

- A top-down, phased-implementation approach requires that development proceed incrementally from a top-level control and data definition downward to functional modules and data structures.
- An important aspect of top-down is an insistence on firm requirements.
- The solution system is defined in terms of functions; data are designed to preserve system functionality and the independence of program modules. Therefore, data requirements are discovered through analysis of functions required by the system.

ponent design and data structure design are performed in parallel, data structure design defers to procedure design to protect the independence and clarity of functional components. Program data requirements are discovered through an analysis of program functional requirements. Thus software engineering emphasizes a functional view of a program.

Figure 3.8 shows the basic steps followed when using a software engineering approach to program development. Notice that the process begins with a dynamic view of data flow before it focuses on functional decomposition. Also, notice that logical design considerations are separated from physical considerations, and logical program design precedes physical program design. The types of structured diagrams that are used to represent a program design with software engineering are listed in Box 3.3.

BOX 3.3 Software engineering diagrams

Types of diagrams needed to support a software engineering approach to system development:

- Data flow diagram: shows top-level functional processes in a system and data flow from acquisition through processing and eventual output
- Hierarchical tree structured diagrams: shows the relationship between program modules and shows hierarchical data structures
- Detailed procedural logic diagram: shows detailed program logic: sequence, selection, loop
- Screen and report layout: shows design of user interface

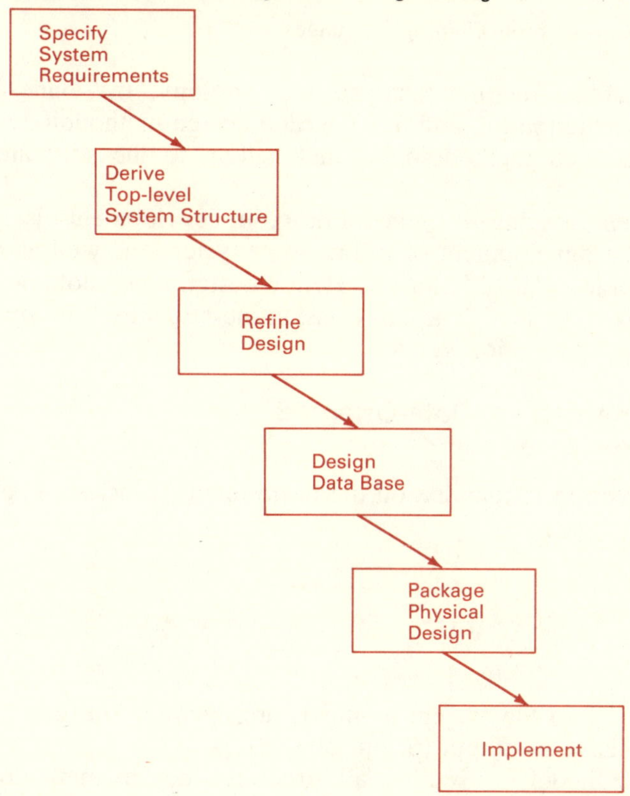

Figure 3.8 Basic steps followed when using a software engineering approach to program development.

Software engineering represents one of the first attempts to structure the software development process. Since the 1960s there has been a move to change software development from a craft-like art to an engineering-like discipline with the objective of introducing a disciplined approach to software development. As Bauer explained, software engineering is "the establishment and use of sound engineering principles (methods) in order to economically obtain software that is reliable and works on real machines" [5, p. 530]. Concepts and techniques that have evolved from the software engineering discipline include:

- Top-down design
- Structured programming
- Modularity

- Stepwise refinement and functional decomposition
- Software quality metrics
- Abstraction of programming languages

The DeMarco structured analysis methodology, the Gane–Sarson structured analysis methodology, and the Yourdon design methodology are examples of popular structured methodologies that belong to the software engineering school.

Software engineering is a general program development discipline that can be applied to the development of information systems as well as real-time systems. For example, Ward/Mellor and Hatley design methodologies for real-time systems are based on the Yourdon–Constantine structured design methodology used to develop information systems.

Procedure-Oriented vs. Data-Oriented Software Development

Software engineering is founded on the basic input–process–output model for a system:

Data are entered into the system as input, are operated on (or transformed) by a process, and leave as output [6, pp. 503–504].

This basic model is used for all structured design methodologies. However, the order in which the model is built depends on the particular structured methodology that is followed. Traditional software engineering views the process part as the fundamental part of the system model and is therefore described as a *procedure-oriented* software development approach. Data follow from function.

A *data-oriented* software development approach views the input and output parts of the model as most important. Therefore, data structures are defined first, and the procedural components are derived from the data structures. Function follows from data. Box 3.4 lists the basic premises of a data-driven development approach. The types of diagrams needed to support a data-driven approach to software development are a hierarchical tree structured diagram for representing both data and program structures and a detailed procedural logic diagram.

The Jackson design methodology is an example of a data-oriented methodology. In the Jackson approach, input and output data structures are defined first. Then the program structure is defined by merging together all the program data structures.

BOX 3.4 Data-driven approach to system development

Basic premises:

- The program control structure should be hierarchical and should be derived from the program data structures.
- The design process consists of first defining the data structures, next merging them to form a single, hierarchical program structure, and then ordering the detail procedural logic to fit this structure.
- Logical design should be separate from and precede physical design.

Types of diagrams needed to support a data-driven approach to software development:

- Hierarchical tree structured diagram
- Detailed procedural logic diagram

The Warnier–Orr design methodology is another example of a data-oriented approach. But unlike the Jackson approach, the Warnier–Orr approach is to focus on the program output. It is an *output-oriented* methodology. Using the Warnier–Orr approach, the program developer begins by defining the system output and works backward through the basic system model to define the process and input portions of the design:

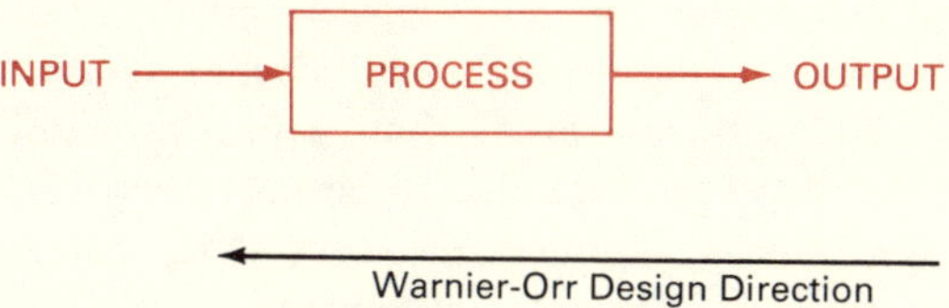

Information-Centered Development Approach

In an *information-centered approach* to system development, a logical data model representing information usage across an organization is the starting point for all system development. The process begins with a high-level analysis of a corporation, its business objectives, and strategic information needs. A global view of information needs is represented in a model showing all the organization's basic data entities and their relationships to each other. Then, based on this model, the individual information systems for the organization are built. Thus procedures follow from data.

Information Engineering

Information engineering is an example of an information-centered development approach. Box 3.5 lists the basic premises of information engineering [6, pp. 651–665].

BOX 3.5 Basic premises of information engineering

- An overall system development strategy that focuses on strategic planning and business goals is needed to build systems that better meet corporate needs.
- Information systems can be better integrated if data that are shared are controlled centrally by being part of the same logical data model.
- Logical representation of data is relatively stable, whereas procedures that use the data change frequently. Therefore, the logical data model, which reflects what the organization is, not how it currently operates, should be the base for system development.

Information engineering is both a business approach and an engineering approach to building software systems. It is a business approach because it begins with strategic information planning for an organization. It is an engineering-like approach because it provides a step-by-step procedure for building information systems. Figure 3.9 describes the basic steps in an information engineering approach.

Information engineering is a newer discipline than software engineering. In one sense, information engineering has a broader focus than software engineering. It is a system building, rather than a program building discipline. It begins at a higher level (with strategic planning) than software engineering. However, at the program design phase, its approach to program development is basically the same as that of software engineering.

In another sense, however, information engineering has a narrower focus than software engineering. Information engineering is used to build information systems, whereas software engineering is used to develop all sorts of systems—both real-time and commercial systems.

Information engineering is an information-oriented approach to software development, and as such it differs from data-oriented approaches such as those of Jackson and Warnier–Orr. Information engineering has been designed to develop database systems and can work with nonhierarchical data structures. Logical data modeling and normalization are required steps in information engineering. Information engineering builds information systems that are integrated because they are built on top of the same logical data model. Also, the emphasis

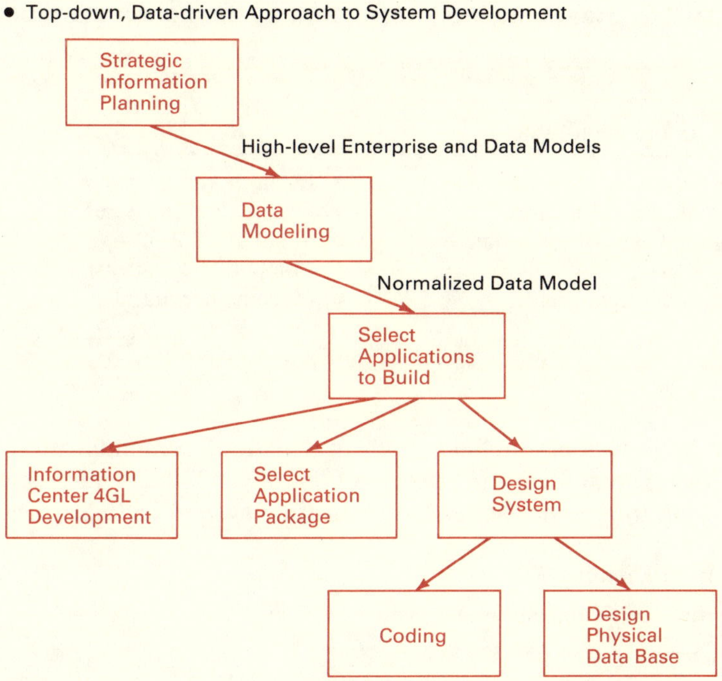

• Top-down, Data-driven Approach to System Development

Strategic Information Planning

High-level Enterprise and Data Models

Data Modeling

Normalized Data Model

Select Applications to Build

Information Center 4GL Development

Select Application Package

Design System

Coding

Design Physical Data Base

Figure 3.9 Basic steps of an information engineering approach to system development.

of information engineering is on data from the standpoint of business requirements, not software system requirements. The entire information engineering development approach centers on a logical view of how the system uses data. Information engineering is discussed later in this chapter in the section entitled "Martin Information Engineering Methodology."

Real-Time vs. Information System Support

Different types of systems require different types of development support. Two examples of system types are real-time/embedded systems and information systems. Box 3.6 outlines their major differences [3].

Real-Time Systems

Real-time systems typically are systems that control and are controlled by external events. Responding to these events (e.g., signal, trigger, or enable/disable) in a timely manner is one of the primary functions of a real-time system [3]. When the system recognizes an event by receiving an input signal, it performs certain calculations and logic to respond to the event by producing its output. Exam-

BOX 3.6 Real-time vs. information system characteristics

Information System	Real-Time System
• Data driven	• Event driven
• Complex data structures	• Simple data structures
• Large volumes of input data	• Small amount of input data
• I/O intensive	• Computational intensive
• Machine independent	• Machine dependent

ples of real-time systems include: flight navigation, communication networks, systems software, manufacturing process control, and chemical processing.

Specifying the requirements for a real-time system includes concerns for:

- Interrupt handling
- Intertask communication and synchronization
- Concurrent processing
- Response timing to external events
- Hardware system requirements and constraints
- System/environment interactions
- Continuous or discrete data

A real-time system design must be able to represent processes that can be interrupted by external events and that can run concurrently on different computers [7].

Special types of structured diagrams are used to represent real-time system requirements. They include control flow diagrams, state transition diagrams, context graphs, state-event matrices, and decision tables. For example, the control flow diagram is used to show the system processes, data input/output signals passed between processes and process timing relationships. The state transition diagram shown in Figure 3.10 is used to show the conditions and actions that cause a system to change from one state to another. The matrix provides more detailed information by describing the conditional logic used within a system state. The context diagram, as shown in Figure 3.11, depicts the boundaries of the system. The block diagram illustrates signal flow between system software and hardware.

Most of these diagrams are variations of structured diagrams used to describe information systems. Similarly, the analysis and design methodologies used for real-time systems are variations of structured methodologies for infor-

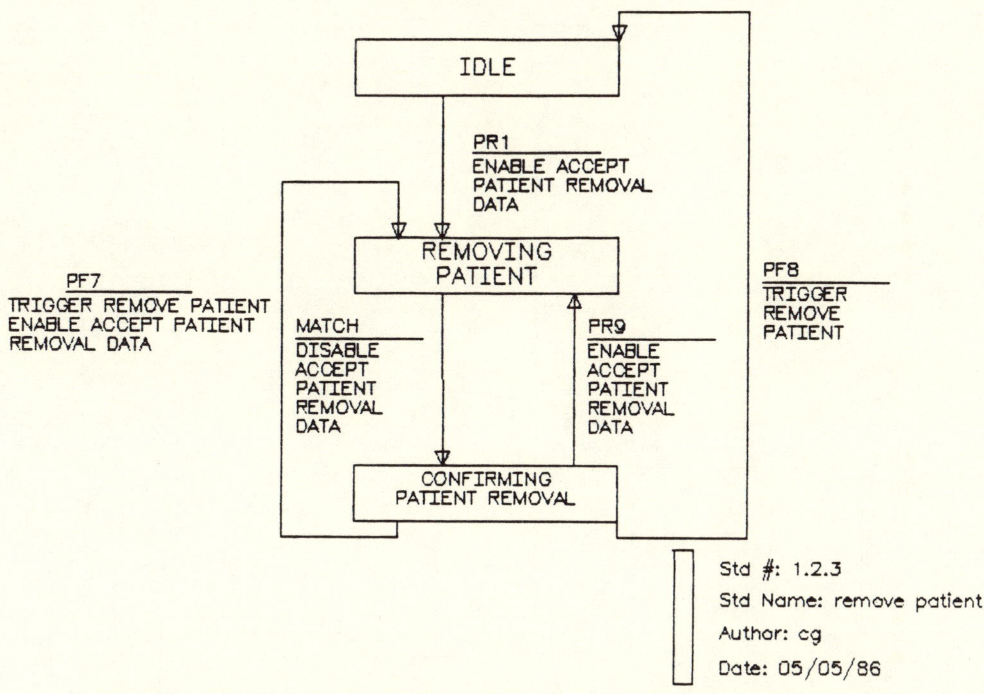

Figure 3.10 This state transition diagram, used to show the conditions and actions that cause a system to change from one state to another, was drawn by the ANALYST/DESIGNER TOOLKIT from the Yourdon Software Engineering Company.

mation systems such as DeMarco, Yourdon, and Jackson. For example, the Hatley methodology is an extension of the Yourdon–Constantine design methodology. The Jackson system design methodology can be used to design either real-time or information systems.

WIDELY-USED STRUCTURED METHODOLOGIES

Box 3.7 lists the most often used structured development methodologies according to a survey of over 1000 U.S. organizations [8]. Box 3.7 also lists the top structured methodologies that organizations plan to adopt as their standard methodology according to the same survey [8]. Notice that information engineering, although not among the most often used methodologies, is one of the methodologies that organizations plan to adopt as their standard. This is probably because information engineering is a much newer methodology relative to the others listed in Box 3.7. It is gaining widespread acceptance because of its incorporation of data modeling and strategic planning into its methodology.

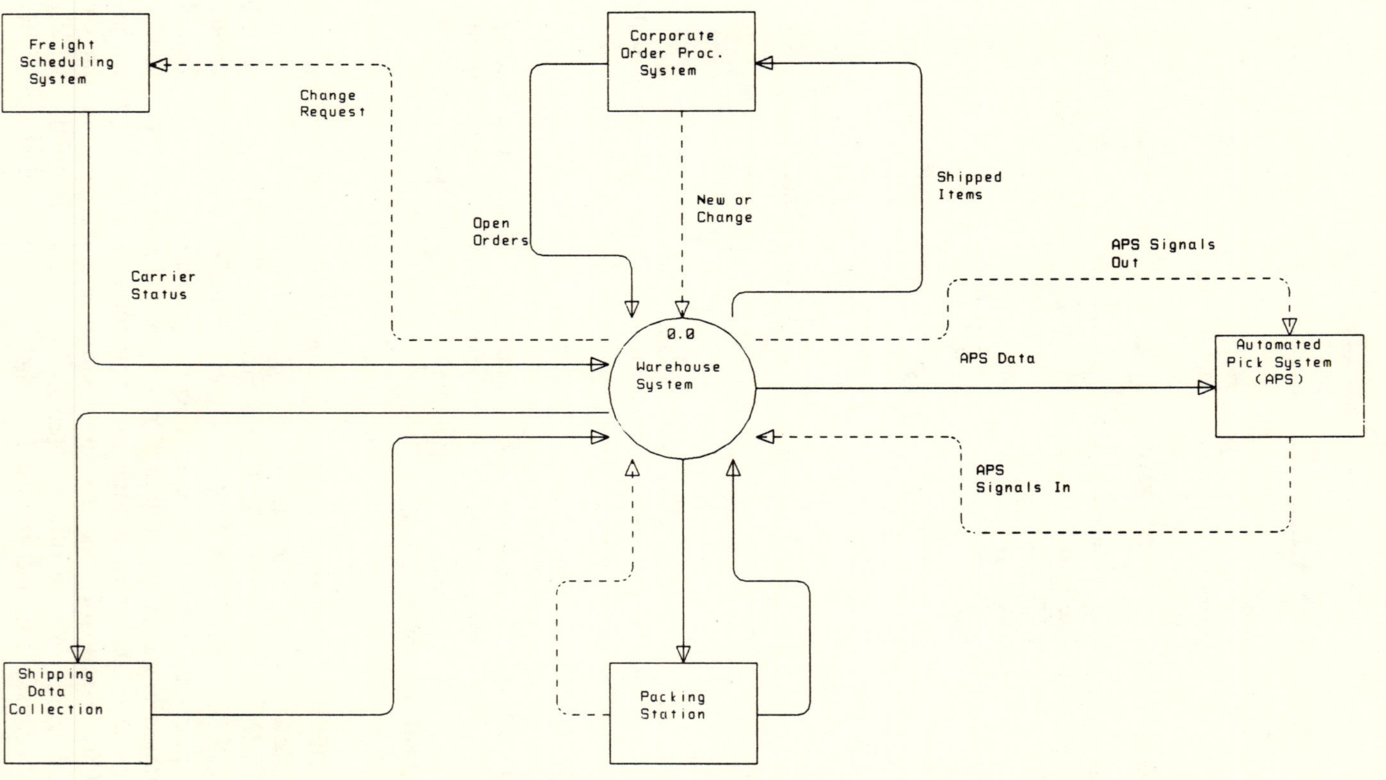

Figure 3.11 The context diagram is a type of control flow diagram that depicts the boundaries of the system. It was drawn by EXCELERATOR/RTS from Index Technology Corporation.

BOX 3.7 Most-often-used methodologies

Most often-used application development methodology in the United States

Yourdon structured design	29.1%
Gane–Sarson structured analysis	13.8%
DeMarco structured analysis	12.3%
Orr structured design	7.2%
Jackson structured design	2.4%

Development methodology standardization choice

Yourdon	24.9%
Gane–Sarson	11.2%
Information engineering	11.2%
DeMarco	9.5%
Orr	7.1%
Jackson	3.6%

The remainder of the chapter is devoted to a brief discussion of the process steps in each of these methodologies. Box 3.8 classifies each of these structured methodologies.

STRUCTURED ANALYSIS

Structured analysis proposes a systematic, step-by-step approach to performing system analysis and producing a system specification [6, pp. 407–416]. There are two similar versions of structured analysis:

- Gane and Sarson
- DeMarco

Both represent a structured discipline based on the following structuring concepts:

- Top-down hierarchical organization
- Graphic communication/documentation tools

Structured analysis uses the top-down, functional decomposition method to define system requirements. The system specification produced by the struc-

BOX 3.8 Methodology classification

Methodology	Classification
Demarco Structured analysis	• Software engineering • Procedure-oriented • Information systems • Informal (real-time extensions)
Gane-Sarson Structured analysis	• Software engineering • Procedure-oriented • Information systems • Informal (real-time extensions)
Yourdon Structured design	• Software engineering • Procedure-oriented • Information systems • Informal (real-time extensions)
Jackson Structured design	• Software engineering • Data-oriented • Information systems • Informal (real-time extensions)
Orr Data structured systems development	• Software engineering • Data-oriented • Output-oriented • Information systems • Informal
Martin Information engineering	• Information engineering • Information-oriented • Information systems • Informal

tured analysis process is a top-down, partitioned model of the system to be built. Providing a description of the requirements of the system to be built, it is the link between analysis and design.

The primary purpose of analysis is to produce a system specification that defines the structure of the problem to be solved as the user views it. The purpose of design is to define the structure of a solution in a form that is compatible with the structure of the problem and with the users' requirements. Advocates of structured analysis suggest that by using the same construction method (top-down functional decomposition) for both the specification and the design, the two can be brought closer together and are more likely to represent a system that will meet the users' needs and expectations.

Structured Specification

The system specification produced by structured analysis is a graphic, partitioned, top-down, hierarchical, and logical model of the system processes and data used by these processes. It is composed of data flow diagrams, a data dictionary, and process specifications.

Data Flow Diagram

A *data flow diagram* is a structured diagram that represents the processes (functions or procedures) in a system and the data connecting them. It is the central modeling tool of structured analysis and is used to partition the system into a process hierarchy. At lower levels, the higher-level processes are exploded so that we can look inside a process to see what more detailed processes and data flows are involved. Figure 3.12 is an example of a data flow diagram.

Data Dictionary

The *data dictionary* is a set of definitions of all data appearing on a data flow diagram in data stores or as data flows. The definition of each data item consists of the data components that make up the data item and the relationships among them.

```
CUSTOMER FILE   = [customer records]
CUSTOMER RECORD = customer-name +
                  customer-address +
                  payment-information +
                  outstanding-orders +
                  customer-type
```

Process Specification

A *process specification,* or minispec, describes what happens inside a process box in a data flow diagram. A minispec is usually about one page long and

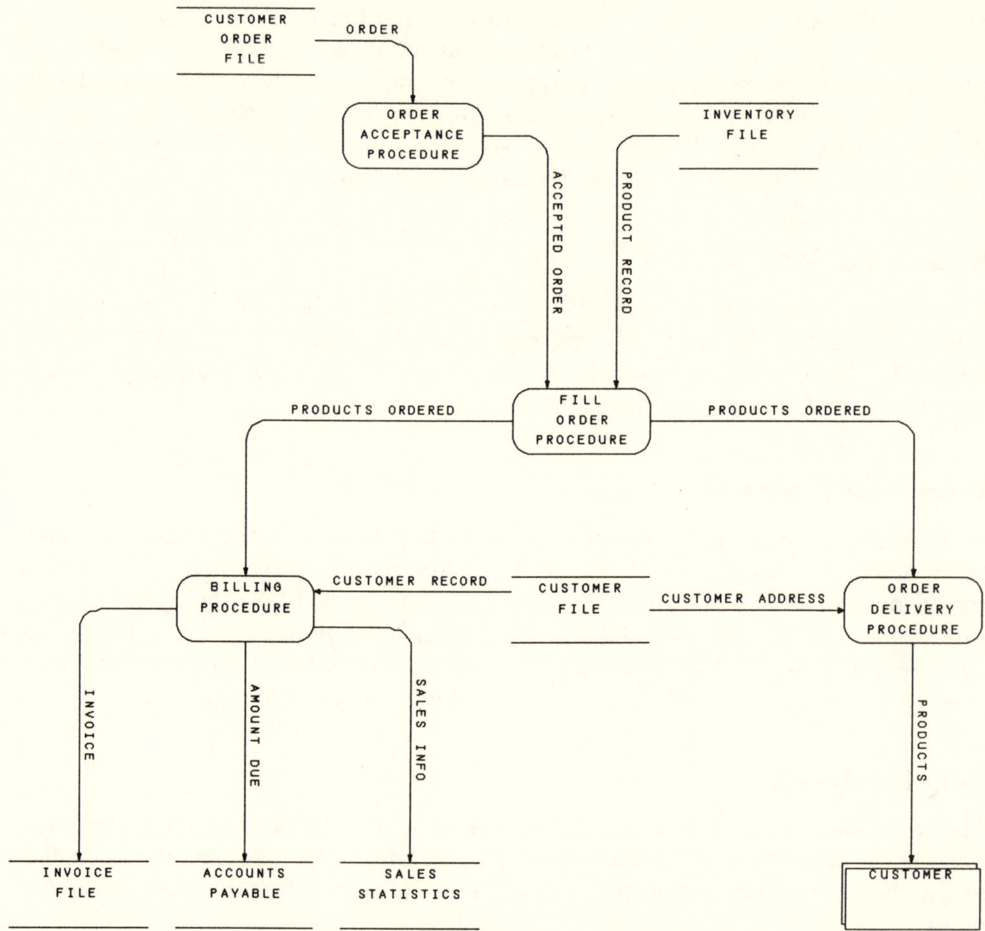

Figure 3.12 Data flow diagram showing the processes in the sales distribution system drawn by the INFORMATION ENGINEERING WORKBENCH from KnowledgeWare.

explains how input data are transformed into output data. A minispec is written in structured English (pseudocode) as a decision table or as an action diagram. Figure 3.13 is an example of a minispec. A minispec is created for each process defined in the lowest-level data flow diagram on the system specification.

Steps of Structured Analysis

As shown in Box 3.9, DeMarco defines structured analysis as a seven-step process:

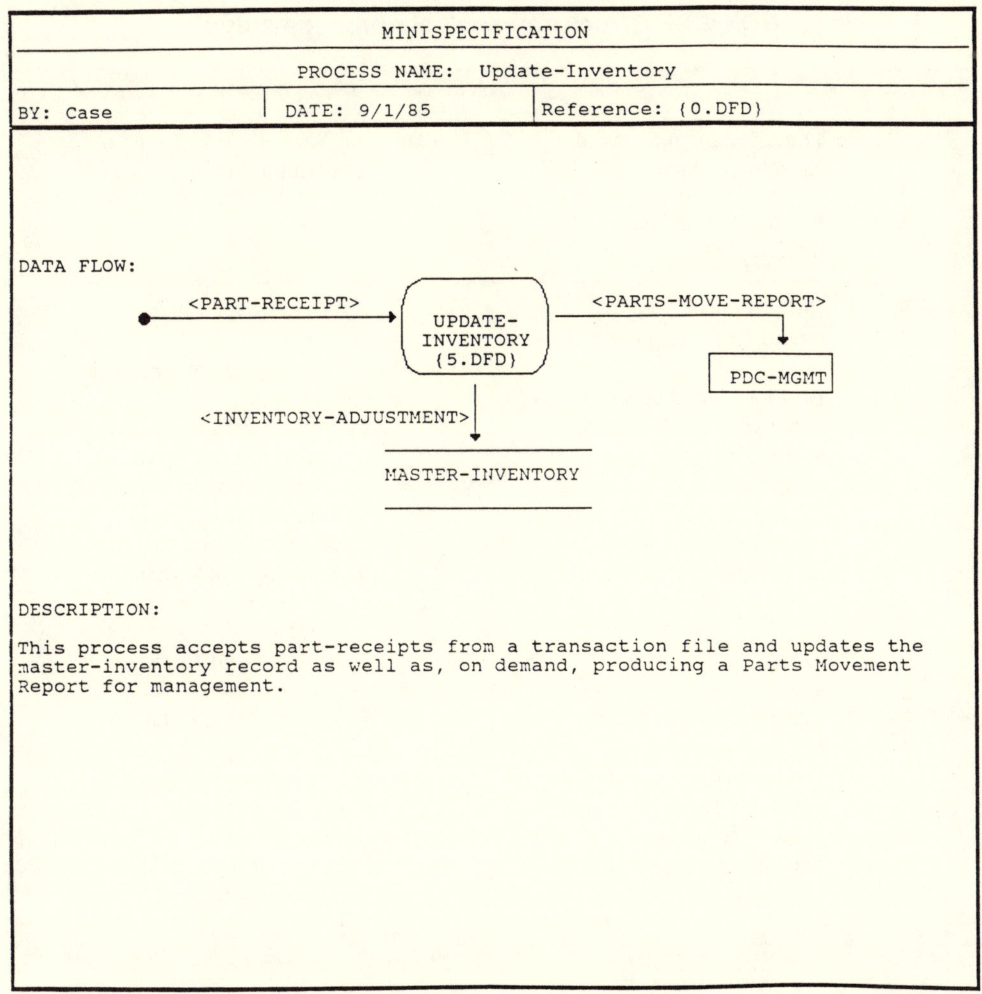

MINISPECIFICATION

PROCESS NAME: Update-Inventory

BY: Case | DATE: 9/1/85 | Reference: {0.DFD}

DATA FLOW:

DESCRIPTION:

This process accepts part-receipts from a transaction file and updates the master-inventory record as well as, on demand, producing a Parts Movement Report for management.

Figure 3.13 This example of a minispec was produced by DESIGNAID from the Nastec Corporation.

Step 1

Document the current way things are done in the present user environment. The output of this step is the current physical data flow diagram(s). It shows locations, personnel, names, and manual and automated procedures, and uses the users', terms.

Step 2

Use the current physical data flow diagram from Step 1 to create the logical model of the current system. The logical model, like the physical model, is

BOX 3.9 Structured analysis process steps

De Marco's Seven Steps of Structured Analysis	Gane and Sarson's Five Steps of Structured Analysis
Step 1: Build a current physical model.	
Step 2: Build a current logical model from the physical model. Step 3: Build a logical model of the new system to be built. • Build a structured specification consisting of data flow diagrams, a data dictionary, and process specifications.	Step 1: Build a current logical model. Step 2: Build a logical model of the new system. • Build a structured specification consisting of data flow diagrams, a data dictionary, and process specifications. • Build a logical data model by expressing the contents of data stores in third-normal form.
Step 4: Create a family of new physical models. Step 5: Produce cost and schedule estimates for each model. Step 6: Select one model. Step 7: Package the specification into subsystems.	Step 3: Design a physical database. Step 4: Create a new physical model of system. Step 5: Package the specification into subsystems.

represented as a set of hierarchically leveled data flow diagrams. The difference between the two models is that the physical model shows the physical details of how particular users currently do things, while the logical model portrays what is done at an abstract level, separating out any current particulars from the fundamental business procedures.

Step 3

Develop the new logical model for the system to be built. The logical model from Step 2 is the starting point. It is modified to incorporate the changes for the new system. It indicates both manual and automatable processes and is represented as a set of leveled data flow diagrams describing the system at varying levels of detail. Step 3 involves the major part of the work effort for the structured analysis process.

Step 4

Create the new physical model for the system to be built by identifying the human–machine interface. More than one possible model is created to represent varying degrees of automation.

Step 5

Produce cost and schedule estimates for each alternative physical model developed in Step 4.

Step 6

Based on the estimate produced in Step 5, select one physical model to be used to specify the functions and requirements of the system to be built.

Step 7

Package the structured specification into its final form, which includes a set of leveled data flow diagrams, a data dictionary, and minispecs.

Gane and Sarson define a similar process for structured analysis (see Box 3.9). The major difference is that Gane and Sarson include a data modeling step in which the contents of the data stores shown in the data flow diagrams are defined, possibly in third-normal form. Gane and Sarson include data modeling in Step 2 of their version of structured analysis. Then in Step 3, the logical data model is used as input to physical database design. Also, as shown in Box 3.10, Gane and Sarson use a slightly different set of graphic symbols in their version of data flow diagrams.

YOURDON STRUCTURED DESIGN

The Yourdon structured design methodology provides a step-by-step design process for system design and detail program design [6, pp. 425–453]. Some steps involve developing the design, some involve documenting the design, and still others involve measuring and improving the quality of the design. Each step is supported by a set of design strategies, guidelines, and documentation techniques. For example, design strategies such as transform analysis and transaction analysis guide the designer in ordering design decisions. Design measures such as coupling and cohesion provide the designer with techniques for measuring the quality of the design. The principal product

BOX 3.10 Symbols used on data flow diagrams

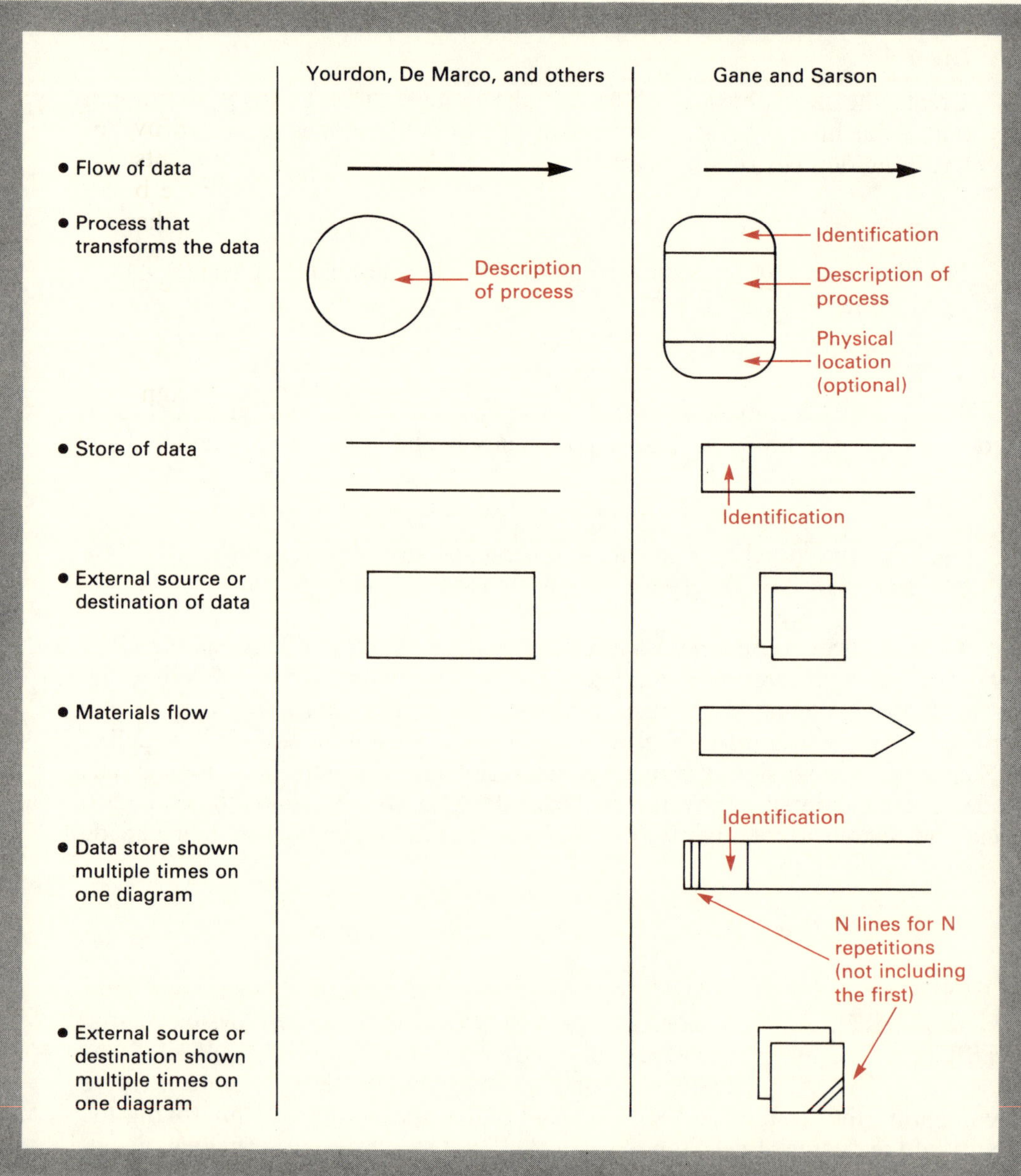

produced by the structured design process is a structure chart showing the programs' procedural components, their hierarchical arrangement, and data connecting them.

Structure Chart

The *structure chart* is a tree or hierarchical diagram that defines the overall architecture of a program by showing the program procedural components and their interrelationships. The basic building blocks of structure charts are boxes representing procedural components and arrows connecting them. Data that are passed between the procedural components are called couples and are written alongside the connecting arrows. Figure 3.19 is an example of a structure chart.

Steps of Yourdon Structured Design

Figure 3.14 shows the four basic steps of the Yourdon structured design process.

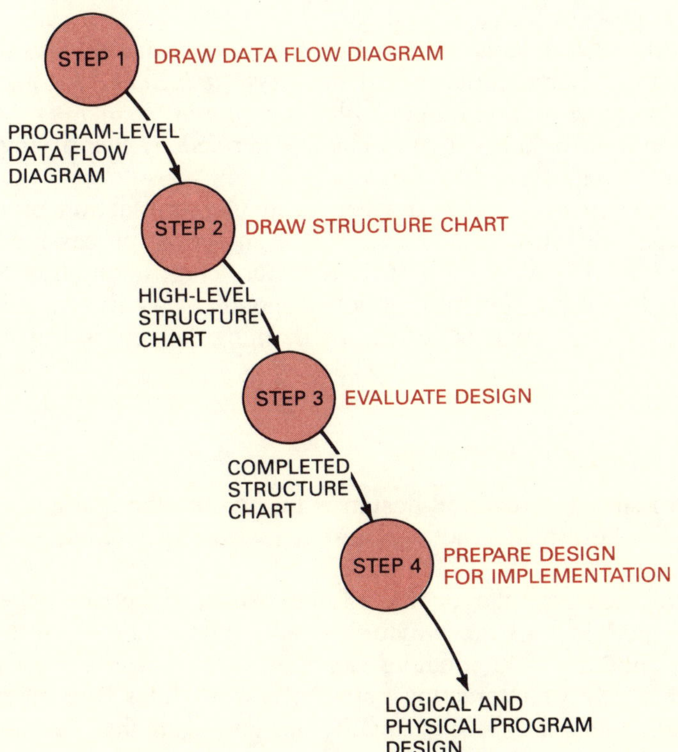

Figure 3.14 The structured design process consists of four sequential steps in the Yourdon structured design methodology.

Step 1: Draw the Data Flow Diagram

The first step in the structured design process is to represent the design problem as the flow of data through a system. The system is composed of processes that operate on (or transform) the data. These processes and the data linking them become the basis for defining the program components. A set of leveled data flow diagrams is used to represent this first view of the program design.

Step 2: Draw the Structure Chart

The second step is to represent the program design as a hierarchy of procedural components. A structure chart is used to show this view of the design. The structure chart is derived from the data flow diagram produced in Step 1. Structured design provides two design strategies to guide the transformation of a data flow diagram(s) into a structure chart: transform analysis and transaction analysis. These two strategies provide two structure models that can be used singly or in conjunction to drive a hierarchical design as well as a step-by-step transformation process for each strategy.

Transform analysis is an information-flow model that divides the data flow diagram into three parts: input called the *afferent branch*(es), logical process called *central transform,* and output called the *efferent branch*(es). As shown in Figures 3.15 and 3.16, the structure chart is derived by identifying these three basic parts in the data flow diagram.

Transaction analysis is used when designing transaction processing programs. The general structure chart for a transaction processing program is shown in Figure 3.17. At the top of the structure chart is one transaction-center module and below it are several transaction modules. As shown in Figures 3.18 and 3.19, the structure chart is derived by defining the central transform and the transactions.

Step 3: Evaluate the Design

The third step in structured design is to measure the quality of the design. Coupling and cohesion are the two design measuring techniques provided by structured design.

Coupling measures the degree of independence between the procedural components (modules) in the structure chart. When there is little interaction between two modules, the modules are described as *loosely coupled.* When there is a great deal of interaction between two modules, the modules are described as *tightly coupled.* A high-quality design means that the modules are as loosely coupled as possible. There are five levels of coupling: data, stamp, control, common, and content. Data coupling is the loosest and the best type of coupling; content coupling is the tightest and the worst type of coupling.

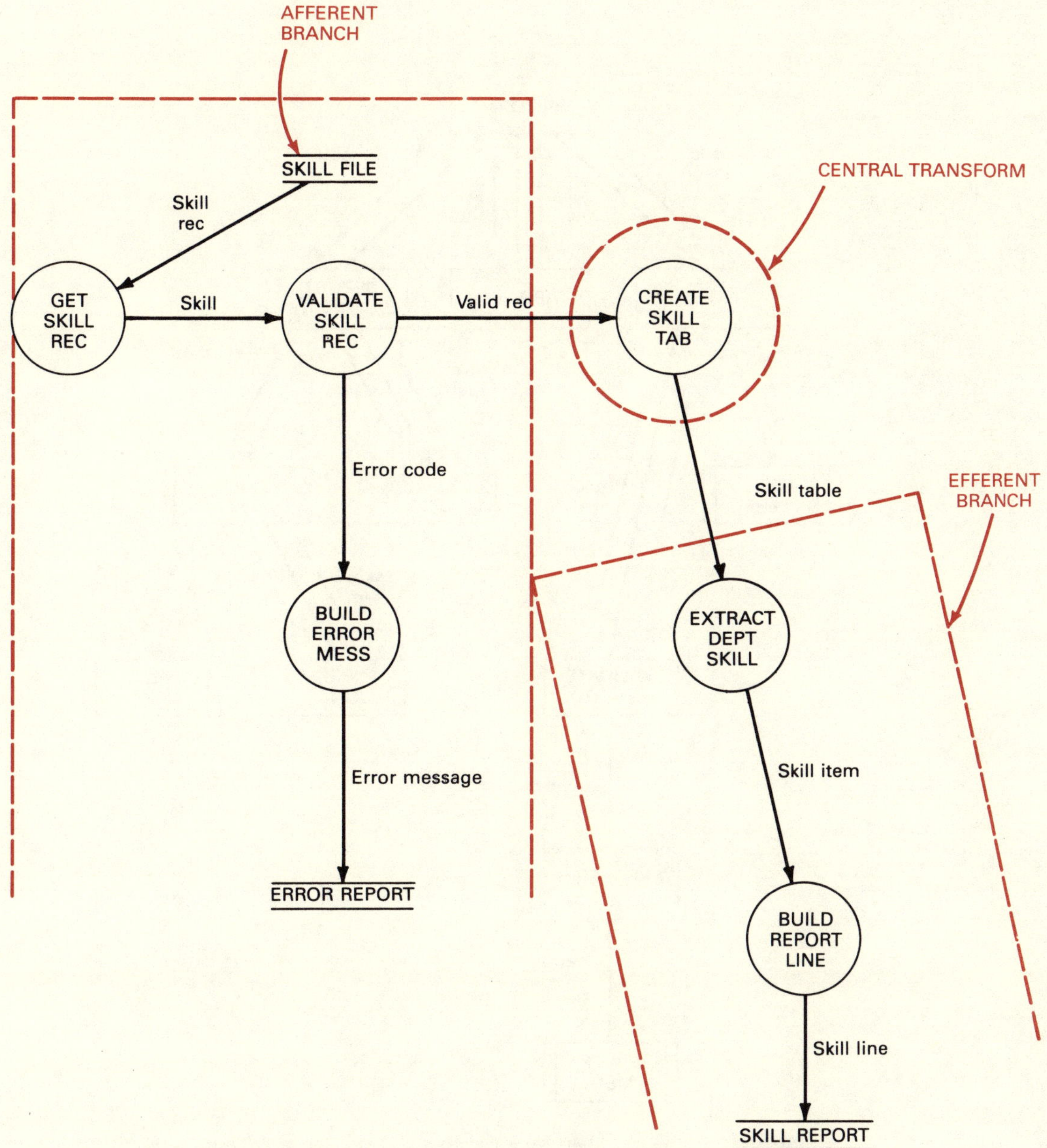

Figure 3.15 Data flow diagram for the employee skills system with afferent branches (input), efferent branches (output), and central transform (logical processing) indicated.

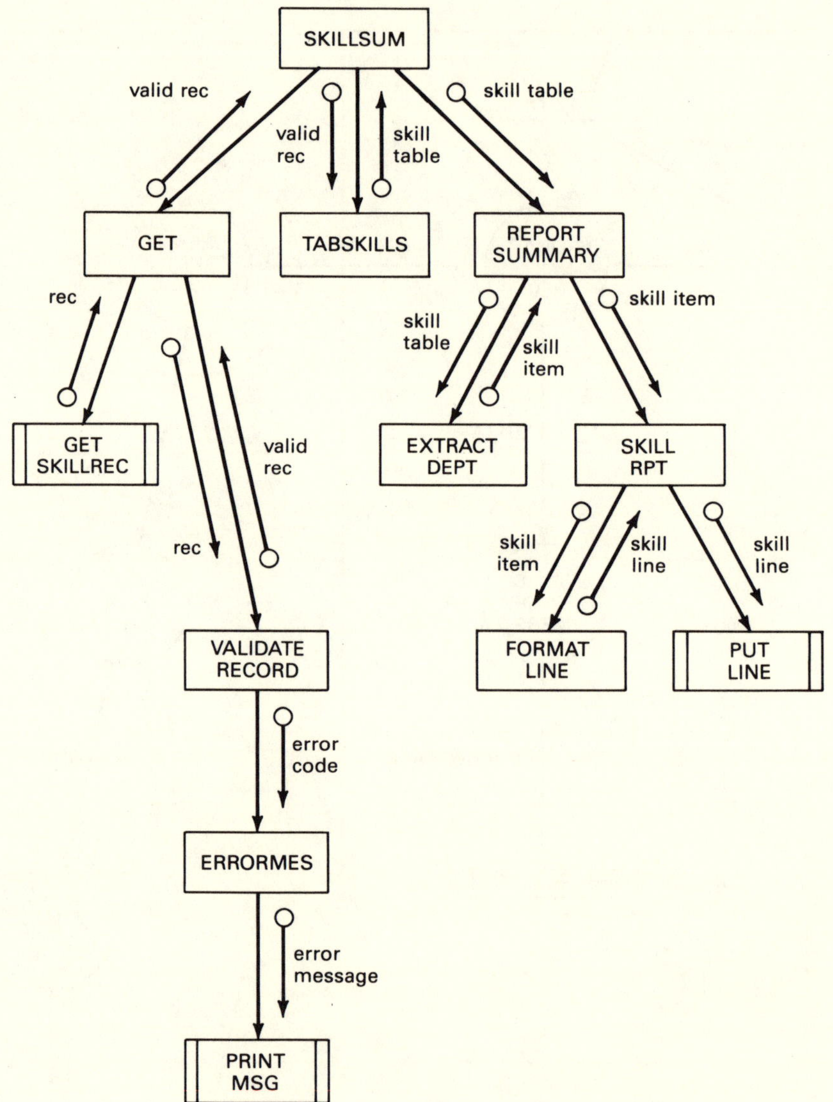

Figure 3.16 Structure chart for the employee skills system derived from the employee skills system data flow diagram shown in Figure 3.15.

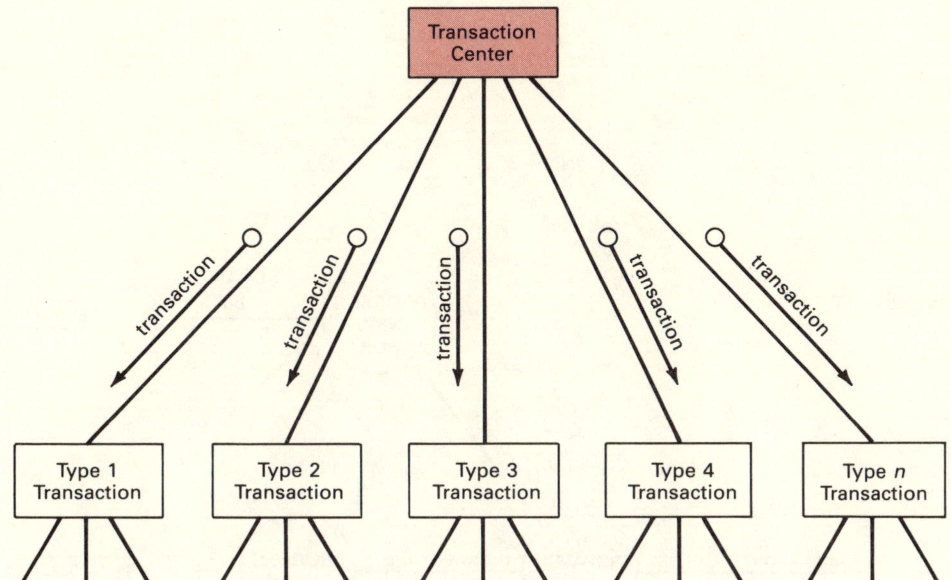

Figure 3.17 The general structure-chart model for a transaction processing program has one transaction-center module at the top and below it one transaction module for each transaction type.

Cohesion measures how strongly the elements within a module are related—the stronger, the better. There are seven levels of cohesion: functional, sequential, communicational, procedural, temporal, logical, and coincidental. Functional cohesion is the best type of cohesion; coincidental cohesion is the worst.

Step 4: Prepare for Design Implementation

The last step of structured design is to prepare the design for implementation. This is called *packaging* the design. Packaging is the process of dividing the logical program design into physical implementation units, called *load units*. This is physical program design.

This is a description of the traditional Yourdon structured design methodology. There are variations and updates, some of which have extended the Yourdon design methodology (which was intended primarily for the design of information systems) to support the design of real-time systems.

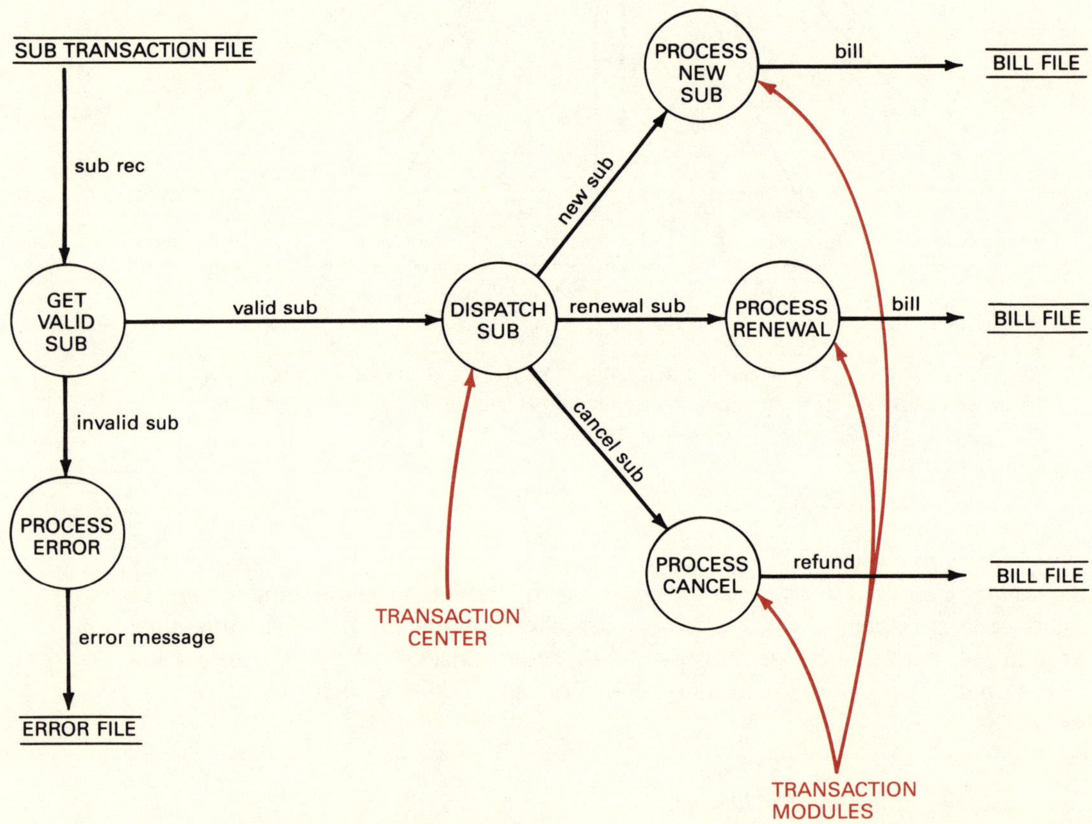

Figure 3.18 Data flow diagram for a subscription system, showing the transaction center and transaction modules.

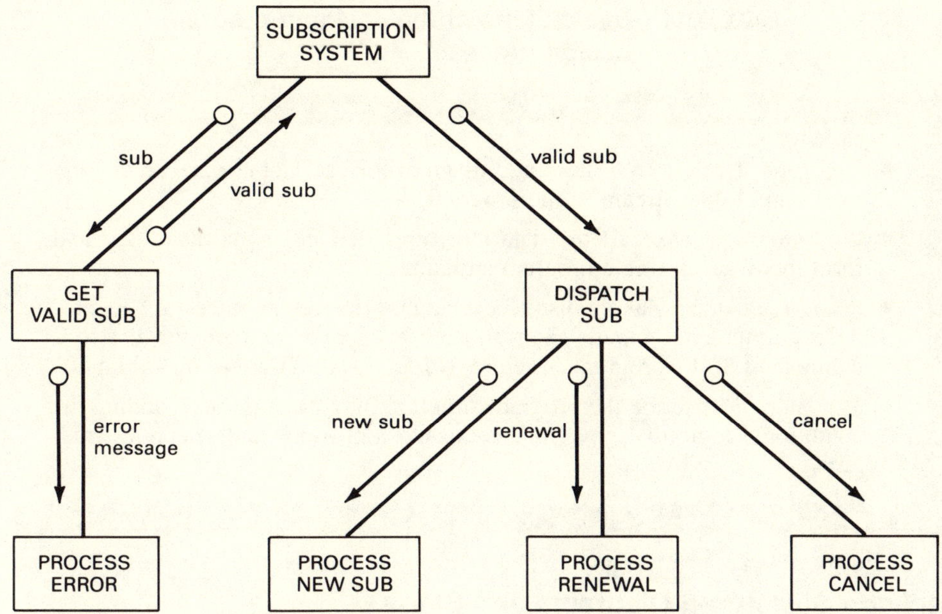

Figure 3.19 High-level structure chart derived from the data flow diagram using the transaction design strategy.

JACKSON PROGRAM DESIGN METHODOLOGY

Like the Yourdon structured design methodology, the Jackson design methodology provides a top-down, step-by-step design process [6, pp. 455–487]. The major difference between the two is that the Jackson design methodology is based on an analysis of data structure, whereas the Yourdon approach is based on analysis of data flow. Jackson is data oriented; Yourdon is procedure oriented. The Jackson approach advocates a static view of structures, whereas the Yourdon approach uses a dynamic view of data flow.

The Jackson program design methodology is a data-driven program design technique. Its approach is to derive the program structure from the data structure(s). It assumes that the problem has been fully specified.

Jackson views a program as a sequential process. It has inputs and outputs that are viewed as sequential streams of records. The design process consists of first defining the structure of the data streams and then ordering the procedural logic (operations) to fit the data structures. As shown in Box 3.11, the Jackson program design process consists of four steps.

BOX 3.11 Basic steps of the Jackson program design process

- Data step: Draw a tree structured diagram for each input data stream and each output data stream in the program.
- Program step: Take all the data structures defined in the data step and form them into a single program structure.
- Operations step: Make a list of executable operations necessary to produce output from input. Then allocate each operation on the list to a component of the program structure. (Progress from output toward input.)
- Text step: Transcribe the program structure into structure text, adding the conditional logic that governs the execution of loops and selection structures.

Jackson Structured Diagrams and Steps

The Jackson design methodology uses three structured diagramming techniques to describe a program design:

- System network diagram: flow of data streams between programs (see Figure 3.20)
- Tree structured diagram: hierarchical representation of program and data structures (see Figures 3.21 and 3.22)
- Structure text: form of pseudocode (see Figure 3.25)

Step 1: Data Step

First, a system network diagram showing all data streams in and out of the program is drawn (see Figure 3.20). Then, each data stream is represented as a hierarchical structure. A tree structured diagram is used.

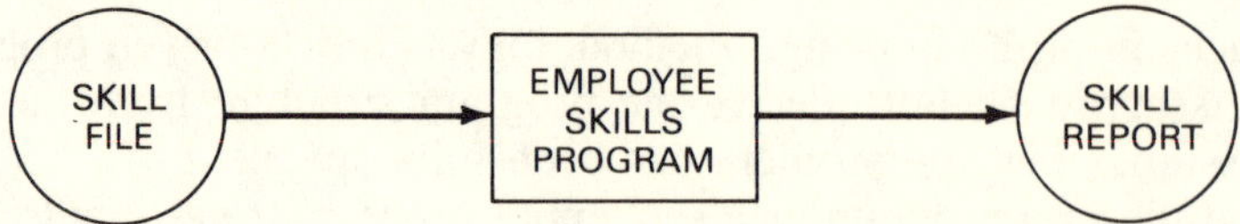

Figure 3.20 The system network diagram for an employee skills system shows that there is one input data stream, SKILL FILE; one output stream, SKILL REPORT; and one program, EMPLOYEE SKILLS PROGRAM. In Jackson terminology, SKILL FILE is consumed by the EMPLOYEE SKILLS PROGRAM to produce SKILL REPORT.

Step 2: Program Step

The second step is to combine data structures into one program structure. There are two parts to the program step. First, all correspondences between the components of the data structures are identified by finding the consume–produce relationships between data structure components (see Figure 3.21). The program structure is built to correspond to these relationships (see Figure 3.22).

The second part of the program step is to verify the correctness of the program structure. This is done by reducing the program structure into its indi-

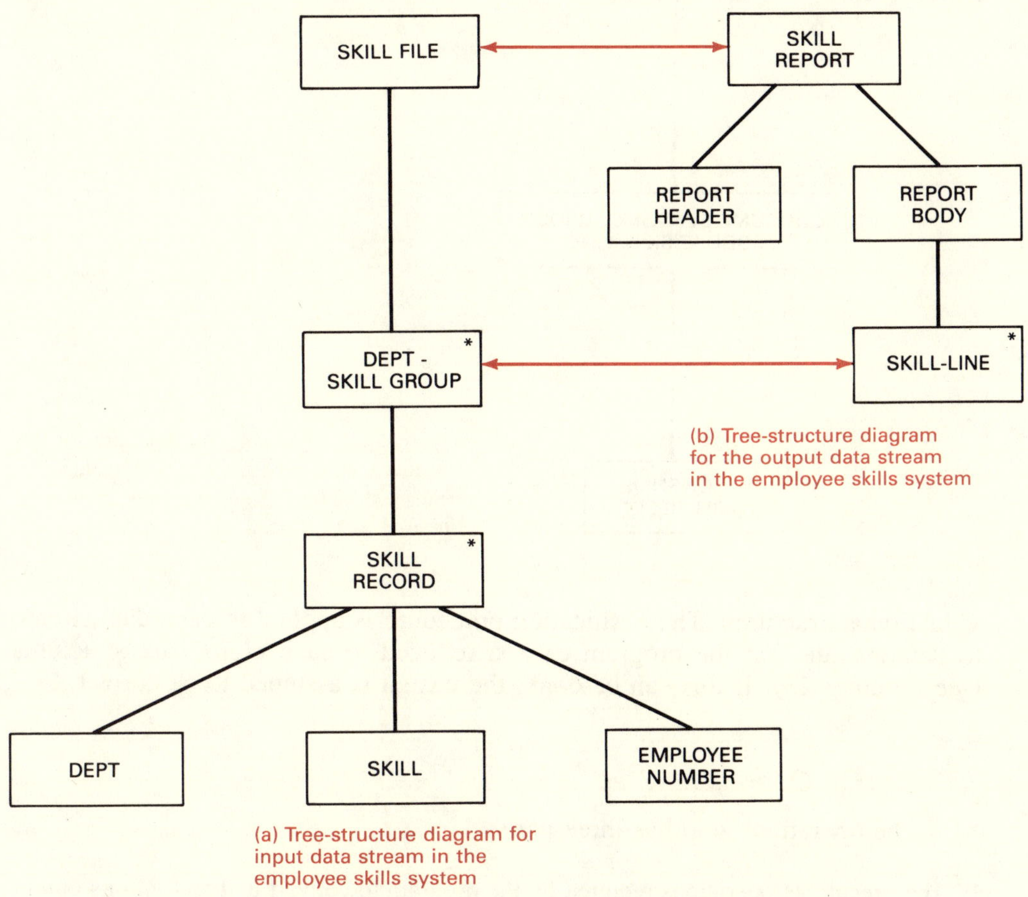

Figure 3.21 The employee skills program has one input data stream and one output data stream. A tree structured diagram is used to represent each data structure. The red arrows show the consume–produce relationships between components in the data structures.

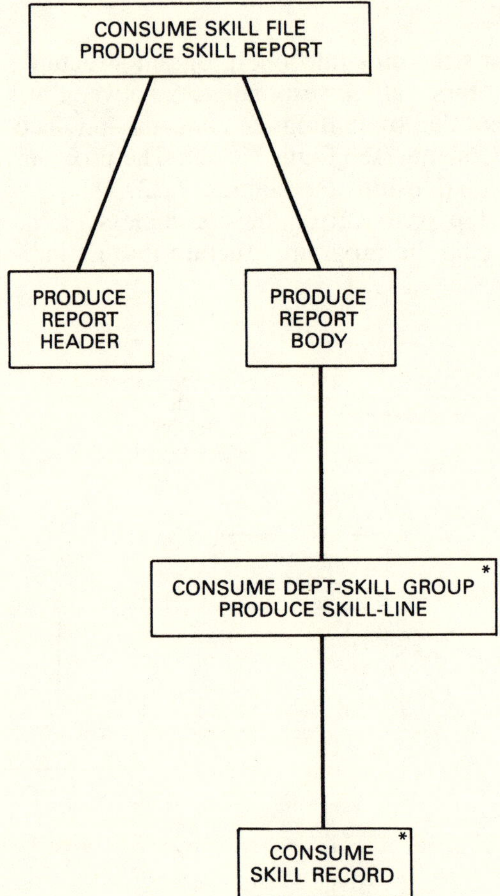

Figure 3.22 The program structure for the employee skills program is a composite of its input and output data structures shown in Figure 3.21.

vidual data structures. The verification procedure is applied to each data stream to demonstrate that the program can be reduced to each of its data structures (see Figure 3.23). If this can be done, the design is assumed to be correct.

Step 3: Operations Step

The operations step has three parts:

1. The executable operations required by the program to convert its input into its output are listed. The list is derived by starting with the output and working back toward the input. Operations are determined by referring to data structures, which in turn are reflected in the program structure.
2. Each operation is allocated to the appropriate place in the program structure.

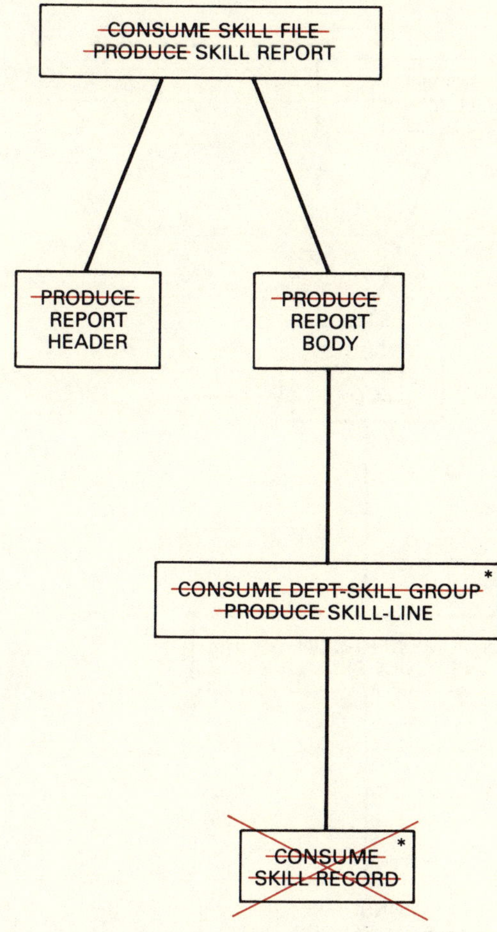

Figure 3.23 The correctness of the program structure is demonstrated by reducing it to its data structures. In this example, the program structure for the employee skills program is reduced to its output data stream, SKILL REPORT. The data structure for SKILL REPORT is shown in Figure 3.21.

3. Correctness is verified by checking that all outputs are produced and all inputs are consumed. Figure 3.24 shows the program structure augmented with its operation steps.

Step 4: Text Step

The last step in the Jackson program design process is the text step. In the text step, the program structure diagram, along with its accompanying operations, is translated into structure text (see Figure 3.25).

Structure text is a formal type of pseudocode. It has strict rules for writing the control constructs of sequence, selection, and iteration, but elementary programming-level instructions are written informally.

The control conditions governing the execution of the select and iteration structures are added to the structure text in this step. At the end of the text step,

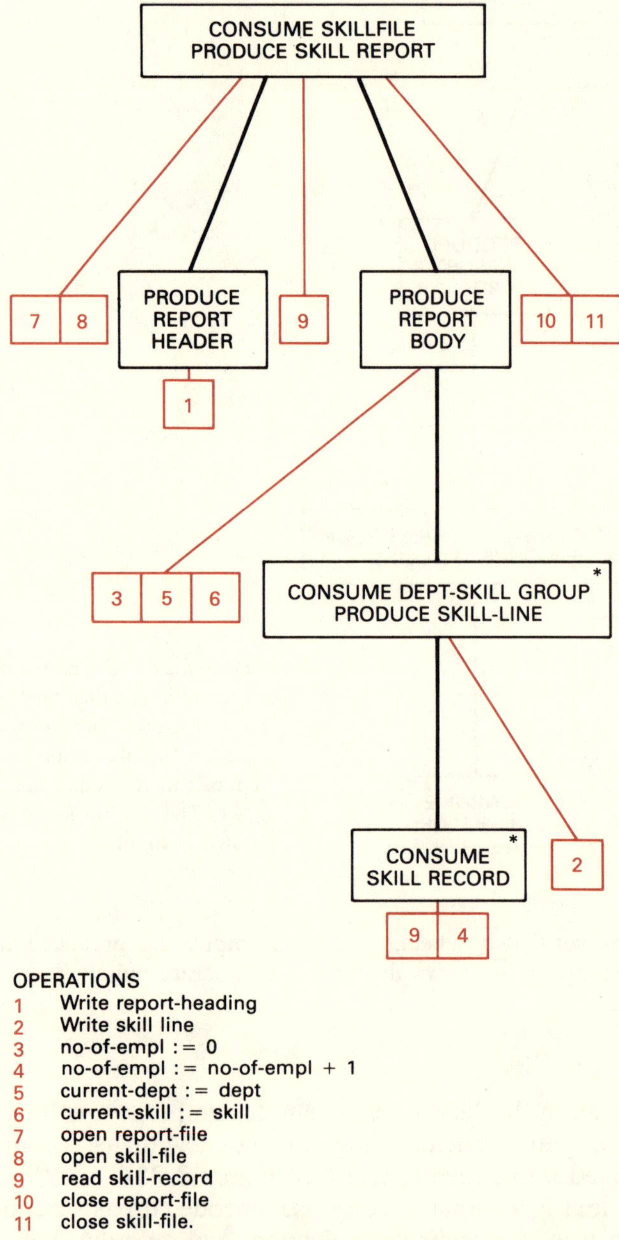

Figure 3.24 The operations step lists the executable operations required by the program and allocates them to the appropriate program component. This is the program structure for the employee skills program.

```
SKILL-REPORT seq
  open skillfile;
  open reportfile;
  write report-header;
  read skill-record;
  REPORT-BODY iter while (not end-of-file)
    DEPT-SKILL-GROUP seq
      no-of-empl := 0;
      current-dept := dept;
      current-skill := skill;
      SKILL-RECORD iter while (dept = current-dept
        and skill = current-skill)
        no-of-empl = no-of-empl + 1;
        read skill-record
      SKILL-RECORD end
      move no-of-empl to skill-line;
      write skill-line;
    DEPT-SKILL-GROUP end
  REPORT-BODY end;
  close skillfile;
  close reportfile;
SKILL-REPORT end
```

CONDITION LOGIC

Figure 3.25 The last step in the Jackson program design process is to translate the program structure into structure text, a formal version of pseudocode. This is the structure text for the employee skills program.

the program design is ready for implementation. The system network diagram, the data-structure trees, the program-structure tree, and the structure text form the complete design package.

Basic Design Procedure

The Jackson design process described above is called the *basic design procedure*. It can be used to design simple programs but is not directly applicable to complex programs. A complex program must first be divided into a sequence of simple programs, each of which can then be designed using the basic design procedure. Resolving structure clashes and program inversion are techniques that are included in the Jackson design process to guide the design of complex programs. Figure 3.26 gives a more complete view of the steps in the Jackson program design process.

The basic Jackson program design process has been extended to handle the design of systems as well as programs and the design of real-time as well as information systems.

MARTIN INFORMATION ENGINEERING METHODOLOGY

The information engineering methodology espoused by James Martin is a top-down, step-by-step approach to information system building [9]. The first steps of the methodology focus on information and enterprise modeling at a high level. The objective is

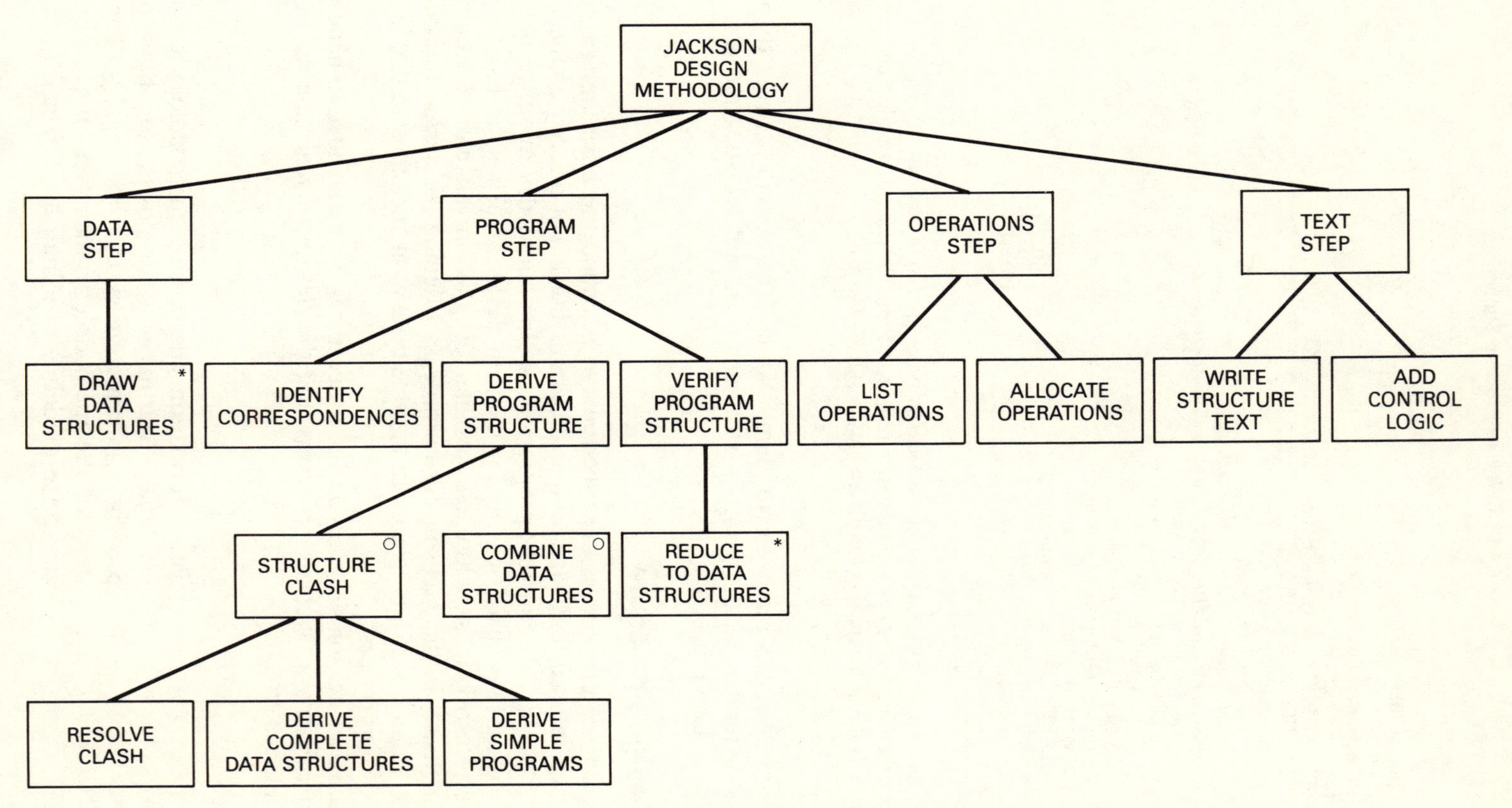

Figure 3.26 Tree structured diagram used to define the Jackson program design process.

to manage system development and interaction through data control. Data that are shared across information systems are defined in one logical data model and are controlled centrally. Thus the Martin methodology looks across all systems in an enterprise to identify how information is used and shared. High-level business functions are defined along with business information. In later steps, data and functions are defined in more detail. At the last step, program data and program logic are defined and implemented.

Program structures are built on top of an enterprise-wide model that establishes a common information infrastructure for uniting information systems used throughout an organization. Thus, procedures follow from data. Logical design is separate from and precedes physical design.

Figure 3.27 outlines the four major stages of Martin's information engineering methodology [10]. Box 3.12 summarizes the types of structured diagrams used in the Martin information engineering methodology.

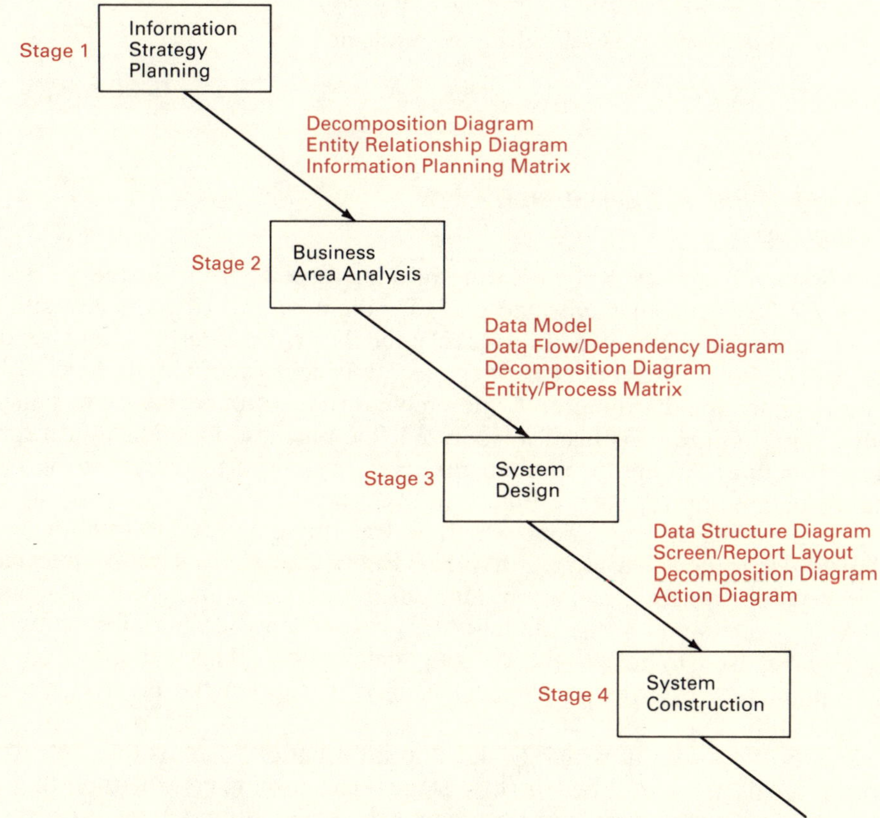

Figure 3.27 Martin information engineering methodology divides the software development process into four basic phases.

BOX 3.12 Information engineering diagrams

Types of diagrams needed to support an information engineering approach to system development:

- Entity relationship diagram: shows entity types and their relationships
- Data structure diagram: shows entity types, their attributes, and their relationships
- Hierarchical tree structured decomposition diagram: shows high-level corporate model, and hierarchical architectural structure of business functions and processes, application systems and procedures, and programs
- Data flow diagram/dependency diagram: shows flow of data between processes
- Screen and report layouts: shows design of user interface
- Action diagram: shows detailed program logic

Stage 1: Information Strategy Planning

This stage begins with the creating of a strategic plan for business systems in which the business objectives and goals for the next 5 to 10 years are defined. Along with the strategic plan, high-level models of the enterprise and its data are built. The enterprise model defines basic business functions (e.g., SALES) and the organizational structure. A hierarchical tree structure diagram, called a *decomposition diagram,* is used to represent the business functions and organizational structure. An entity relationship diagram is used to represent the organization's data entity types (see Figure 3.28).

An entity is anything about which an enterprise stores information (e.g., employee, department, customer, invoice). Entities are discovered by interviewing information system users. Individual user views are analyzed and merged together to create a composite model. Also, reverse engineering of existing systems may be used to reveal the existing data model. This can be used as a starting point to create the data model needed to support the enterprise's strategic direction.

Finally, the order in which to develop information systems to meet overall enterprise goals is determined in this stage. The user plays an important and active role during this stage and throughout the information engineering system development process.

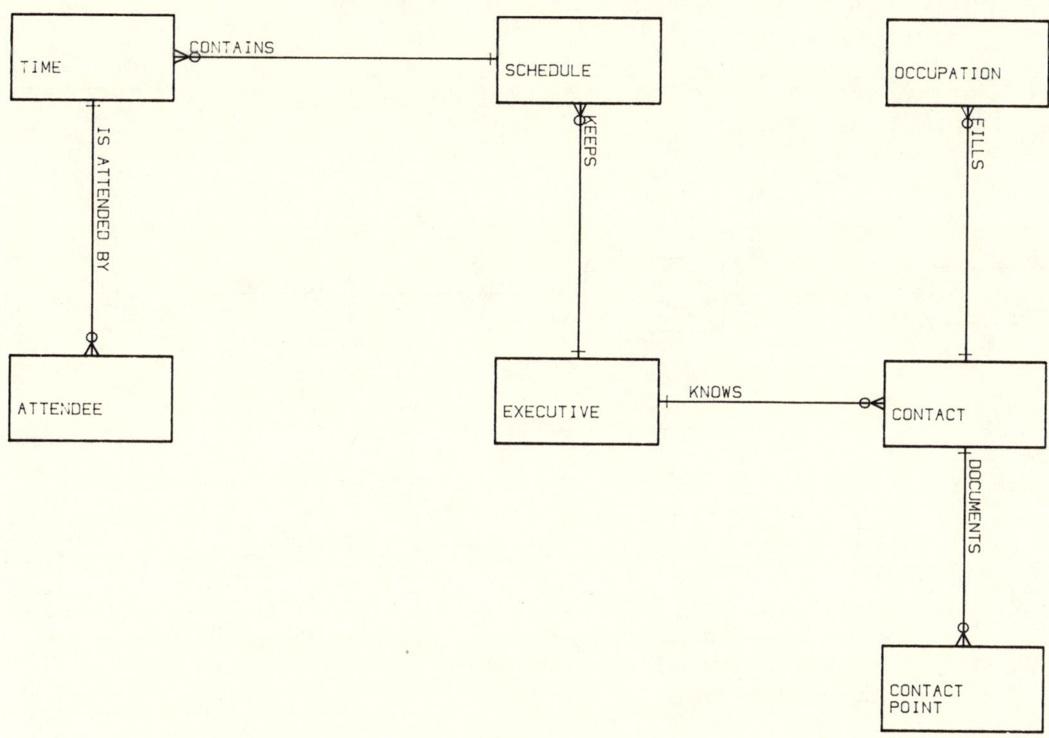

Figure 3.28 Entity relationship diagram produced by the INFORMATION ENGINEERING FACILITY™ from Texas Instruments Incorporated.

Stage 2: Business Area Analysis

The business functions defined in Stage 1 are used to divide the enterprise into logical business areas (e.g., purchasing). Then the information systems needed to support a particular business area can be defined and built.

This stage concentrates on defining the data and processes needed to meet the enterprise goals within a particular business area. That part of the entity relationship diagram developed in Stage 1 that is concerned with a particular business area is extracted and developed into a fully *normalized* data model. Data entities, their attributes, and their relationships to each other are fully defined. The decomposition diagram from Stage 1 representing the business functions is decomposed into business area processes that perform these higher-level functions. The processes can be represented in dependency diagrams (a type of data flow diagram), data flow diagrams, or decomposition diagrams (see Figure 3.29). An entity/process matrix is used to relate data and the processes in which they are used.

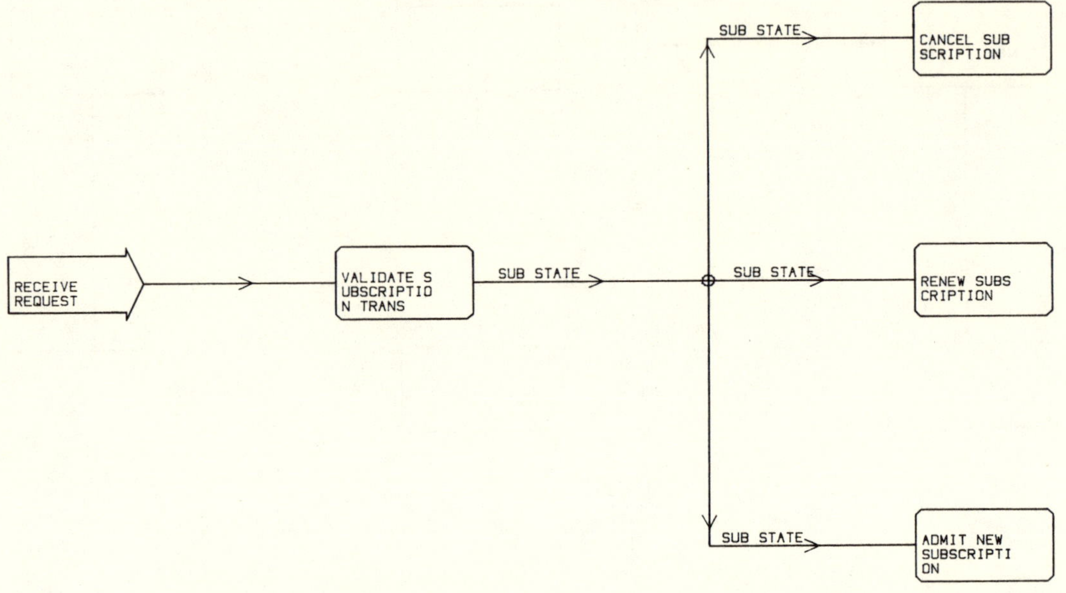

Figure 3.29 Dependency diagram, which is a type of data flow diagram. It was produced with the INFORMATION ENGINEERING FACILITY™ from Texas Instruments Incorporated.

Stage 3: System Design

Stage 3 is concerned with logical system design considerations. The business processes defined in Stage 2 form the basis for system design in this stage. The procedures needed to perform the processes and their logical data structures are designed. Top-down, functional decomposition is used to guide the design process. At this stage the information engineering methodology becomes similar to traditional software engineering methodology for program development. The system design is represented by data structure diagrams, screen/report layouts, decomposition diagrams, and action diagrams. Action diagrams show detailed procedural logic and database accesses (see Figure 3.30).

Prototyping of the user interface with screen, dialogue, and report painters is used to discover user requirements. User involvement is needed to help build and check the validity of the prototype models.

Stage 4: Construction

Whereas Stage 3 was concerned with logical system design, Stage 4 is concerned with physical system design and program implementation. During Stage 4, the completed information system is delivered as a logical database,

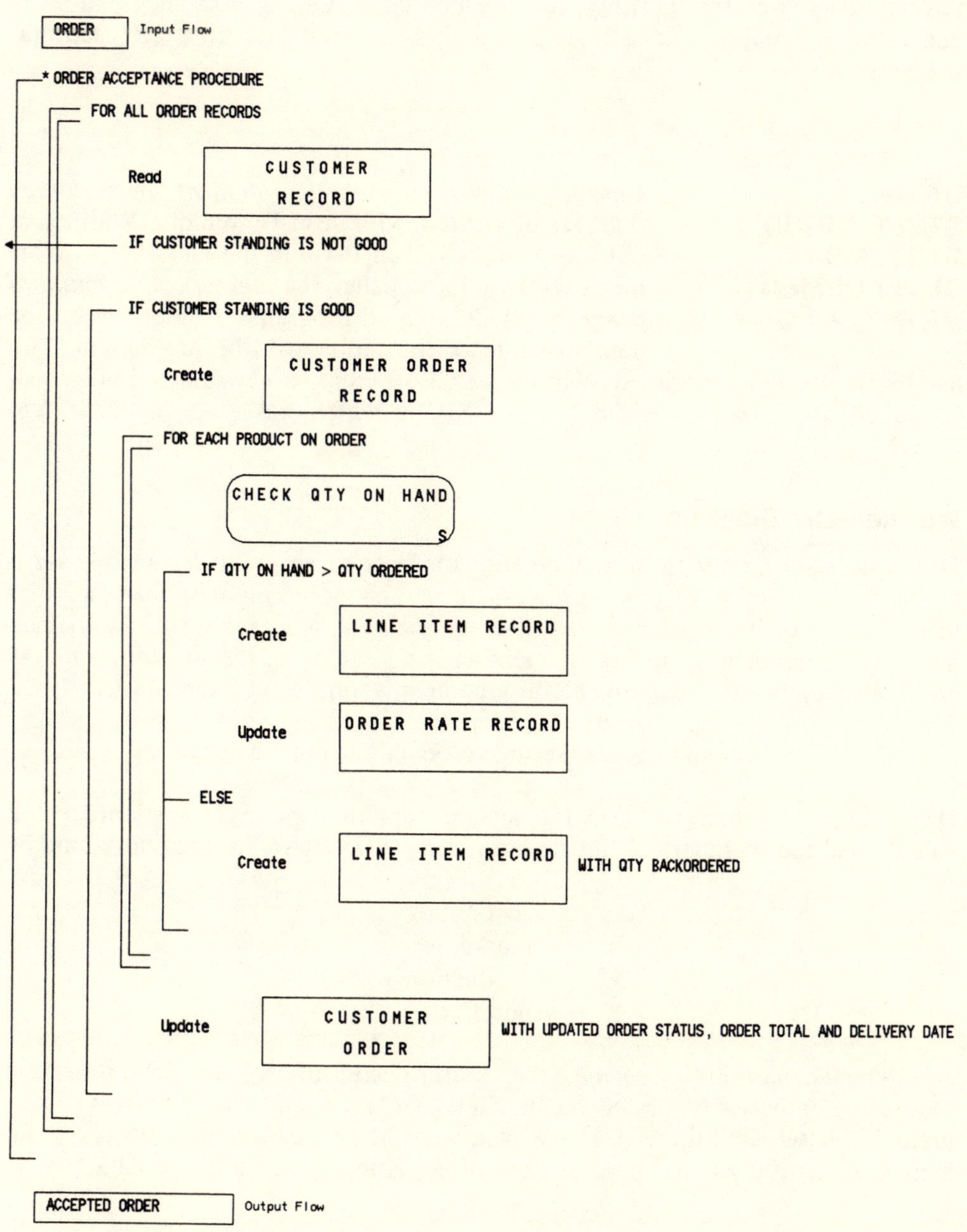

Figure 3.30 Action diagram drawn by the INFORMATION ENGINEERING WORKBENCH from KnowledgeWare for the order acceptance procedure in the sales distribution system.

physical database, and working, documented code. CASE tools such as fourth-generation languages, decision support tools, and code generators are used during Stage 4.

DATA STRUCTURED SYSTEMS DEVELOPMENT METHODOLOGY

Data structured systems development methodology (DSSD) originated with Jean-Dominique Warnier at CII Honeywell-Bull in Paris in the late 1950s. Warnier's methodology, called the *logical construction of programs* (LCP), based program development on the data structure of the problem to be programmed. In the 1970s, Ken Orr modified Warnier's LCP to create a new methodology that he called *structured program design* (SPD), which has since evolved into DSSD.

Warnier–Orr Diagram

DSSD uses set theory from mathematics to describe program designs. A *set* is an ordered collection of objects that share one or more common characteristics (e.g., the set of integers or the set of departments in a company). In mathematics, a set is denoted by listing its members and enclosing the list within brackets. For example, the departments in a company form a set indicated by

{accounting, marketing, production, purchasing}

DSSD uses a similar notation for sets, except that the right-hand bracket is deleted and the members of the set are listed vertically rather than horizontally:

$$\left\{\begin{array}{l}\text{accounting}\\ \text{marketing}\\ \text{production}\\ \text{purchasing}\end{array}\right.$$

The *Warnier–Orr diagram,* the central design tool of the DSSD methodology, is composed of nested set brackets. An example of a Warnier–Orr diagram is shown in Figure 3.31. Warnier–Orr diagrams are used to show the hierarchical structure and process flow of activities, procedures, or data.

Output-Oriented Approach

Data structured system development is a methodology for building information systems. It is similar to the Jackson design methodology in that both are data-driven approaches. They both derive the program structure from the data struc-

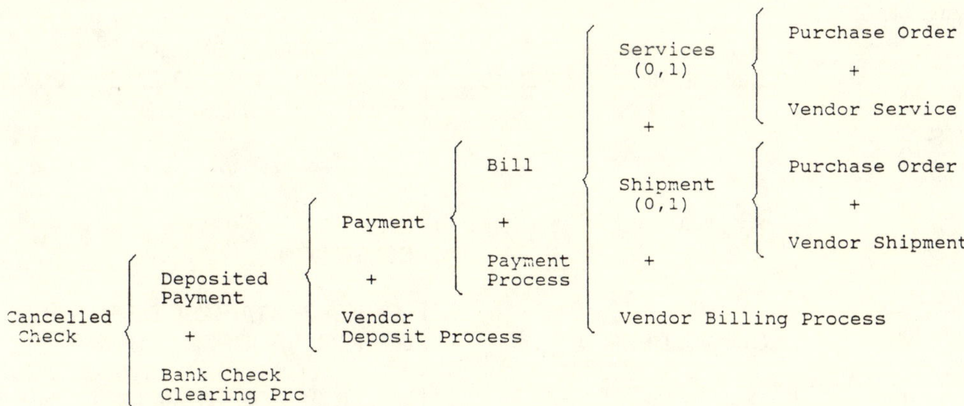

Figure 3.31 The Warnier–Orr diagram is used for hierarchical representation of plans, procedures, and data structures. This Warnier–Orr diagram was drawn by DESIGNAID from Nastec Corporation.

ture. Also, they both stress that logical design should be separate from and precede physical design.

The major difference between the two is that the Jackson approach is to merge all input and output data structures to form a single program structure, whereas the Warnier–Orr approach is to derive the program structure *and* the input data structures from the output data structures. The Warnier–Orr philosophy is that the program/system output completely and absolutely determines the data structure, and the data structure, in turn, determines the program structure [11]. "By working backward from the output, it is possible to determine exactly the minimal database and inputs for the system," according to Ken Orr [12].

Basic Steps of DSSD

As shown in the Warnier–Orr diagram in Figure 3.32, the DSSD methodology consists of nine phases.

Project Planning Phase

During this phase, the project plan is developed by linking the overall business goals with the system objectives. Expected business results that the system will provide and business constraints on the system are defined.

Requirements Definition Phase

During this phase, the user and organizational requirements for the system are defined. Also, the computer environment needed for the system is defined. The requirements definition phase is divided into two subphases: logical requirements and physical requirements; and in turn, each of these subphases is further

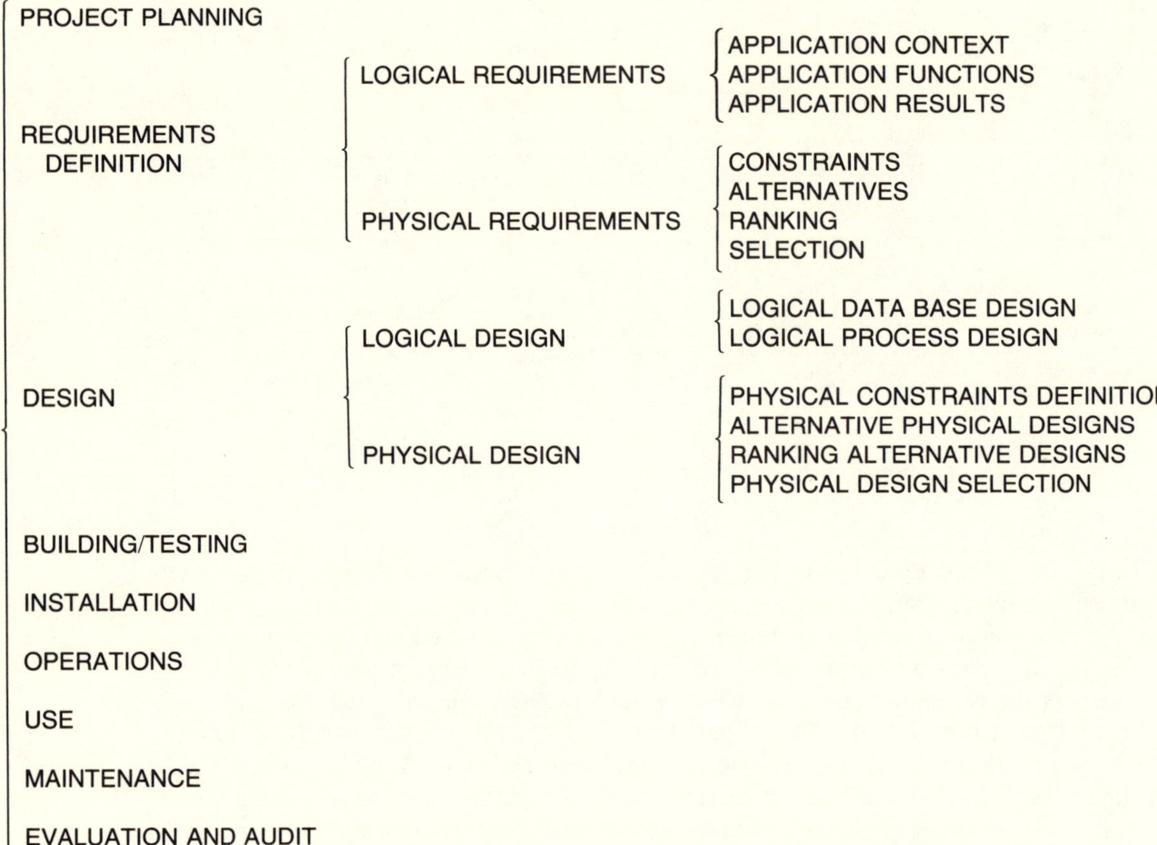

Figure 3.32 The data structured systems development methodology is represented here by a Warnier–Orr diagram.

divided into steps. The primary purpose of this phase is to define the principal outputs that the system is to produce. These outputs provide the basis for database and process design in the design phase of DSSD.

An *entity diagram,* which is a type of data flow diagram, is used to define system entities and the transactions that pass between them. The entity diagram is used to determine the scope of the system. An *assembly-line diagram,* which is a type of Warnier–Orr diagram, is used to define the functional processes (i.e., transformation of a set of inputs to a set of outputs). The outputs needed to support the processes and to define the logical output base are represented in a Warnier–Orr diagram and a data dictionary. Figure 3.33 is an example of a logical output base.

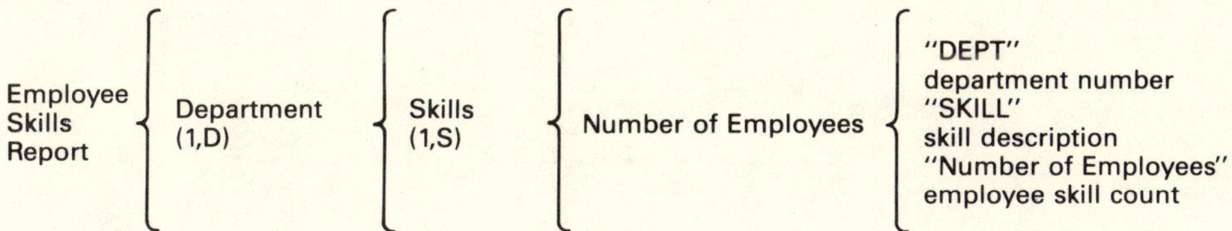

Figure 3.33 The Warnier–Orr diagram is used to represent the logical output base for the employee skills system.

Design Phase

The DSSD methodology divides the design phase into two parts: logical design and physical design.

1. Design the logical database.
2. Design the logical process.

Using the logical output base from the previous phase as input, logical database design begins by developing the logical data structures that contain the minimum data required to produce an output. Next, logical basis files representing a normalized data architecture are developed. It can be demonstrated that each system output can be produced from the logical basis files and that all data in the basis files are needed to produce the system output. Next, logical data updates and edit and input transactions are defined.

In the final steps of logical database design, the logical update base and the logical input base are developed. They are used later to guide physical database design.

The logical data structures, the logical update base, and logical input base are all represented using Warnier–Orr diagrams. Figure 3.34 is an example of a logical data structure.

During the process logic design step, the logical process base is developed. It is also represented as a Warnier–Orr diagram. The purpose of the logical process base is to define the mappings needed to produce the system output from the input.

During the physical design phase, physical environment constraints, such

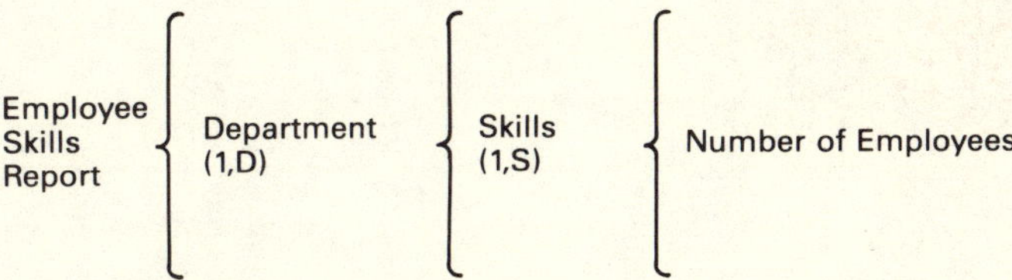

Figure 3.34 A Warnier–Orr diagram is used to represent the logical data structure for the employee skills system.

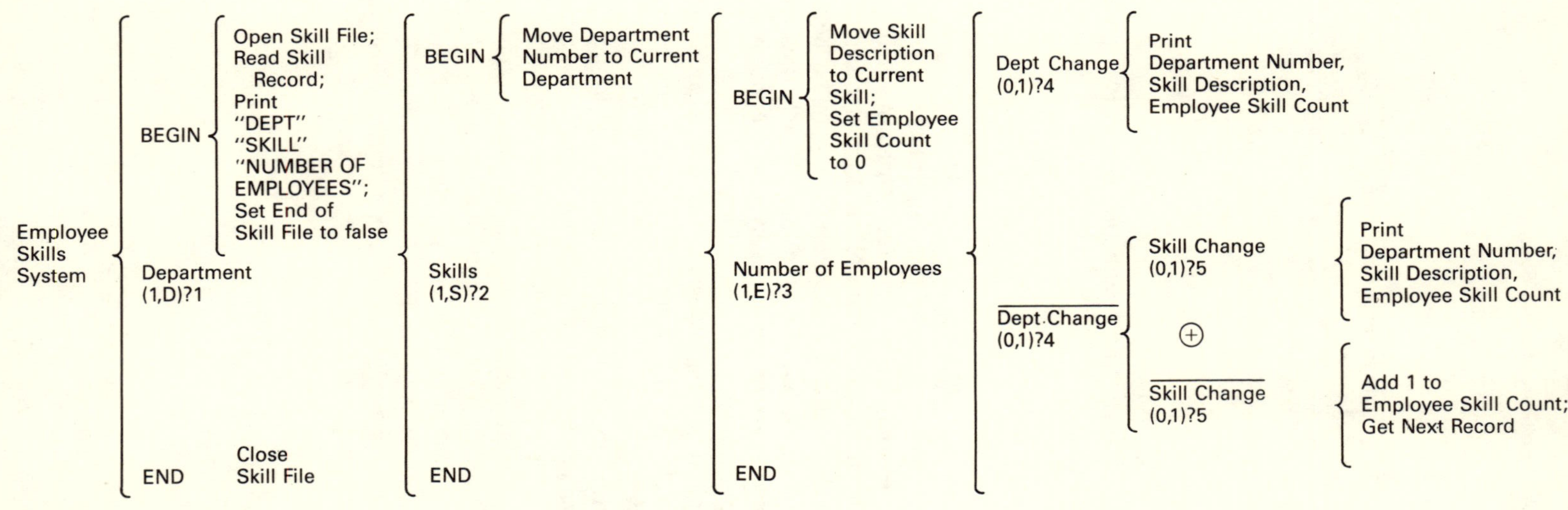

Figure 3.35 The complete program design for the employee skills system is represented here by a Warnier–Orr diagram.

as those imposed by a programming language, are added to the logical process base.

Figure 3.35 is a Warnier–Orr diagram representing the complete design for an employee skills system.

REFERENCES

1. V. Haase and G. Koch, "Developing the Connection between User and Code," *Computer,* Vol. 15, No. 5, May 1982, pp. 10–11.

2. B. Boehm, R. McClearn, and D. Unfrig, "Some Experiences with Automated Aids to the Design of Large-Scale Reliable Software," *IEEE Transactions on Software Engineering,* Vol. 1, No. 1, March 1975, pp. 125–133.

3. S. Houtchens and J. Pollock, "Developing Real-Time Software without Writing Source Code," *Internal Report*. Santa Clara, Calif.: Integrated Systems, Inc., 1987.

4. J. Emos and R. Van Tilburg, "Software Design," *Computer,* Vol. 14, No. 2, February 1981, pp. 61–83.

5. F. L. Bauer, *Software Engineering*. Amsterdam: North-Holland, 1972.

6. J. Martin and C. McClure, *Structured Techniques: The Basis of CASE*. Englewood Cliffs, N.J.: Prentice-Hall, 1988.

7. R. Pressman, "Meeting the Challenge of Real-Time Software Engineering," *The CASE Report*. Southfield, Mich.: Nastec Corporation, March 1987, pp. 1–3.

8. "CASE 1987 Survey Report," *Software News*. Westborough, Mass.: Sentry Publishing Company, 1987.

9. J. Martin, *"Information Engineering," Savant Technical Report*. Carnforth, Lancashire, England, 1987.

10. J. Martin and E. A. Hershey, "Information Engineering Whitepaper," *Technical Report*. Atlanta, Ga.: KnowledgeWare, 1986.

11. D. Higgins, *Program Design and Construction*. Englewood Cliffs, N.J.: Prentice-Hall, 1979.

12. K. Brown and R. Whinery, editors, *Data Structured Systems Development Methodology*. Topeka, Kans.: Ken Orr & Associates, Inc., 1986.

4 CASE HARDWARE PLATFORMS

REDEFINING THE SOFTWARE SUPPORT ENVIRONMENT

"It is becoming a requirement . . . to offer a totally integrated environment that provides a swift and effective path from the [software] problem description to a running solution" [1]. However, the CASE technology is not merely an approach for assembling a set of related software life cycle tools. It is a redefinition of the whole software development and support environment. As such, tools, methodologies, and the hardware platform must be addressed by the CASE technology.

In Chapters 2, 3, and 5 we consider how CASE redefines software tools and methodologies. In this chapter we discuss the CASE system hardware platform.

ALTERNATIVE HARDWARE PLATFORMS

As shown in Figure 4.1, there are three alternative hardware platforms for the CASE software support environment:

1. Individual (standalone) workstation
2. Two-tiered architecture consisting of a central host and individual workstations
3. Three-tiered architecture consisting of a host, intermediate department-level or project-level host, and individual workstations

Standalone Workstation Platform

Standalone workstations provide a highly interactive, responsive, and dedicated platform on which to carry out software life cycle tasks. In particular, their powerful graphics capabilities enable easy creation and manipulation of struc-

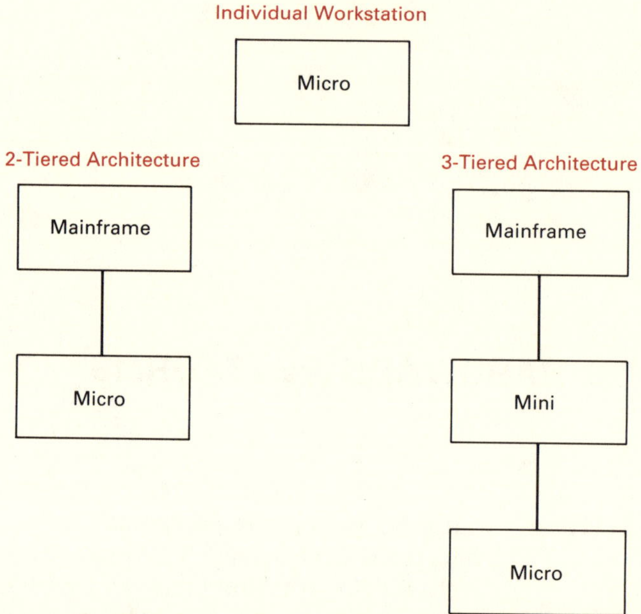

Figure 4.1 There are three alternative hardware platforms for a CASE software support environment.

tured diagrams used to specify and document software systems. Also, they enable rapid prototyping for creating system models to help discover and clarify user requirements. They are the perfect platform for analysis and design tasks. Standalone workstations provide the maximum possible support for each person involved in software development, maintenance, or project management work.

The hardware architecture for the CASE workstation is either a 32-bit technical/engineering workstation such as a HP9000, SUN-2 and 3, Apollo Series 3000, DEC VAXstation II, IBM RT PC, or a personal computer such as an IBM PC AT/XT, PS/2, Macintosh, TI Professional PC, or Wang PC. Most CASE systems that support the development of real-time/embedded systems run on a 32-bit technical workstation, while most CASE systems that support the development of MIS application systems run on a personal computer.

In both cases, considerations for choosing workstation hardware focus on:

- Memory and processing capabilities
- Quality of graphics
- Networking capabilities
- Multiuser/multitasking capability
- Connectivity

For most of these capabilities, the 32-bit technical workstation, although more expensive, is superior to the personal computer. The 32-bit technical workstation has more power and more reliability than a personal computer. Its greater memory and processing capabilities enable the developer to work on larger systems and have faster access to more system information. Because a 32-bit workstation can offer a true multiuser, multitasking environment, the developer can work on multiple system tasks simultaneously. Also, 32-bit workstations can offer high-quality graphics with higher resolution and a larger display (e.g., Apollo Series 3000 offers 1280 × 1024 pixel resolution). Finally, the 32-bit workstation can provide networking support. For example, the DEC VAXstation has networking through DECnet; the SUN through Ethernet and Network Software Environment (NSE), and Apollo through Domain.

Bridges Between Workstations

In practice, however, the CASE workstation cannot exist in isolation. Bridges must be provided to connect the individual developer's workstation to other workstations and to other hardware systems. This enables communication and information sharing between project team members and data exchange between the CASE system and existing data dictionaries, databases, and outside tools such as fourth-generation languages and code generators.

Connectivity of workstations is accomplished by the use of a local-area network (e.g., IBM token ring, PC Net, and Novell). The purpose is to share system information stored in the CASE repository. To enable system information sharing at the workstation level, one workstation can act as a file server that is designated as the master CASE repository (e.g., the project library holding all information associated with the entire project). Developers maintain working project libraries on their individual workstations by importing selected pieces to their local workstation-based CASE repository. The contents of the master CASE repository are protected by restricting the update privileges of individual developers. A multiuser data storage structure provides record-lockout capabilities that allow multiple users to access the same file concurrently without conflicts.

Multiple-Tiered Hardware Platform

Although connectivity of workstations can support many software life cycle tasks and some forms of team communication, it cannot support the entire software job. A mainframe or large minicomputer is still a necessary component of the CASE hardware platform. Some tasks, such as code generation, analysis of existing source code, and program testing, require the power of a large computer. Also, information storage requirements and information consolidation and analysis tasks require the power of a large computer (see Box 4.1).

The supporting hardware architecture for a full-function CASE workbench

BOX 4.1 CASE functions

Function	Host	Workstation
Diagram creating, manipulating and updating		×
Screen and report painting		×
Menu definitions		×
Prototyping/simulation	×	×
Specification checking	×	×
System information storage, management, and reporting	×	×
Documentation generation	×	×
Code generation	×	
System testing	×	
Database generation		×
Data reformatting	×	
Program analysis	×	×
Data analysis and consolidation	×	
Canonical synthesis and normalization	×	

(e.g., TI's INFORMATION ENGINEERING FACILITY, KnowledgeWare's INFORMATION ENGINEERING WORKBENCH) has two or three tiers. The two-tiered architecture consists of workstations (either a personal computer or a 32-bit technical engineering workstation) connected to a host (either a mainframe or a large mini). The two hardware levels are connected via file transfer, uploading/downloading facilities.

Some CASE systems employ an intermediate hardware level between a host mainframe computer and individual PC-based workstations. The intermediate level is a file server supporting a department or a project team. For example, in Softlab's Maestro system, a Motorola 5000 system is the file server, acting as a database on a local-area network to archive all project documents [2].

Distributing system tasks among the tiers reduces contention for expensive mainframe resources and allows tasks to be executed on the hardware system that is most expedient.

Considerations for a two-tiered or three-tiered CASE hardware platform include:

- Connectivity between levels and between workstations
- Multiuser support

- Interfaces to corporate dictionaries and databases
- Bridges to fourth-generation languages (4GLs)
- Linking multiple system information repositories

Bridges to Dictionaries, Databases, and 4GLs

Connecting CASE workstations to host computers where existing corporate data dictionaries (e.g., IBM DB/DC Data Dictionary and MSP Data Manager) and database management systems (e.g., Cullinet IDMS/R) reside reduces the need to enter redundant system information. To access standard corporate data definitions, an import/export path is needed between the CASE workstation and host-based dictionaries and databases. This micro-mainframe link is provided by file transfer, 3278/79 emulation boards, and so on. For example, through importing facilities, a CASE repository could be populated with existing IBM IMS Program Specification Blocks (PSBs), COBOL data structure descriptions, CICS BMS screens, VSAM file descriptions, and DB2 catalogs. Through exporting facilities from the CASE workstation repository, high-level design information can be passed to code generator mainframe-based dictionaries. To simplify data transfer, the file format of the dictionary and the CASE repository may be the same (e.g., dBASE III).

Connecting the CASE workstation to a mainframe/minicomputer also provides a bridge to fourth-generation languages and database management systems. This enables the use of CASE technology in the development of fourth-generation applications and databases. Analysis and design work for the 4GL application can be performed on the CASE workstation. Then files containing the application's specification (e.g., screen, report, and record descriptions) can be transferred to the mainframe environment, where they become the input to the 4GL application generator or code generator. In the case of databases, strategic data planning, logical data modeling, and logical and physical database design can be performed at the workstation level. Then files containing the database schema syntax can be transferred to the mainframe for normalization and database generation.

BASIC CASE SYSTEM COMPONENTS

As shown in Figure 4.2, we can divide a CASE system into three basic components:

1. Front end
2. Central repository
3. Back end

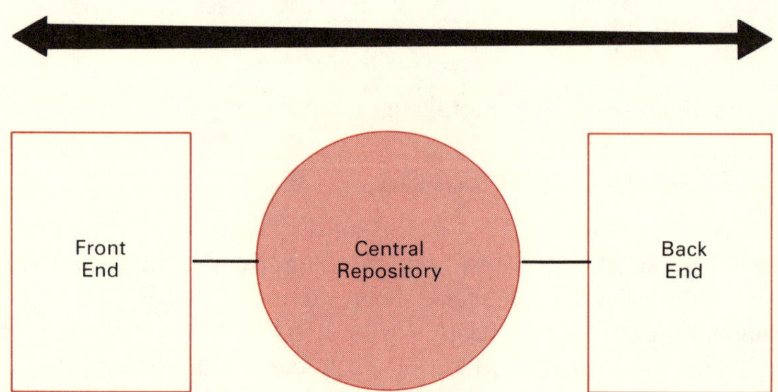

Figure 4.2 The basic components of a CASE workbench are: a front end, a repository, and a back end.

The *front-end component* corresponds to the front end or early phases of the software life cycle: namely, analysis and design. The *front end* can also correspond to the PC or workstation component portion of the CASE hardware platform. Front-end CASE tools provide functions to support analysis and design activities such as diagramming, prototyping, and specification checking. These activities are best performed on a dedicated personal machine with rapid response time, bit-mapped, high-resolution graphics, and a mouse.

The *back-end component* corresponds to the back end or latter phases of the software life cycle: namely, program implementation and maintenance. The *back end* also corresponds to the mainframe portion of the CASE hardware platform. Back-end CASE tools automate coding, testing, database generation, data normalization, and existing system impact analysis tasks. These tasks require the power and storage capability of a large mainframe or minicomputer.

Multiple Repositories

The information repository is the link between the front-end and back-end components of a CASE system. It is the communication vehicle by which all system information collected during the software life cycle can be managed and shared. It is also the vehicle by which system work from different team members can be combined, analyzed, and consolidated into one consistent, complete, and ongoing representation of the system. The CASE repository is the underlying life-cycle integrator that enables CASE tools used at one phase of the life cycle to pass data on to the next phase.

Logically, the CASE repository is divided into project libraries and system models. Physically, the CASE repository is divided into levels that correspond to each hardware platform of the CASE system. At the workstation level, a local repository exists to support the individual developer. At the host level, a mainframe-based repository exists to hold all corporate systems information. At the department or project level, an intermediate repository exists to hold all project information.

Links between the physical repositories must exist so that data can be uploaded and downloaded between the levels. For example, the host repository contents can be selectively or entirely downloaded to a project-level or workstation-level repository; and the workstation-level repository contents can be uploaded and merged with repository data on the levels above. Links are provided by communication facilities such as Ethernet, TCP/IP, NFS, Domain, DECnet, SNA, and 3270 protocol.

However, the real issues concerning transporting system information between CASE hardware environments involve not simply the ability to transfer data, but rather how easy it is to select and reformat the necessary data. How easy is it to extract the data needed and to determine their physical availability and integrity? Can the data be compressed when they are moved? How easy is it to restructure the data into a format in which they can be used? Thus connectivity issues between hardware systems include:

- Selective data download
- Data upload and consolidation
- Data reformatting requirements
- Data security and control
- Speed
- Efficiency
- Multiple-user file access
- Backups

Transparent Interfaces

Figure 4.2 showed the basic components of a CASE system. Figure 4.3 shows another, perhaps more realistic view of the basic components of a CASE system. Notice that the CASE system in Figure 4.3 has multiple repositories. There are several reasons for multiple repositories:

1. A local repository is needed to hold all the working information sets for each team member. Each local repository will reside physically on a workstation hardware platform.
2. A host repository is needed to hold all corporate-level systems information. The host repository will reside on a large mainframe or mini.

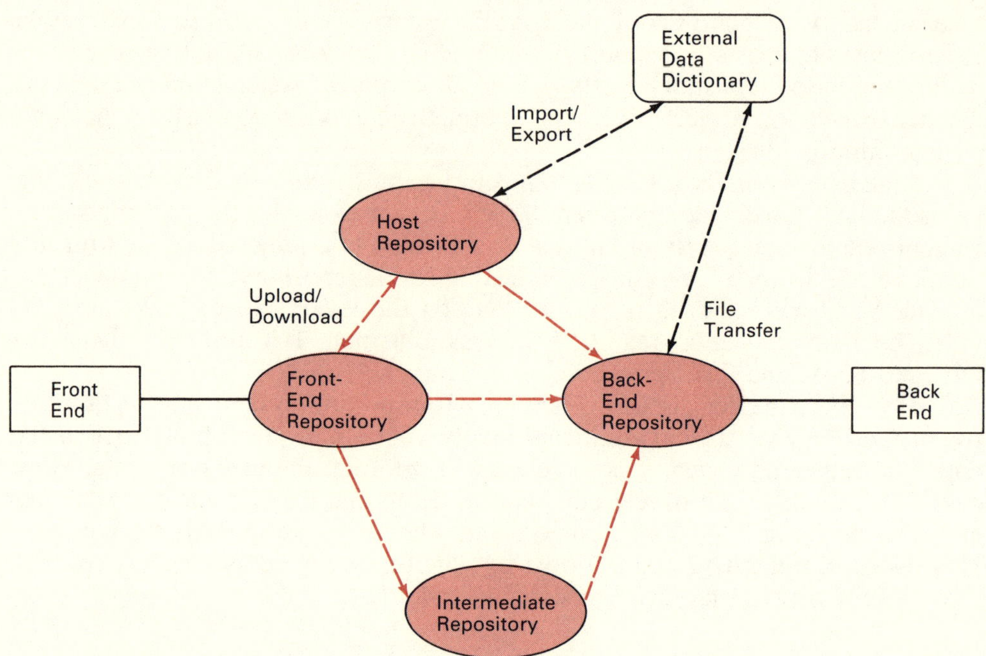

Figure 4.3 A more complete picture of the basic components of a CASE workbench shows that it has multiple repositories.

3. Multiple vendors may supply CASE tools to support the various phases of the life cycle. For example, one vendor may supply front-end CASE tools with their own repository, and another vendor may supply back-end CASE tools with their own repository.

An important element in integrating CASE tools consists of the interfaces between the multiple repositories. To create interfaces that are as transparent and efficient as possible will require cooperation between vendors and standards.

For example, vendors may set up proprietary gateways to other vendor products (e.g., APS/PC EXCELERATOR Integrator connecting EXCELERATOR to APS) or institute an open architecture policy in which they publish interface requirements (e.g., XL/INTERFACE TELON from Pansophic to allow users of various front-end CASE tools to connect to the code generator TELON). In the CAD/CAM world, there now exists a standard method of linking CAD/CAM tools. It is the Electronic Document Interchange Form (EDIF), which is a protocol for exchanging data between tools. It is possible that EDIF will also become a standard in the CASE world (e.g., Cadre's TEAMWORK supports the EDIF standard).

SUMMARY

A complete CASE system that supports the entire software job resides on multiple hardware platforms:

1. Workstation
2. Mini
3. Mainframe

Sharing information and tools across these hardware platforms is a major issue in making the CASE technology practical and efficient. Connectivity between hardware systems and interfaces between tools are important capabilities to examine when selecting or evaluating a CASE system. Box 4.2 summarizes the CASE hardware platform considerations.

BOX 4.2 CASE system hardware platform considerations

Considerations at Workstation Level

- Memory and processing capabilities
- Quality of graphics
- Networking capabilities
- Multitasking capability
- Connectivity

Considerations for a Two-/Three-Tiered Platform

- Connectivity between tiers and between workstations
- Multiuser support
- Interfaces to corporate dictionaries and databases
- Bridges to 4GLs
- Linking multiple system information repositories
- Speed and efficiency
- Security and control
- Backups
- Concurrent file access with record/field-lockout capabilities

REFERENCES

1. William Suydam, "CASE Makes Strides toward Automated Software Development," *Computer Design,* January 1, 1987, pp. 49–70.
2. "An Overview of Structured Analysis and Design Tools," *CASE Outlook,* Vol. 1, No. 2, August 1987, pp. 1–14.

5 CATEGORIES OF CASE TOOLS

DISTINGUISHING CASE TOOLS

Different CASE tools focus on the support of different phases of the software life cycle or on the development of different types of software systems. To more easily distinguish CASE tools, we categorize CASE tools in this chapter.

As defined in Box 5.1, there are three basic categories of CASE tools:

1. CASE toolkits
2. CASE workbenches
3. CASE methodology companions

Toolkits are the simplest type of CASE tools. They are a set of integrated tools that automate one type of software life cycle task, such as system design

BOX 5.1 CASE tool categories

- Toolkit: sets of integrated tools that support one type of software development function or job class
- Workbench: general-purpose software development environment supporting the full range of the software job
- Methodology companion: computerized assistance for a particular software development methodology
  - Methodology companion toolkit
  - Methodology companion workbench

or program maintenance, or one type of job class, such as system analyst. *CASE workbenches* are composed of a set of integrated tools that automate tasks across the entire software life cycle. A *CASE methodology companion* provides computerized assistance for a particular software development methodology, such as DeMarco structured analysis, Jackson structured design, or Martin information engineering. Each CASE tool category is discussed in detail in this chapter.

CASE TOOLKITS

CASE toolkits can be described as phase-level tools because they focus on the support of one particular phase of the life cycle or the development of one type of software system. As shown in Figure 5.1, there are analyst, designer, programmer, and maintainer toolkits. Also, there are toolkits that focus on the design of real-time systems, MIS on-line systems, or project management.

CASE toolkits can be further classified in terms of the hardward and operating system environment in which they run, the product line to which they belong, whether they have an open or closed architecture, and the methodologies they support.

For example, many CASE toolkits run on an IBM PC under MS-DOS or PS/2. Others run on 32-bit workstations such as SUN, Apollo, or DEC VAXstation II. Some run on the Macintosh, Wang, PC, and TI Professional PC. Finally, some run on an IBM or Data General mainframe or across the DEC VAX family.

Some toolkits are part of a family of software products. They can be used alone or in conjunction with other tools within the family. For example, Texas Instruments offers the Planning, Analysis, Design, Code Generation, and Data-

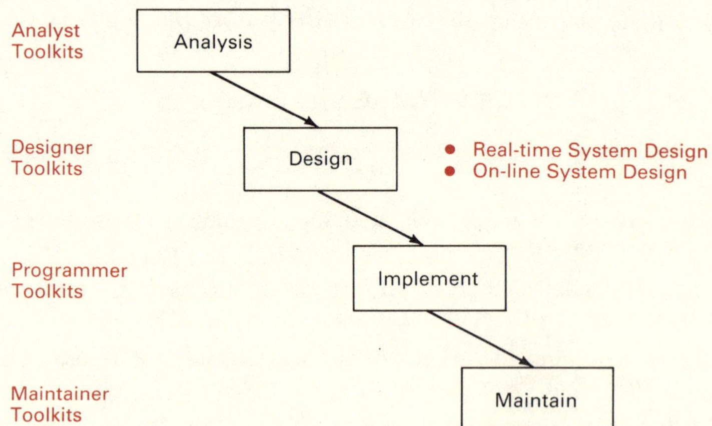

Figure 5.1 CASE toolkits are called phase-level CASE tools because they focus on the support of one particular phase of the software life cycle or the development of one type of system.

base Generation Toolsets in its INFORMATION ENGINEERING FACILITY product line, and Nastec offers DESIGNAID, LIFE CYCLE MANAGER, and REQUIREMENTS MANAGEMENT SYSTEM in its CASE 2000 product line.

Also, some toolkits are open architecture products that can be used with CASE tools offered by various vendors. For example, EXCELERATOR from Index Technology is an analysis toolkit that can be used with other CASE tools, such as TELON from Pansophic or APS from Sage. Other examples include DESIGNAID from Nastec and TEAMWORK from Cadre.

Many open architecture products are not tied to specific hardware, operating system, target programming language, or development methodologies. Whereas toolkits such as the ANALYST/DESIGNER toolkit from Yourdon, Inc. supports only the Yourdon structured design methodology, and DESIGN MACHINE from Ken Orr & Associates supports only the data structured systems development methodology, other toolkits, such as the DEVELOPER from Asyst, PROKIT*ANALYST from McDonnell-Douglas, DEFT from Disus, TekCASE DESIGN from Tektronix, and PROMOD from Promod, Inc. are more generic toolkits supporting multiple structured methodologies. IDMS/ARCHITECT from Cullinet is a database design toolkit primarily for IDMS, but AUTO-MATE PLUS from Learmonth and Burchett, and SCHEMAGEN from Chen & Associates are more generic data design toolkits.

SOFTWARE THROUGH PICTURES from Interactive Development Environments, PROMOD from Promod, Inc., STATEMATE from i-Logix, Inc., and TAGS from Teledyne Brown Engineering are examples of toolkits that target Ada development support.

TEAMWORK/RT from Cadre and EXCELERATOR/RTS from Index Technology are examples of CASE analysis toolkits that support the development of real-time systems. DESIGNAID from Nastec and ANALYST/DESIGNER TOOLKIT from Yourdon, Inc. are examples of toolkits that support the development of both business systems and real-time systems.

Box 5.2 summarizes the classifications for CASE toolkits.

ANALYSIS TOOLKITS

Analysis toolkits make it easier to follow the principles of good systems analysis and design by automatically taking care of burdensome paperwork and countless system details. The purpose of an analysis toolkit is to automate the creation of a system specification describing the system requirements. The output produced by an analysis toolkit is a system specification consisting of the following:

- Screen and report definitions
- Data structure definitions
- Functional component descriptions

BOX 5.2 Classifications of toolkits

1. Phase level
   _____ Analysis
   _____ Programming
   _____ Design
   _____ Maintenance
   _____ Project management
2. Part of a product line
   _____ Part of a family of products
   _____ Standalone product
   _____ Methodology independent
3. Open architecture
   _____ Open front-end interfaces
   _____ Open back-end interfaces
   _____ Framework
4. Hardware environment/operating system
   _____ PC/workstation
   _____ Mini
   _____ Mainframe
   _____ MS-DOS
   _____ Unix
   _____ Ada
   _____ MVS
   _____ VM
   _____ VAX/VMS
5. Application class
   _____ Real-time/embedded
   _____ On-line
   _____ High-volume transaction, processing
6. Software job class
   _____ Analyst
   _____ Designer
   _____ Programmer
   _____ Project manager
   _____ Maintainer
7. Methodologies supported
   _____ Yourdon/Constantine
   _____ DeMarco
   _____ Gane–Sarson
   _____ Orr
   _____ Jackson
   _____ Bachman
   _____ Chen
   _____ Merise
   _____ Martin
   _____ Ward and Mellor
   _____ Hatley
   _____ Other _______________
   _____ DOD Standard 2167

An analysis toolkit is made up of four basic components:

1. Structured diagramming tools
2. Prototyping tools
3. Repository
4. Specification checker

Diagramming Tools

The first component, structured diagramming tools, is a set of computerized tools for drawing, manipulating, and storing structured diagrams such as data flow diagrams, dependency diagrams, and entity relationship diagrams. Often, these tools reside on personal computers or workstations that support graphics manipulations. Diagramming capabilities for CASE tools are discussed in Chapter 2 in the section entitled "Graphics Capability."

At minimum, an analysis toolkit should provide diagramming tools that draw, update, and store at least one version of each of these types of structured diagrams:

- Data flow diagrams
- Entity relationship diagrams

Real-Time Analysis Toolkits

To represent real-time system specifications, this basic diagram set must be expanded. Diagrams that show sequence and timing relationships between system processes and the effect of external events on the system must be included. Control flow diagrams and state transition diagrams are typically used to model real-time systems and therefore should be added to the diagram set of an analysis toolkit that supports real-time systems analysis and design tasks.

Prototyping Tools

Prototyping tools are the second component of an analysis toolkit. They are used to help determine system requirements and answer questions about the performance capabilities of the system before it is even built.

An analysis toolkit should provide two types of prototyping tools:

1. User interface painters (screen painters, report painters, menu builders)
2. Executable specification languages

The prototyping capability of CASE tools is discussed in Chapter 3 in the section entitled "Prototyping."

Repository

The third component of an analysis toolkit is the repository. All system specification information is stored in the repository. The capabilities of a CASE repository are discussed in Chapter 2 in the section entitled "CASE Information Repository."

Specification Checker

Automatic checking of the system specification begins as soon as an analyst starts drawing a structured diagram or entering information into the repository. Structured diagrams are checked for adherence to the syntax rules of that diagram. They are also checked for completeness and consistency with other system specification information. Automatic checking provided by CASE tools is discussed in Chapter 2 in the section entitled "Error Checking."

Design Extensions

Analysis toolkits are sometimes extended to support the design phase as well as the analysis phase of the software life cycle. For this type of toolkit, the analysis diagramming toolset is expanded to include diagramming and checking capabilities for:

- Hierarchical tree structured diagrams
- Procedural logic diagrams

Box 5.3 summarizes the description of a CASE analysis toolkit.

BOX 5.3 Analysis toolkit

Purpose: define system requirements and properties that system must possess to meet these requirements
Output: specification of system components and interfaces connecting these components

- Screen, report definitions
- Data structures
- Databases and files
- Functional components

Facilities

- Diagramming tools
  —Data flow diagrams
  —Entity relationship diagrams

BOX 5.3 *(Continued)*

- Prototyping tools
  —Screen and report painters
  —Executable specification language
- Information repository with reporting capability
- Import/export capabilities between repository and outside dictionaries
- Specification analyzer and checker

Real-time extensions

- Control flow diagrams
- Finite-state diagrams
- Decision tables

System design extensions

- Hierarchical diagram
- Procedural logic

Design purpose: create a design of software system to be built to meet specification requirements
Design output: architectural structure for system and detailed blueprint of program design, including program algorithms and data structures

DATA DESIGN TOOLKITS

CASE data design toolkits support the logical and physical design of databases and files. They support logical data modeling, the automatic conversion of data models to third-normal form, the automatic generation of database schemes for particular database management systems, and the automatic generation of program-code-level file descriptions.

Examples of CASE data design toolkits include AUTO-MATE PLUS from Learmonth & Burchett, SQL*DESIGN DICTIONARY from Oracle, IDMS/ARCHITECH from Cullinet, and the CHEN toolkit from Chen & Associates.

PROGRAMMING TOOLKITS

Box 5.4 is a list of tools included in a CASE programming toolkit to support program implementa-

BOX 5.4 Programming toolkit

Purpose: produce a tested, documented software program that meets program specification requirements

Tools

- Hierarchical tree structured diagramming tools with syntax and consistency checker
- Procedural logic diagrammer and on-line editor
- CASE repository with information manager
- Code generator
- Code analyzer
- File manipulator
- Test data generator
- Test coverage analyzer
- File comparer
- Abend debugger
- Performance monitor
- Run environment generator and verifier
- Target environment simulator

tion. Many of these tools are familiar and are already widely used by programmers. The difference is that the tools in the programming toolkit are packaged to be compatible with one another. In other words, they have been designed or customized to share common interfaces and to call, use, and feed one another easily. Unix programming environments and the Interlisp programming environments are two good examples of earlier programming toolkits.

Code Generators

One important tool in the CASE programming toolkit is a code generator. A code generator enables automatic code production from a program design. Code generators offer several benefits:

- Increased productivity over manually writing program code
- Increased program reliability because of automatically produced code

- Prototyping support through screen and report painters
- Generation of compiled, structured code such as COBOL, PL/1, Fortran, C, or Ada
- Reduced maintenance costs because the code is maintained through the generator

COBOL Code Generators

Box 5.5 summarizes the benefits offered by widely used COBOL code generators such as TELON from Pansophic, APS from Sage Software, PACBASE from CGI Systems, TRANSFORM from Transform Logic, and GAMMA from KnowledgeWare. They all run in an IBM DOS and MVS environment, and support major database access methods such as IMS, CICS, VSAM, and DB/2. They all offer screen and report painting, prototyping, custom logic handling, and code, database, and documentation generation. The COBOL Code Generator from Digital Equipment Corporation and Netron/CAP are examples of COBOL code generators that run on the DEC VAX system.

BOX 5.5 COBOL code generator benefits

- Support detail design and programming of *custom* applications
- Safe way to achieve productivity gains
- Full functional replacement for manually written COBOL
- Compatible with existing systems
- Fit in with existing procedures and standards
- Minimal training
- Tool-independent code

In general, COBOL code generators support the program design through the maintenance phases of the software life cycle. They provide three capabilities:

1. Manage program specification and design information.
2. Generate program code and documentation.
3. Support ongoing program maintenance.

The program development process typically followed when using a COBOL code generator to build a business application program is as follows. First, the developer creates the screens and/or reports required by the application. The developer stores information about the format of the report and the individual data items appearing in the report in the generator's dictionary. Similarly, the developer stores information about screen literals, data items, and ordering of screens in the dictionary. This information will be used to generate source code and to build prototype models of the program.

Next, the developer defines the contents of each screen and report in more detail. For example, each data element in the screens is identified as input or output. Editing, validation, and the internal data form of each data element is specified. Also, each report data field is completely defined. Then any additional program logic is specified. Custom logic is added through the use of subroutines, macros, or high-level procedural logic facilities provided by the generator. When all the necessary program specification and design information is complete, the generator can produce source code, database definitions, JCL, and documentation.

MAINTENANCE TOOLKITS

Maintenance currently dominates the software life cycle. Over $30 billion per year is being spent on software maintenance worldwide [1]. It is estimated that there are over 100 billion lines of existing code supporting current business application systems that must be maintained. Of that 100 billion lines of code, over 70 billion lines are COBOL code [2]. In many MIS organizations, more time is spent maintaining existing systems than in developing new ones [3]. In a recent survey of over 1000 MIS organizations, software maintenance was cited most frequently (72% of the respondents) as the major cause of software backlogs [4].

Maintenance is also a major concern in the world of real-time/embedded systems. For example, the estimated software development cost for the U.S. Airforce F-16 jet fighter plane is $85 million. However, the estimated lifetime software maintenance cost is $250 million [5]. According to a former U.S. Pentagon chief, "If anything kills us before the Russians, it'll be our software" [6].

Tools to analyze, document, reverse engineer, reengineer, and convert existing systems are desperately needed. As shown in Box 5.6, these are the types of tools that are packaged in a CASE maintenance toolkit.

For example, the U.S. General Services Administration of the Federal Software Development Center has put together a CASE maintenance toolkit called the Programmers Workbench (PWB) for use by federal agencies and private contractors using federal funds. The PWB consists of 11 tools integrated

BOX 5.6 Maintenance toolkit

Purpose: correct, change, enhance, analyze, revalidate, convert, and reengineer existing systems

Facilities

- Tools for system evaluation and assessment
  - —Program management facility to maintain audit trail of all system documents, including program code, specifications, JCL, test cases
  - —Maintenance estimator to predict effort to maintain, effort to change, error-proneness
  - —Test coverage monitor to prepare test data and to determine the degree to which a program has been tested
  - —Performance monitor
  - —File comparer to determine portions of files that do not match
- Tools for analysis and reengineering
  - —Static program analyzers to produce logic schematics, where-used, how-used, and cross-reference information from scanning existing source code, and to evaluate impact of a program change on program, data structures, and JCL

    Examples:

    *What are the sequential order of processes and the links between them?

    *How does a given data field travel through the system, and under what aliases?

    *What fields are shared by a record in a customer file and a record in a transaction file?

    *Can a change to a city field in a transaction file cause a change in a post-code field in a customer file?

    *Is any code unreachable?
  - —Dynamic program analyzers such as compilers and interpreters with interactive debugging facilities, fast syntax checking, one-step compile and run, forward and backward program path/variable/procedure call tracers, execution suspension, and restart
  - —Documenter to produce updated documentation from existing source code

BOX 5.6 *(Continued)*

—Reformatter to reformat and rename source code for an existing program

—Restructurer to reformat, redocument, and replace source code for an existing program with well-structured code

—On-line, fast, full-function program editor, including a zoomout capability to exclude detail lines in a program listing to highlight structure

—Code generator to enable specification-level maintenance of generated code

—Reverse engineering tools to translate a system back into its specification for query and analysis

- Tools for migration

—Translator, data converter, and manipulator to migrate to new operating and hardware environments; provide the capability of editing, browsing, extracting, and reformatting data

into an IBM/MVS/TSO-based workbench to support the maintenance of COBOL programs. The tools included in the PWB are:

- Tool integrator, the RAND DEVELOPMENT CENTER, supplied by Rand Information Systems, Inc.
- Test coverage monitor, ANALYZER, from Aldon Computer Group
- COBOL translation system, TRANSIT, from UCCEL Corporation
- COBOL cross-referencer, DCD II, from Marble Computer, Inc.
- COBOL restructurer, RETROFIT, from Peat, Marwick, Mitchell & Company
- Data name standardizer, CSA, from Marble Computer, Inc.
- COBOL reformatter, HAWKEYE, from Blackhawk Data Corporation
- Data manipulator, DATA-XPERT, from XA Systems Corporation
- Documentation analyzer, PATHVU, from Peat, Marwick, Mitchell & Company
- Source and file comparer, COMPAREX, from Sterling Software Marketing
- COBOL source code analyzer, VIA/INSIGHT, from ViaSoft, Inc.

Restructuring and Reverse Engineering Existing Systems

Hartford Insurance Company expects to reduce its software maintenance costs by 25 to 75 percent after it automatically restructures millions of lines of existing COBOL code in its current business application systems [1].

In general, the cures for software maintenance problems include:

- Reformatting: reorganizing source code by introducing indentation and renaming variables and procedures in the source code
- Restructuring: hierarchically restructuring, analyzing, and documenting source code
- Reengineering: redesigning, rearchitecturing, and adding functions to existing programs
- Replacing: replacing existing programs with newer technologies and preprogrammed packages or retiring existing programs that are no longer used
- Reverse engineering: translating an existing program back into its design specification, including its program architectural structure, data structures, and logical data models

Fortunately, many of these maintenance cures can be applied through the use of automated maintenance tools. Some examples of automated maintenance tools are listed in Box 5.7. They are some of the most powerful, useful types of tools in the maintenance toolkit.

For example, automatic program restructuring tools can be substantially cheaper than manual rewrites and can provide the following benefits:

- Reduce future program maintenance costs.
- Facilitate program reengineering.
- Enforce structured programming and documentation standards.
- Generate program documentation, including graphic views of the program data structures and procedural structure.
- Extend the program's useful life.

Program restructuring tools transform unstructured source code into well-structured, documented code. The resulting structured program is executionally equivalent to the prestructured program since both programs perform the same sequence of operations on the same data. Of course, any logic errors contained in the prestructured program will be transferred to the newly structured version. Now, however, they probably will be easier to identify and correct.

The restructuring process consists of five steps. First, the unstructured program is analyzed automatically to review structured program deficiencies, dead

BOX 5.7 Maintenance tool examples

Documentation/restructuring

- PATHVU/STRUCTURED RETROFIT from Peat, Marwick, Mitchell & Company
- SCANCOBOL/SUPERSTRUCTURE from Group Operations, Inc.
- INSPECTOR/RECODER from Language Technology
- COBOL/SF from IBM
- SYSDOC from Syncsort, Inc.
- VERIFY from OnLine Software International

Program analyzers/reverse engineering tools

- PM/SS from Adpac
- MAESTRO from SoftLab
- DIALOGIC WORKBENCH from Dialogic Systems
- PSL/PSA from MetaSystems
- VIA/INSIGHT from ViaSoft
- FASTBOL from Tasco
- COMPAREX from Sterling Software

code, nonstandard language usages, and so on. Second, the programmer reviews the analysis information produced in the first step and makes corrections necessary for automatic restructuring. Next, the code is restructured and documented automatically. Fourth, the source code is recompiled with the aid of an optimizing compiler to enhance its efficiency. Finally, the newly structured program is revalidated.

PROJECT MANAGEMENT TOOLKITS

Good project management is one of the most important factors in improving software development and maintenance efforts. Automated project management tools can help project managers to improve tracking, control, and reporting on software projects. To be most effective, project management tools should be part of a CASE system with access to the CASE repository in which all system information is stored. The CASE repository is the up-to-date, central source for all technical system information and should also serve as the up-to-date, central source for all project status, estimation, budget, and quality assurance information.

Box 5.8 lists the types of project management tools that should be included in a CASE project management toolkit. LIFE CYCLE MANAGER from Nastec, PROJECT WORKBENCH from Applied Business Technology, MULTI/CAM from AGS Management Systems, MAESTRO PLUS from SoftLab, Inc., and LIFE CYCLE PROJECT MANAGER from American Management Systems are examples of CASE project management toolkits.

BOX 5.8 Project management toolkit

- Word processing
- Interface to electronic mail
- Spreadsheets
- Project management forms
- Configuration management for change, version, and access control
- Project plans
- Calendar and task assignment system
- Estimater tool
- Timetables and scheduling tools
- Quality control metrics
- CASE Repository with audit trail of all system information

FRAMEWORKS

A *framework* is a type of CASE toolkit that provides an infrastructure for fitting together, customizing, and managing individual software tools. With a framework, old, new, and multivendor-supplied tools that otherwise would be incompatible are assembled into an environment in which they are easy to use with one another. For example, CASE tools, traditional program implementation tools, and database management tools all can be integrated within the framework infrastructure. Frameworks can enhance the portability of tools, allowing tools to run across different hardware platforms. Tools within the framework infrastructures appear to the user to present a common user interface, share common data interfaces, and run in the same hardware environment.

Examples of CASE framework toolkits include SOFTWARE BACKPLANE from Atherton Technology, RULE TOOL from Cadware Group, RAND DEVELOP-

MENT CENTER from Rand Information Systems, LIFE CYCLE PRODUCTIVITY SYSTEM from American Management Systems, and CUSTOMIZER from Index Technology.

Box 5.9 summarizes the characteristics of a CASE framework toolkit.

BOX 5.9 Framework toolkit

Purpose: infrastructure designed for tool integration, management, and customization

- Support in the following areas of toolkit/workbench design and development:
  —Menu structure
  —Help function
  —Documentation format
  —Diagramming symbols and syntax rules
  —Workstation-to-mainframe communications
  —System configuration management
  —Form templates
- Framework should be usable in a wide range of development environments
- Framework should be built on an open architecture so that new tools and tools from different sources can be added incrementally

CASE WORKBENCHES

A *CASE workbench* is an assembly of integrated tools whose function is to automate the development and maintenance of software systems as well as software project management activities. A CASE workbench contains tools that integrate the basic phases of the software life cycle: namely, analysis, design, and implementation. The tools are integrated to the level that the output of one life cycle phase is directly and automatically passed on to the next phase. The final product of a CASE workbench is an executable software system and its accompanying documentation. The characteristics of a CASE workbench are discussed in detail in Chapters 2 and 3.

The INFORMATION ENGINEERING FACILITY (IEF) from Texas Instruments is an example of a CASE workbench. The IEF supports the information engineering methodology. It automatically transforms the information represented by diagrams created in one stage of information engineering into information and diagrams used in the next stage of information engineering. The INFORMATION ENGINEERING WORKBENCH (IEW) from KnowledgeWare is another CASE workbench that supports information engineering and that automatically passes information on to the next phase. For example, the IEW automatically transforms business activities represented in decomposition diagrams at the information strategy planning stage into a fully leveled set of data flow diagrams which are then used in the business area analysis stage of information engineering.

TekCASE tools from Tektronix support the development of real-time systems. TekCASE DESIGNER transforms the real-time system model produced with TekCASE ANALYST/RT into alternative structured designs, preserving data and control information to establish requirements traceability from the analysis phase to the design phase. Then the Tektronix PICKBOSS tool can be used to identify the best design by automatically evaluating the complexity of each design alternative. PICKBOSS recommends the design that can be represented by the least complex structure chart.

PROMOD from Promod, Inc. is also used for the development of real-time systems. The PROMOD/MODULAR DESIGN TRANSFORMATION PROCESS converts a data flow model created during the analysis phase into a control hierarchy of subsystems, modules, and functions to begin the program design phase.

Other examples of CASE workbenches include CORVISION from Cortex, EXSYS from Exsys, Inc., and AUTOCODE from Integrated Systems.

Different CASE workbenches run in different hardware and operating system environments, support different structured development methodologies, and support the development of different types of target systems. Box 5.10 lists how CASE workbenches can be further classified.

BOX 5.10 Classifications of workbenches

1. Hardware environment/operating system

_____ Mainframe	_____ MVS	_____ MS-DOS
_____ Mini	_____ VM	_____ Unix
_____ PC/workstation	_____ VAX/VMS	_____ Ada

2. Open architecture

_____ Alternative front-end interfaces
_____ Alternative back-end interfaces

3. CASE information repository

_____ Centralized		_____ Local	
_____ Dictionary	_____ DBMS		_____ Knowledge base
_____ Interfaced		_____ Fully integrated	

BOX 5.10 *(Continued)*

4. Application class

_____ Real-time	_____ COBOL	_____ PL/1
_____ On-line	_____ 4GL	_____ Ada
_____ High-volume transaction	_____ Fortran	_____ Other

5. Methodology supported
   - _____ Software engineering
   - _____ Information engineering
   - _____ Generic structured—methodology independent
   - _____ Structured—methodology specific ____________________
   - _____ Formal structured

CASE METHODOLOGY COMPANIONS

A *CASE methodology companion* is either a CASE toolkit or a CASE workbench that structures the software development process according to the steps and rules of a particular structured methodology. Information about the methodology is embedded into the methodology companion by means of help panels, menu choices, forcing functions, and quality assurance checks. For example, help screens and menus inform the developer of the next step to be done, what input is needed to perform this step, and what output is to be produced. Forcing functions do not allow the developer to proceed to the next step in the methodology until the methodology companion judges that the current task is complete, and certifies that the outputs from this task are correct and comply with current standards.

Embedding methodology information in CASE tools makes more extensive user help and system checking possible. It also minimizes the information that the developer must enter to perform tasks since information can be transformed automatically and passed on to subsequent tasks in the exact form required by the tasks based on the methodology's rules.

Examples of CASE methodology companions are listed in Box 5.11, and classifications for CASE methodology companions are listed in Box 5.12. The methodology driver, which is an expert-system-based CASE methodology companion, is discussed in Chapter 12.

BOX 5.11 Examples of CASE methodology companions

Tool	Type of Tool	Methodology Supported
DATA RESOURCES LEVERAGE WITH JANUS from D. Appleton Company	Data design toolkit	Prototype development methodology
FOUNDATION from Arthur Andersen	CASE workbench	METHOD-1
DESIGN MACHINE from Ken Orr & Associates	Analysis/design toolkit	Data structured systems development
SQL*DESIGN DICTIONARY from Oracle	Data design toolkit	SQL development method
AUTO-MATE PLUS from Learmonth & Burchett	Data design toolkit	L&B structured development method
INFORMATION ENGINEERING FACILITY from Texas Instruments	CASE workbench	Information engineering methodology
TAGS from Teledyne Brown	CASE workbench	TAGS/IORL
ANALYST/DESIGNER TOOLKIT from Yourdon, Inc.	Analysis/design toolkit	Yourdon structured design methodology

BOX 5.12 Classifications of CASE methodology companions

1. Methodology supported
   - _____ Software engineering
   - _____ Information engineering
   - _____ Structured technique
   - _____ In-house methodology
   - _____ Formal structured
   - _____ Specific _______________
   - _______________________

BOX 5.12 *(Continued)*

2. Hardware environment/operating system

_____ Mainframe	_____ MVS	_____ MS-DOS
_____ Mini	_____ VM	_____ Unix
_____ PC/workstation	_____ VAX/VMS	_____ Ada

3. Level of support

_____ Documentation production
_____ Guidance system
_____ Intelligent methodology driver

4. Application class

_____ Real-time	_____ COBOL	_____ PL/1
_____ On-line	_____ 4GL	_____ Ada
_____ High-volume transaction	_____ Fortran	_____ Other

REFERENCES

1. Girish Parikh, "Restructuring Your COBOL Programs," *Computer World Focus,* February 19, 1986, pp. 39–42.
2. *ViaSoft News Release*. Phoenix, Ariz.: ViaSoft, December 2, 1986.
3. Stan Kolodziej, "Gaining Control of Maintenance," *Computer World Focus,* February 19, 1986, pp. 31–36.
4. "CASE 1987 Survey," *Software News*. Westborough, Mass.: Sentry Publishing Company, 1987.
5. William Suydam, "CASE Makes Strides toward Automated Software Development," *Computer Design,* January 1, 1987, pp. 49–70.
6. *Atherton Technology White Paper*. Sunnyvale, Calif.: Atherton Technology, August 1987.

PART III USE OF COMPUTER-AIDED SOFTWARE ENGINEERING

6 CASE STUDIES ON CASE

INCREASING SOFTWARE PRODUCTIVITY

The key to productivity is automation. This applies to software development as well as to other types of product manufacturing. Computer-aided software engineering is the automation of many of the tasks in the software life cycle. The CASE technology is the focus of productivity improvements for software in the late 1980s.

The proof that computer-aided software engineering works is already coming from many companies for which dramatic software productivity increases are being reported. Although very different, these companies share their successful use of CASE tools for increasing productivity. In each case they have chosen tools that help automate structured methodologies.

Structured methodologies, many of which were developed in the 1970s, provide a proven way for producing high-quality, reliable software systems. The failure of structured methodologies, however, has been the time-consuming manual effort they require. Automated tools solve this problem by taking over many of the burdensome details and paperwork of applying these methodologies. This frees the software developer to concentrate on the creative part of the software development process. The result is a very significant increase in each individual developer's ability to produce more and better-quality software systems.

The basic idea behind CASE is to support each phase of the life cycle with a set of laborsaving tools. Some CASE tools concentrate on supporting the early phases of the life cycle. They give automated assistance in the form of automated diagram drawing, screen painting, and correctness checking. Others focus on the implementation phases of the life cycle. They include automated code and test case generators.

In some cases, these tools are used in conjunction with third- and fourth-generation languages. In other cases they replace them by allowing the devel-

CASE productivity statistics

	Excelerator	IE workbench	Factory
Type	Analysis toolkit	CASE specification workbench	CASE generator workbench
Primary use	Systems analysis and documentation	Systems analysis and design	System development and maintenance
Reported productivity increases	Factor of 2 to 10 times	Factor of 2 to 4 times	Factor of 2 to 20 times

Figure 6.1 Productivity improvements reported by users of CASE tools.

oper to create high-level program specifications from which program code can be generated.

In this chapter we look at how companies have improved software productivity with the use of three different CASE tools: EXCELERATOR from Index Technology Corporation, the INFORMATION ENGINEERING WORKBENCH from KnowledgeWare, and the APPLICATION FACTORY from Cortex. Companies using these tools reported productivity improvements across various phases of the life cycle that ranged from a factor of 2 to a factor of 20 times (see Figure 6.1).

EXCELERATOR PRODUCTIVITY EXPERIENCES

EXCELERATOR, from Index Technology Corporation, is a productivity tool aimed at designing and documenting information systems and real-time systems. It is a PC-based tool to be used by a professional systems analyst or designer.

EXCELERATOR has four basic facilities:

1. An automated diagramming tool for drawing structured diagrams, like data flow diagrams, structure charts, data models, control flow diagrams, and finite-state diagrams
2. Screen and report painters for specifying and prototyping the user interface of an information system
3. An integrated repository for storing and cross-referencing all systems analysis and design information
4. An automated analysis tool for checking and reporting the syntactic correctness, completeness, and consistency of structured diagrams

EXCELERATOR is best described as an *analysis toolkit* because it provides an integrated set of tools for automating systems analysis and design tasks.

EXCELERATOR provides its user with three major benefits. First, EXCELERATOR makes structured methodologies such as DeMarco structured analysis and Yourdon structured design practical to use. Automated drawing and redrawing of structured diagrams, capturing of design information in the automated repository, and automated tracking and maintaining of all design details allow the analyst to concentrate on the design problem rather than on paperwork.

Second, EXCELERATOR improves overall system design quality. Keeping all design information on the computer and then checking its consistency and completeness automatically assures the highest-quality design information.

Third, EXCELERATOR speeds up the design process. With EXCELERATOR's automated assistance, major design modifications can be made in seconds, work can be checked at the same time that the design is being developed, and designs can be reused by retrieving them from EXCELERATOR's repository.

Recent case studies from 12 organizations using EXCELERATOR in systems analysis and design work cited productivity increases ranging from a factor of 2 to a factor of 10 times. The 12 organizations have a similar development environment:

- IBM mainframe shop using VM and/or MVS
- Installed database management systems such as IMS and DB2
- Use of fourth-generation tools such as FOCUS, DATA DICTIONARY, and DATAMANAGER
- Use of COBOL for large mainframe-based applications

At each organization, EXCELERATOR was used mainly in new system development efforts as a tool for automating currently used structured methods. The primary user was a systems analyst, and the primary use was for system requirements specification. EXCELERATOR users reported an average of 8 to 30 hours to become proficient using the tool. They were already trained in structured methods.

U.S. Government EXCELERATOR Experiences

One of the 12 case studies came from a U.S. government organization, which reported that with the aid of EXCELERATOR, it could reduce the length of the development cycle to a point where a system could be implemented before it became obsolete. Analysts completed system specifications in four months instead of the estimated two years if done manually.

ARCO EXCELERATOR Experiences

Another EXCELERATOR case study came from ARCO. At ARCO most software development for mainframe applications is done using COBOL and the SDM structured development methodology. ARCO chose EXCELERATOR because they were looking for a tool to automate the data modeling process. They needed a way to enhance the productivity of software developers since due to a restructuring of the business, their development staff size had been greatly reduced. ARCO began using EXCELERATOR in 1984. By mid-1986, ARCO had 23 copies of EXCELERATOR installed.

On a major production redevelopment project ARCO reported that systems analysts using EXCELERATOR prepared logical data models of information systems with a 10-to-1 gain in productivity over doing it manually.

ARCO enhanced EXCELERATOR's import/export capability by writing its own software that enables importing and exporting of information from EXCELERATOR's dictionary to and from IBM's Data Dictionary. From a data administration viewpoint, this means that data can be better controlled. To ARCO this is just as important as performing software tasks faster.

Touche Ross EXCELERATOR Experiences

Touche Ross, one of the first users of EXCELERATOR, was the subject of another case report. They chose EXCELERATOR because EXCELERATOR supports the Yourdon structured methodology. Touche Ross has used EXCELERATOR to design many different types of applications, such as order entry, inventory control, criminal justice, and bidding systems. The primary user of EXCELERATOR at Touche Ross is a systems analyst trained in Yourdon structured techniques. There are four personal computers each with a copy of EXCELERATOR at Touche Ross. One personal computer is assigned to a project where one person is responsible for entering and updating all system information in the EXCELERATOR dictionary.

They reported that EXCELERATOR dramatically changes the way they do systems analysis. They use EXCELERATOR down to system design level. System specification quality is greatly improved, user involvement is made practical, and automated drawing of diagrams make changes easy to do. Although the primary use of EXCELERATOR is for system requirements specification, Touche Ross has also used EXCELERATOR in some usual ways that have nothing to do with software development. They have used EXCELERATOR to describe all sorts of systems (both automated and manual) for the purposes of better understanding the systems and streamlining the systems, rather than with the intention of eventually automating the systems. For example, the chief justice of Milwaukee County, Wisconsin, said that after 31 years on the bench, he finally understood the criminal justice system because Touche Ross, with the help of EXCELERATOR, described it in pictures rather than in words. The system was described with 287 data flow diagrams after an 8½-month system requirements definition effort.

Touche Ross feels that a major productivity advantage of using EXCELERATOR is that it is easy to review system requirements because it is easy to revise automated diagrams with EXCELERATOR. Another advantage is the consistency of the output it produces.

The consensus among EXCELERATOR users is that the key to productivity successes is good management, a solid understanding of structured analysis and design, and powerful automated tools.

APPLICATION FACTORY PRODUCTIVITY EXPERIENCES

The APPLICATION FACTORY from Cortex Corporation is a productivity tool for generating on-line, multiuser information systems. The core of the FACTORY is its automatic code generator. The FACTORY runs on DEC VAX computers.

The APPLICATION FACTORY includes five basic facilities:

1. Screen and report painters for specifying and prototyping the system's user interface
2. A repository for storing all information about a system
3. Automated checking for completeness and consistency of program specifications
4. A code generator capable of automatic generation of 95 percent of the program code from program specifications
5. An automated program documentation generator

The APPLICATION FACTORY is used by systems analysts and programmers to develop and maintain medium-sized-to-large information systems. The FACTORY is appropriate for building medium-sized-to-large production systems in high-volume transaction environments interfacing to real-time devices.

Users noted three major benefits. First, developers are more productive with the APPLICATION FACTORY than programming in third-generation languages such as COBOL and FORTRAN. Also, developers are more productive with the APPLICATION FACTORY than programming in fourth-generation languages. The FACTORY generates highly efficient code and has the power to handle large as well as small application systems. Unlike fourth-generation languages, the FACTORY has been used successfully to build high-volume transaction systems. With the FACTORY, the bigger, the better in terms of application size. The FACTORY has been used to build systems with 2500 function points handling 15,000 transactions daily and 300 users.

Second, the APPLICATION FACTORY makes rapid, iterative prototyping a practical way of building systems to meet user requirements. A series of prototype models of the system are built as a way of more clearly identifying user requirements. The final system eventually evolves from the prototypes. The APPLICATION FACTORY makes this process quick and easy by generating code automatically from the prototype specifications.

Third, the APPLICATION FACTORY greatly simplifies program maintenance because the program specification, not the code, is maintained. When there is a need to change a system, its specification is changed and then the code and its documentation are regenerated automatically from the system specification. In this way, documentation is a by-product of development and maintenance and is always kept up to date.

Case studies of system development with the APPLICATION FACTORY reported an average productivity increase of a factor of 13 times with FACTORY over COBOL. The case studies included the development of 26 application systems at 22 separate locations. Productivity increases were measured with function points by comparing the *estimated* COBOL effort to the *actual* FACTORY effort. System size ranged from 78 to 2418 functions points, which is approximately the size range of 8300- to 253,000-line COBOL programs. In addition, the case studies showed that the FACTORY productivity relative to COBOL increases as application size and complexity increases. Experiences show that project size and developer experience significantly affected productivity, and that developer experience had the greater effect of the two.

DuPont FACTORY Experiences

At the DuPont Textile Fibers Plant, the Information Systems Group uses FORTRAN and COBOL to develop application systems. At the time of the case study, they were in the process of converting from a DEC PDP-11 and IBM mainframe system environment to a DEC VAX environment. Also, they have developed their own methodology, called RIPP (Rapid Iterative Production Prototyping), for system development (see Figure 6.2). RIPP limits all system development projects to a maximum of 90 days, including system specification, system prototyping, and system implementation. Sixty of those 90 days are spent in the prototyping step. Their charter is to:

1. Automate as much of the software development process as possible.
2. Improve the quality of information systems.
3. Improve software productivity over the entire life cycle.
4. Integrate data management and software development.

The DuPont productivity goal is to improve productivity by a factor of 10 over the entire life cycle. DuPont is literally exploding with software systems projects because of corporate changes and a move toward greater automation in the plants.

DuPont reported some very impressive cost savings when the APPLICATION FACTORY was used to develop systems. In nine system development projects, DuPont saved almost $2 million by using the FACTORY rather than third-generation languages such as COBOL and FORTRAN (see Figure 6.3). With the FACTORY, the number of staff days to develop the system was reduced substan-

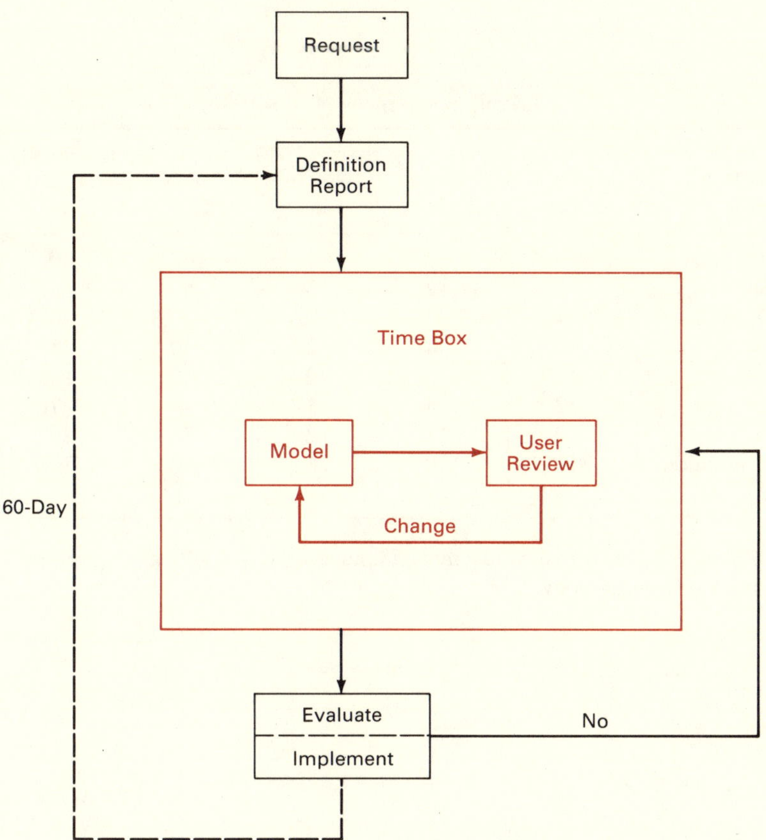

Figure 6.2 DuPont RIPP methodology, 90-day projects.

tially. FACTORY's automatic code generator had the greatest impact on reducing the staff effort in the programming and testing phases (see Figure 6.4). DuPont said that the FACTORY helped them get the systems built faster even when they used less experienced developers. Many of their developers were right out of college. The learning curve for the FACTORY was three months to reach competence level, and six months to reach expert level.

The FACTORY is helping DuPont achieve its productivity goals because, on average, the development effort can be cut in half when the FACTORY is used. One example is the Bulk Continuous Filament Project, which is part of the Inspection and Packing System for the DuPont Waynesboro Textile Plant. The project requirements were to use fourth-generation techniques, use structured techniques, use a database management system run on a DEC VAX computer, and finish a critical subset of the system in 1986. Preliminary analysis of the project had been done using Yourdon structured techniques to produce project-size estimates. Use of the FACTORY along with RIPP enabled DuPont developers

DuPont experiences (1985–1986)

Application System	No. of Screens	No. of Reports	No. of Files	Costs (M)		
				Est.	Actual	Saved
BCF stretch wrap	3	5	11	$ 168.	$ 30.	$ 138.
Suggestion	5	12	3	50.	8.	42.
Training history	4	2	2	0.9	0.9	0.
Spinning 1	16	4	12	50.	25.	25.
Spinning 2	11	5	9	29.	14.6	14.4
Feedstock	12	4	11	45.1	7.5	37.6
Transfer	12	11	12	125.0	20.	105.0
Kevlar information system	313	119	76	1472.9	420.8	1052.1

Figure 6.3 Reported productivity improvements at DuPont achieved by using CASE technology.

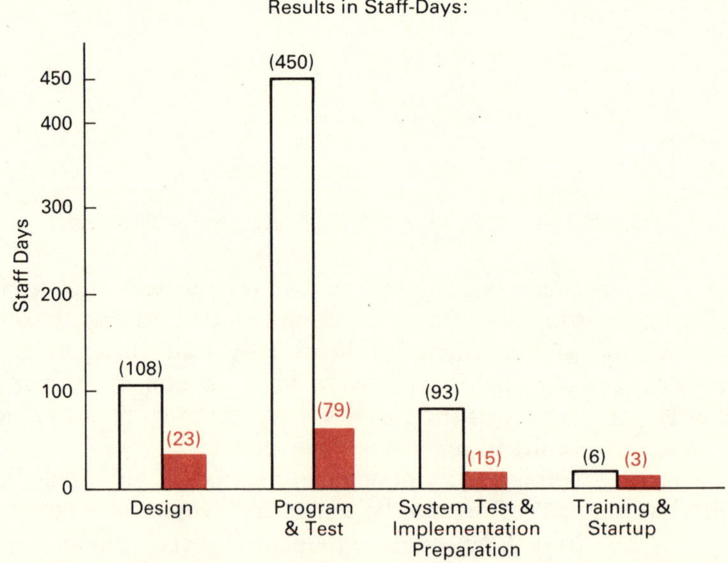

Figure 6.4 The greatest productivity improvements at DuPont occurred during the programming and test phases (results in staff-days). Red: Actual FACTORY Effort White: Estimated COBOL Effort

to satisfy the project requirements. The first version of the system was completed ahead of schedule with a cost savings of $500,000. Not only was the project completed ahead of schedule, but the system had more functionality than the user expected. Although the estimated project time with traditional development methods was 28 to 39 staff months, the project was actually completed in 5 staff months.

DuPont said that if the project had been done using Fortran, the system could not possibly have been completed within the necessary time frame. Besides the use of the FACTORY, DuPont cited two other reasons for project success: RIPP and user involvement. Structured analysis was followed by use of RIPP. Use of the RIPP methodology allowed the system to be developed in versions. The developers were less reluctant to change the system and the users saw results sooner. Also, the project had the full-time commitment of the most experienced plant expert. This was necessary because the system needed to interface with other systems, some of which controlled plant production. The system consisted of 12 subsystems, 7 FACTORY reports, 20 customized reports built in the Cortex BUILDER Language, 65 data sets, and 300 fields.

In general, users seemed happy with the resulting system. They said that they got their system much faster than ever before. What they gave up for this development speed was customization of reports and procedures. For the most part, however, the users were willing to accept this limitation as long as it meant quicker service in developing and maintaining (changing) systems. Users measure success in terms of a quick response to requests for changes: namely, 24 hours in FACTORY instead of 1 week in FORTRAN.

The average productivity increase for this project was a factor of 3 over expected results. DuPont discovered that user expectations increase with more project involvement and positive results, and that developer credibility improves greatly when projects are completed on schedule.

DuPont also discovered that its users could not handle a factor of 10 increase because this creates a new bottleneck—the implementation bottleneck.

According to DuPont, a perfect application fit for the FACTORY is:

- A project that an individual developer can complete in three months (the RIPP development cycle)
- Minimal use of the BUILDER Language, which is the customized procedural language of the FACTORY

Other application development projects under way at DuPont include terminal tracking, toxicology, chemical hazards, key receipts, and waste monitoring systems. DuPont plans to train 12 more programmer/analysts to use the FACTORY and to move 20 to 30 IBM COBOL applications to the DEC VAX environment with the help of the FACTORY.

INFORMATION ENGINEERING WORKBENCH PRODUCTIVITY EXPERIENCES

KnowledgeWare's INFORMATION ENGINEERING WORKBENCH, known as the IEW, is a CASE workbench for the commercial applications systems analyst. The IEW is a CASE workbench and methodology companion that automates a structured methodology called information engineering.

The IEW has three basic facilities:

1. An automated diagramming tool for drawing structured diagrams
2. A CASE repository with its intelligent information management system, called an *encyclopedia,* for storing, analyzing, and coordinating all system information
3. An automated analysis tool called the *knowledge coordinator,* for checking the completeness and consistency of all systems analysis and design information

In these case studies, the IEW was used mainly to provide automated support for the systems analysis and data analysis steps of the information engineering methodology.

IEW users report three major benefits. First, the IEW is an automated companion for information engineering. Besides automating mundane tasks such as drawing and revising structured diagrams, the IEW enforces and standardizes the use of the information engineering methodology. One IEW user commented that enforcing the rigor of a structured methodology is essential in building better-quality systems.

Second, the IEW increases software development productivity by reducing the time to plan for, analyze, design, and build information systems. An IEW user reported that an end-user interview that would have taken four hours normally took only one hour with IEW assistance.

Third, the IEW enhances communication by automatically documenting everything the analyst does. The use of structured diagrams to explain the system specification improves communication with end users, management, and system developers.

Deere & Co. IEW Experiences

At Deere & Co. there are 39 decentralized system development groups and no overall company standards. Because the farm industry has been depressed, there has been a hiring freeze at Deere & Co. since 1979. During this period the addition of multiple database management systems such as DB2, ORACLE, and dBASE III has meant growing complexity for the development organizations, which previously supported only IMS. Also, during this time period, Deere & Co. has developed its own system development methodology based on the information engineering methodology.

The charter of the System Planning and Data Administration Department at Deere & Co. is to:

1. Perform early requirements analysis for projects involving shared corporate data.
2. Improve data administration and its integration with system development.
3. Position the entire organization to improve system development by supporting the Deere methodology with automated tools.

The major productivity issue at Deere & Co. is to achieve a 30 percent software development productivity increase. They want fewer people to do more work in less time. They want to do a better job of specifying system requirements. They want to move analysts more easily from project to project. Finally, they want to reduce their maintenance effort.

Deere & Co. chose the INFORMATION ENGINEERING WORKBENCH (IEW) to help them achieve their productivity goals. Since 1985, there have been 10 copies of the IEW installed at Deere & Co. This is an average of one personal computer per two analysts. The total cost of hardware and software is $15,000 per CASE workstation. It was a two-week effort to integrate the IEW use with the Deere methodology. The primary user of the IEW at Deere & Co. is the systems analyst. The primary use is to design new systems. The time to become proficient with the tool averaged two days, assuming that the user was already familiar with structured analysis techniques.

Deere & Co. plans eventually to have one IEW PC-based CASE workstation for each of its 300 programmers and analysts. Currently, five medium-sized system development projects are using the IEW at Deere & Co. Productivity gains of a factor of 2 for requirements analysis and data analysis tasks using the IEW rather than doing it manually have been reported at Deere & Co. One system under development is the Track Project Development Cycle System. Ninety data flow diagrams and 50 entity relationship diagrams were used to describe its 430 business functions. Automatic diagramming tools make diagrams a practical analysis tool and help improve communications with the users. In addition, Deere & Co. reported that automated checking for design errors in the structured diagrams was the most important factor in increasing productivity. Getting the errors out early in the development process simplified the job down the line in the later development phases.

The Deere philosophy and advice is to have the development methodology in place first. Tools do not provide the methodology, only the automated assistance for the methodology.

Babcock & Wilcox IEW Experiences

There are six divisions in the Power Generation Group at Babcock & Wilcox. They use fourth-generation languages and COBOL to develop batch and on-line systems. They developed their own methodology based on Arthur Young's computer system methodology, information system planning, and information engineering.

Babcock and Wilcox also chose the IEW to help automate their version of the information engineering methodology. They were particularly interested in tools to automate systems analysis and design phases of the life cycle.

The charter of the Data Base and Standards Department at Babcock and Wilcox is to:

1. Perform database administration and implementation.
2. Develop system development standards and procedures.
3. Improve productivity of the system developers, especially in the phases of analysis and design.

Productivity improvements were most needed in analysis and design because Babcock & Wilcox felt that they did an inadequate job in these most important phases of system development.

Since January 1986, four copies of the IEW have been used at Babcock & Wilcox. These four copies are shared among 14 analysts and across many projects. The IEW encyclopedia is populated with the results from the information system planning step, which produced 52 business functions. This then serves as the foundation for all development projects. One of the four IEW workstations has been designated as the master encyclopedia. The primary use of the IEW is to design business application systems. The primary user is a systems analyst, but end users are developing logical data models with the IEW.

Currently, four medium-sized application systems are being designed using the IEW at Babcock and Wilcox. End users are constructing their own structured diagrams with the IEW automatic drawing tools. Babcock and Wilcox expect a threefold productivity increase in analysis and design tasks using the IEW over doing it manually.

Looking to the future, Babcock and Wilcox software developers have a maintenance vision. With IEW, they will be able to maintain systems by maintaining design information in the IEW encyclopedia and automatically generating and regenerating code from the design rather than maintaining the code itself.

SUMMARY

To summarize, the EXCELERATOR, APPLICATION FACTORY and IEW users mentioned in this chapter all reported that the CASE technology plays a major role in increasing productivity. Also, CASE technology has a very positive productivity impact on the development of software systems of all sizes and types.

Finally, they reported that software productivity is likely to be at its highest when the tools automate a structured methodology already accepted and in place in the organization, and when the tools are in the hands of experienced, skilled analysts and programmers.

It is important to emphasize that many of the productivity gains reported in this chapter were confined to specific tasks, such as logical data modeling, rather than stretching across multiple phases of the software life cycle. This suggests that users should take care to select CASE tools that are likely to improve productivity where it is most needed in their particular organization. It is also important to emphasize that methodology training is a critical factor in increasing productivity. Those organizations that achieved the biggest productivity gains had already done methodology training. Many of the users that were interviewed commented that methodology training was far more important and more time consuming than tools training. Choosing the right development methodology is the foundation upon which to build a high-productivity strategy because it is the methodology that drives the software development process.

There is no magic formula for achieving software productivity success, but if you want to stack the deck in your favor: Use the best people, the best methodologies, and the best tools.

REFERENCES

Material for this chapter was obtained by interviews of CASE tool users from the various companies mentioned and the tool vendors. The interviews were conducted by the author. A copy of the interview questions is included in Box 6.1.

BOX 6.1 Productivity questions

1. Company background?
   - Department(s) involved
   - Size of analyst and programmer staff
   - Computers and languages used
   - Types of software systems
   - Productivity issues
2. How is software developer productivity measured?
3. What criteria were used to select productivity tools?

BOX 6.1 *(Continued)*

4. What other software tools and techniques (methodologies) are in place?
5. How was success in improving productivity measured?
   What role did the tools play?
   Return on investment?
6. For what types of application/tasks are the tools applicable?
   Who are the primary users?
   How much time is needed to become proficient in using the tools?
7. How were the tools integrated with the current environment?
8. How was the software development process changed by the introduction of the tools?
   - Impact on maintenance?
   - Role of end users?
9. Case histories of tool use?

7 CASE IMPLEMENTATION CONSIDERATIONS

MULTIFACETED SOFTWARE PROBLEMS AND SOLUTIONS

Although there are many reported software productivity successes with the CASE technology, there also are failures in which the use of CASE did not significantly change or improve software development and maintenance. Why do some organizations fail to use CASE successfully, whereas others achieve dramatic success?

Experience has shown that the use of the CASE technology does not always guarantee success [1]. Some frequent observations from CASE technology users include the following:

- The CASE technology cannot improve software productivity and software quality if it is not used.
- Many system developers have not been trained in and do not use engineering-like development methodologies.
- The CASE technology is not a substitute for good project management.
- The attitude of software developers can greatly affect successful use of CASE technology.
- Software projects are often out of control because management does not enforce development standards and procedures.

A more complete list of causes of failure to use the CASE technology effectively are cited in Box 7.1. However, there is a more basic, more important reason for failure. Organizations that failed did not recognize the full complexity of their software problems and therefore did not fully understand how to use CASE in a solution to their problems.

The software crisis that affects most organizations today is a multifaceted problem to which there is no simple, single solution. The CASE technology can

BOX 7.1 Causes of CASE failures

- Confusion about what individual CASE products actually do
- Using CASE tools to address problems for which they were not intended
- Placing too much emphasis on CASE tools as a whole solution
- Ignoring the importance of good management
- No development methodology or standards in place
- Poorly integrated CASE tools
- Poor tool documentation and training
- Not enough functionality present in CASE tools
- Unclear about which software problem needs to be solved
- No methods for measuring impact of CASE on software development and maintenance
- No software development methodology training
- Indecisive—unwilling to make a decision about how to use CASE technology
- Unwilling to change current way of developing and maintaining software
- View CASE as a high-risk technology
- No plan detailing how to implement CASE technology

address the technical aspects of the software crisis. However, there are serious people and management issues that must be addressed as well. The CASE technology is an important part of the solution to the software crisis but should not be considered the whole solution. Simply buying CASE tools is unlikely to have a significant effect on improving overall software productivity and quality. A total solution to the software crisis must also be multifaceted—addressing management, people, tools, and methodology issues.

CASE OR NO CASE

Whenever a new technology such as CASE becomes available, an organization must make a decision concerning its use of this new technology. The basic choices are simple:

1. Do nothing.
2. Adopt the new technology.

However, arriving at the decision may not be so simple. Decisions should not be based solely on a response to user pressure to build systems more quickly or a developer's desire to try the newest technological advancement.

Some organizations get stuck indefinitely studying various aspects of the new technology and never seem to reach a decision as to whether or not to adopt it. For example, one very large organization, with revenues at $5 billion and an MIS budget of $100 million, spent $500,000 trying out CASE tools. A decision about whether or not to use CASE was never made. The indecisiveness was caused in large part by the perceived risk of failure from making the wrong decision.

After spending over $1 million to formulate its CASE plan, another organization still had no plan, because no CASE tool that could solve *all* their very unique software problems existed and because their software developers were hesitant to use tools developed outside the organization. Organizations waiting for the perfect, easy-to-implement solution to all their software problems probably will be waiting for a very, very long time.

Other organizations jump in too quickly and adopt the technology without considering what the strategy or impact may be. For example, many powerful CASE tools have become "shelfware" and are never really used because the organization bought them without a plan for introducing CASE into their existing software culture. Software developers want to be involved in the selection of tools they are expected to use.

A strategy that can counteract these problems and help an organization reach a reasonable decision about its use of the CASE technology in a reasonable amount of time is to:

1. Establish the organization's needs.
2. Demonstrate that the new technology can meet those needs.
3. Devise a plan for introducing the new technology and implement it.

ESTABLISHING THE NEEDS

Most organizations are now facing a serious software crisis. They have a large backlog of software systems waiting to be developed. According to the findings of a recent survey of over 1000 organizations, the software application backlog averaged 88 months [2]. Also, organizations are not satisfied with the quality of software systems being developed. They cannot change systems fast enough to meet changing user requirements. They face an ever-increasing burden from the maintenance needs of existing systems. In short, most organizations recognize a desperate need to improve the software development and maintenance process significantly. Doing nothing to solve the software crisis is a grave mistake that can only result in escalating software problems and costs.

The need is clear. Organizations need to solve the software crisis immediately. They need to develop better-quality systems in much less time at much lower costs. They need to reduce the software maintenance burden, which is a major cause of large backlogs [2]. Unfortunately, how best to address this need has certainly not been clear. Organizations are suffering burnout as a result of previous failed attempts to alleviate the software crisis. This explains a great part of their reluctance to embrace yet another new technology. An important part of successfully implementing CASE in an organization is to overcome this reluctance by determining what must be done and how CASE can help accomplish it.

BOX 7.2 Determining an organization's needs to improve the state of the art of the software process

Management Questions

- What is the organizational structure for software developers? Is it centralized or decentralized?
- What training in software tools and methodologies has been given to software developers?
- What project management standards and procedures are in place?
- What are the strengths and weaknesses and bottlenecks in the current software life cycle process?
- How is software productivity measured?
- How is software quality measured?

Technical Questions

- Is an established engineering-like process followed for developing software systems? For maintaining systems?
- Is there a disciplined development methodology used to order the software development effort?
- What hardware environment is used as the software development and maintenance platform?
- What software development and maintenance tools (including programming languages) are already in place?
- What technical standards and procedures are followed to ensure software quality?
- What procedures and standards are applied to software maintenance?
- What is the software developers' attitude toward software automation?

Defining the Needs in Detail

Because each organization suffers from its own unique form of the software crisis, there is no universal cure-all. A workable solution must be tailored to each organization. This means that an organization should begin by specifying and prioritizing its needs in detail. Simply stating "We need to improve software productivity and quality" is not adequate specification of the needs to determine a practical solution that involves CASE. Box 7.2 lists questions that must be asked *and* answered to determine the needs of an organization. The questions are divided into management and technical categories because both aspects must be understood to specify the needs completely. An organization must understand its current state of the art of software development and maintenance and the areas of most concern before it can determine a practical CASE solution to its software crisis.

Setting Organizational Goals

Once the organization's needs have been defined and the current state of the art of software development and maintenance within the organization is understood, short-term and long-term goals for meeting these needs can be set. Goals should be prioritized based on the urgency of meeting particular needs and the costs, the training, and the implementation time involved.

MAKING A CASE DECISION

Now that the organization has a clear, detailed understanding of its goals, it can make a determination as to if and how CASE can be used to meet these goals. Both management and technical issues must be considered. There are important management considerations. For example, is the organizational culture open to change? Are software developers now willing to accept CASE, or will they view it with indifference or rejection? How can the CASE concept be sold most effectively to management so that it will be willing to commit the time and money needed to introduce CASE properly into the organization, and later to provide continuing support?

Does the organization accept the concept of standards for both the software life cycle process and product, and how can standards be enforced? Who can make the decision to adopt or not adopt the CASE technology? If adopted, who will be responsible for implementation of the new technology?

Also, there are many important technical considerations. What changes in current standards and procedures are necessary to adopt CASE? Is the current development methodology amenable to CASE automation? If there is no current methodology, which methodology should be chosen? Who will be the primary users of the CASE technology? What technical training will they need to use the CASE technology effectively? What is the learning curve involved? Who will provide the training? How will the use of CASE change the software life cycle process? Where are the strengths and weaknesses in the software life cycle process as it is currently practiced?

CASE IMPLEMENTATION PLAN

If the decision is made to adopt the CASE technology, a plan for implementing CASE must be devised. The plan should propose a phased implementation of CASE because organizations that attempt to implement too much too quickly greatly increase the risk for failure [3]. For example, underestimating the need for methodology training and the learning curve for CASE can lead to failure to adopt CASE successfully. Box 7.3 lists management and technical considerations that should be covered in a CASE implementation plan.

The steps to follow in implementing CASE will vary depending on whether or not satisfactory and automatable standards and procedures for the software life cycle process already exist in the organization. If they do, then as the first step, select CASE tools that support the automation of these standards and procedures to enhance the existing software support environment. If they do not exist, begin by creating standards and procedures where help is most needed to improve the software development and maintenance process. Then as the next step, select CASE tools that automate and support these standards and procedures. It makes sense that one must have a well-defined process in mind before attempting to automate that process through the use of CASE tools. (Structured methodologies were discussed in Chapter 3.)

METHODOLOGY FIRST

Organizations that get the most benefit out of the CASE technology use a set of well-integrated CASE tools that automate and support an integrated software life cycle process. Although this should be viewed as the ultimate goal, it cannot be accomplished in one implementation step. Because a structured development methodology provides the overall framework for defining and linking together the software process steps, selecting a methodology must be the first step in implementing CASE.

Once the whole software process has been defined, a CASE approach can be implemented by applying CASE to the individual methodology steps, one step at a time. The implementation order will depend on an organization's needs and priorities. For example, if an organization has determined that improving the software analysis and design steps is a top-priority need, its first step may be to introduce prototyping and joint-application-design sessions. Next, CASE tools that support these techniques should be selected. Or suppose an organization has determined that it must improve its software review process because the current review methods do not reveal software errors soon enough. Then,

BOX 7.3 CASE implementation plan

Management Considerations

- Commitment and approval for CASE tool purchases, training, and ongoing support
- Setting of goals and budgetary guidelines
- Selling CASE technology to management and to software developers and maintainers
- Creation of CASE technology implementation group and ongoing support
- Assignment of responsibilities for investigating, implementing and evaluating CASE technologies
- Definition of management controls
- Enforcement of standards and procedures
- Creation of CASE tool and methodology training programs
- Creation of timetable for steps of CASE implementation plan

Technical Considerations

- Selection of development methodology
- Definition of technical standards for tool interfaces, DBMS interfaces, 4GL interfaces, dictionary interfaces, and software quality control
- Definition of CASE tool capabilities sought
- Definition of hardware requirements and local area network requirements
- Selection of CASE tools that fit organization's methodology, standards, and procedures
- Definition of technical training needs
- Definition of technical support requirements for CASE tools and methodologies
- Definition of types of systems to be developed and maintained with CASE tools
- Performance of CASE pilot projects
- Configuration management of CASE tools

BOX 7.4 Basic steps for implementing CASE

Step 1: Define the software life cycle process by specifying the steps in the process, the standards and procedures that control the process, and quality assurance checks for the software product.

Step 2: Define the order of applying the CASE technology to the process based on the organization's needs and priorities.

Step 3: Select CASE tools to automate and support the process and to enforce the standards and procedures.

Step 4: Try out CASE tools and methodologies in pilot projects.

Step 5: Introduce proven CASE tools and methodologies on a wide scale throughout the organization by means of training programs and management commitment and enforcement.

Step 6: Evaluate the impact of CASE by applying predetermined success measures; and maintain a commitment to continual improvement of the software life cycle process and software product quality.

this organization should first implement CASE tools that perform continual automatic checking of the software product as it is being developed and provide checking and analysis reports.

The basic steps to follow when implementing CASE are outlined in Box 7.4.

CASE PILOT PROJECT

Those organizations that face reluctance on the part of management and/or software developers to try CASE should begin by setting up a pilot project to prove that CASE can work in their organizations. The pilot should be with a real but noncritical project. The goals of using CASE and how to measure the success of using CASE should be carefully defined before the pilot begins. CASE tools should be selected on the basis of their applicability to meet the stated goals. Alternative tools and/or methodologies can be selected and used in parallel pilots as a way of comparing various CASE approaches. Participants in the pilot should be software developers that are eager to use the CASE technology. At least some of the participants should be experienced software developers. When the pilot is finished, the results can be used to:

1. Suggest which CASE tools and methodologies are most useful.
2. Convince management and developers of the benefits that can be derived by using CASE in their organization.
3. Define standards and procedures that can be used to enforce the use of the CASE technology.

Then, participants in the pilot can go out and become members of other projects in which CASE is used. CASE training programs and a wide-scale plan for using CASE throughout the organization can be instituted.

Even organizations that already have management commitment and software developers open to using CASE may find that pilot projects are a good first step in introducing CASE into the organization.

CASE IMPLEMENTORS

The task of implementing CASE is usually assigned to a special group of software professionals. Some organizations have a development center, a standards and procedures group, an advanced technology group, or a quality assurance group that investigates new technologies. If such a group does not already exist, one should be created. The responsibilities of the group include:

1. Researching new technologies such as CASE
2. Devising a plan to implement appropriate new technologies
3. Introducing the new technology along with appropriate standards and procedures
4. Providing consulting support for the new technology on an ongoing basis

Recall that many of the organizations discussed in the case studies on CASE presented in Chapter 6 had a research and development or standards and procedures group that was responsible for implementing the CASE technology.

CASE TOOL SELECTION

CASE tools should be selected in the context of (1) identified organizational needs and priorities, (2) software tools already in place, and (3) methodologies that structure the process. Box 7.5 lists the technical considerations for selecting CASE tools. (The characteristics of a complete CASE workbench were discussed in detail in Chapters 2 through 4.)

SELLING CASE

Selling the CASE concept to management and software developers is one of the most important ways to make CASE work in an organization. A positive attitude toward CASE ulti-

BOX 7.5 Technical considerations for selecting CASE tools

- Software, hardware, and training costs
- Hardware requirements
- Tools already in place, including dictionaries, DBMS, and 4GLs with which CASE tools must be integrated
- Types of software systems supported by tools
- Tool documentation quality
- Tool customization possibilities
- Tool support and maintenance
- Available tool training and expected learning curve
- Tool demonstration and hands-on experience
- Interviews with current tool users
- Vender reputation and product line
- Organization's future direction and that of the vendor
- Quality of technical capabilities of tool
  —Graphics interface
  —Level of tool integration
  —Interfaces with outside tools
  —CASE repository
  —Coverage of life cycle support
  —Structured methodology support

mately can make the difference between a CASE success and a CASE failure. Software developers must be convinced that the CASE technology is real and can do something worthwhile for them, and is therefore worth learning about and using in real software projects. If they do not understand why it is necessary to change and improve the current software process through the use of CASE, they are unlikely to accept it.

Participation of the eventual players is a good way to sell a new concept. Allowing software developers to participate in the selection and evaluation of CASE tools can help create a corporate spirit and excitement for CASE. Each developer must believe that participation presents him or her with an opportunity to broaden expertise, to contribute to the establishment of corporate standards and procedures, and to be recognized by superiors.

The need to sell CASE does not stop with its introduction and training programs. Project managers must continue to sell the merits of CASE throughout each software project if they expect the CASE technology to be used by software developers.

CASE can be sold in a variety of ways, some of which are listed in Box 7.6.

BOX 7.6 Ways to sell CASE technology

- Pilot projects that demonstrate CASE works in this organization
- Measures of success that demonstrate the positive impact of CASE
- Involvement of targeted CASE users in the tool selection process and formulation of standards and procedures
- Training in CASE tools and structured methodologies
- Never stop selling

EVALUATING CASE

Because most software projects fall behind schedule and because management is anxious to see work begin on the next software system awaiting development, no time is taken to look back. Software developers and maintainers seldom look back to learn from past successes and failures. The pressures to meet growing demands for more software and to remain at the state-of-the-art level have overshadowed the importance of evaluating how well software technologies work in practice.

Using software tools and methodologies is only the first step in improving the software process. Their utility in practice must also be evaluated. A major problem blocking software improvements is the lack of reported software project case studies. It is difficult to convince management of the value of trying new software technologies when there is no supporting evidence to draw upon. Also, it is difficult to speculate where further change and improvement are needed. In Chapter 6, case studies on the CASE technology were presented to demonstrate that CASE has worked in real organizations. Studying how software tools and methodologies work in practice may be the best way of preparing for higher levels of software automation.

This is not a new philosophy. It has often been advocated in software engineering literature. For example, the final principle listed in Boehm's seven basic principles of software engineering in 1977 is [4]:

Maintain a commitment to improve the process.

Boehm explains that fundamental to the process of producing quality software is a continuing commitment on the part of the software developer and maintainer to seek ways in which to improve the software product and its production. New software methodologies and tools should be tried in actual projects. Methods to evaluate the effect of these tools should be defined. Data should be collected and analyzed to determine production bottlenecks, poor schedule and cost estimates, and error frequencies.

Although advocated for over a decade, this principle is seldom practiced today. To emphasize its importance, it should be considered a fundamental step in implementing the CASE technology in any organization. The reason is to provide information that can be used to improve future software projects and products:

- What worked?
- What did not work?
- What is the next step in attempting to do a better job of developing and maintaining software systems?

REFERENCES

1. Jim Huling, ''Tools of the Trade: Is CASE Really a Cure-All?'' *Computerworld,* April 20, 1987, pp. 73–86.
2. ''CASE 1987 Survey Executive Summary,'' *Software News*. Westborough, Mass.: Sentry Publishing Company, 1987.
3. Roger S. Pressman, ''Making Software Engineering Happen,'' *The CASE Report*. Southfield, Mich.: Nastec Corporation, July 1987, pp. 1–3.
4. Barry Boehm, ''Seven Basic Principles of Software Engineering,'' in *Infotech State of the Art Reports: Software Engineering Techniques*. Maidenhead, England: Infotech International, 1977, pp. 77–113.

8 SOFTWARE LIFE CYCLE CHANGES

STREAMLINING THE SOFTWARE LIFE CYCLE

The use of the CASE technology affects all phases of the software life cycle, from requirements definition through analysis, design, coding, testing, and into maintenance. The use of CASE also changes and streamlines the software life cycle.

As shown in Figure 8.1, the software life cycle can be viewed as a series of transformations. First, the requirements of the system are defined. Next, the requirements are transformed into a design specification for a system that meets

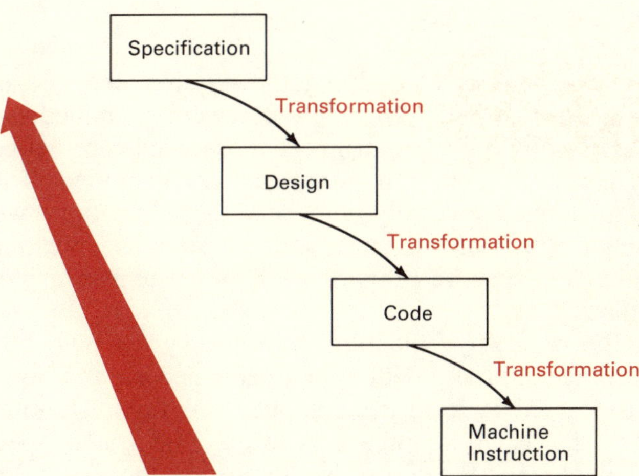

Figure 8.1 The development portion of the software life cycle can be viewed as a series of transformations where system objectives are transformed into specification requirements, then into a design specification, next into program code, and finally into machine instructions.

those requirements; then the design is transformed into programs; and finally, the programs are translated into machine-readable instructions. The most creative part of the process is system requirements definition, which is a type of problem solving. Thereafter, the transformations are quite straightforward and automatable. The final transformation (at the machine instruction level) is of course already automated by compilers and assemblers. The CASE technology proposes to streamline the software life cycle by automating the higher-level transformations as well.

A UNIFYING CONCEPT

A fundamental, unifying concept in software engineering is the traditional software life cycle. It describes the sequence of stages for developing, using, and maintaining software systems. In essence, it is a management technique for structuring software development and maintenance.

The software life cycle is a multiphase process beginning with problem definition and continuing to system obsolescence, replacement, or legitimate consumption (e.g., during warfare). The software life cycle typically is defined as consisting of five basic phases (see Figure 8.2):

- Analysis
- Design
- Coding
- Testing
- Operation and maintenance

Analysis is the process of defining the requirements for a solution to a problem. During analysis the needs of the users are examined, and the properties that the system should possess to meet those needs are defined. Also, system constraints and performance requirements are identified. The functions to be performed are defined precisely, but how these functions work is not addressed. The major output of this phase is the system specification. Ideally, the specification states the specific properties of the system in a precise, testable, and formal manner.

Design is the process of planning how the system will be built; that is, determining the procedural and data components needed and how these components will be assembled to form the computer solution. Algorithms are developed to describe what each component is to do. The system specifications, the problem requirements, and the constraints defined in the analysis phase are used as input to the design phase.

Coding is the process of transforming the design into computer instructions. The objective of the coding phase is to produce correct and efficient programs. Unit testing of coded modules is usually performed during this step.

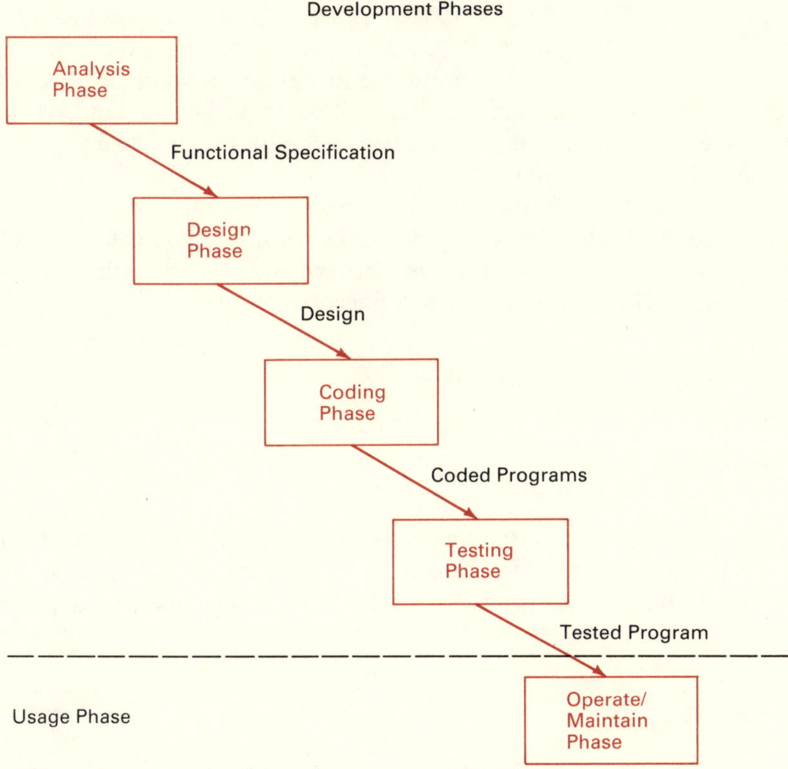

Figure 8.2 The traditional software life cycle is defined as consisting of five sequential phases: analysis, design, coding, testing, and operation/maintenance.

Testing is the process of demonstrating that a software system conforms to problem requirements and performs correctly for all possible input data. The goal of testing is to eliminate unexpected program conditions and failures and to discover any incorrect implementations of problem requirements. Tested modules are integrated and tested in larger and larger groupings until the system as a whole is tested.

Operation and maintenance is the process of executing a software system in a production mode and keeping it in good operating order. This involves

1. Correcting errors and inadequacies that were not discovered during system development.
2. Modifying the system to meet changing requirements, adapting it to changes in the operating environment, and improving its operating efficiency and overall quality. All resources and activities required to ensure that the software continues to meet or exceed required operational capabilities are considered part of the maintenance process.

TRADITIONAL LIFE CYCLE MODEL

In the 1970s, most organizations developed a software life cycle model to describe the actions and decisions required to define, develop, test, deliver, operate, and maintain a software system. The model was derived from the hardware model, which includes phases for requirements, design, fabrication, test, and operations/maintenance.

Some organizations formalized their life cycle model by expanding it into a complete methodology. The life cycle methodology includes tools, techniques, and methods to provide guidelines for ordering and controlling all software-related activities. These activities are defined in terms of:

- The resulting products and deliverables
- Required resources
- Methodologies used

A key aspect of the software life cycle methodology is formal management control. It is the primary means of evaluating and regulating life cycle activities to assure the achievement of life cycle objectives and development schedules.

Coding Too Soon

Figure 8.3 shows that in the traditional software life cycle, the later phases were emphasized. Because system developers were anxious to begin coding and project managers were anxious to show tangible results of progress to management and users, less than 35 percent of the development effort normally was spent on the analysis and design phases [1, pp. 1–44]. This distribution of effort across the development phases of the life cycle results in poorly specified, high-cost systems.

Defining requirements is often a difficult task because it is difficult to describe users needs in precise, technical terms. Furthermore, requirements are not stable; they change with people and over time. In practice, the analysis phase must be performed repeatedly as users and developers learn more about the system. Requirements specification errors spill over and compound themselves in later phases of the life cycle. "More than any other single factor a specification that inadequately defines system requirements can jeopardize a project's success" [2].

Front-End Loading

When it was discovered that the most serious and most costly errors occur in the early stages of software development, the early phases of the software life

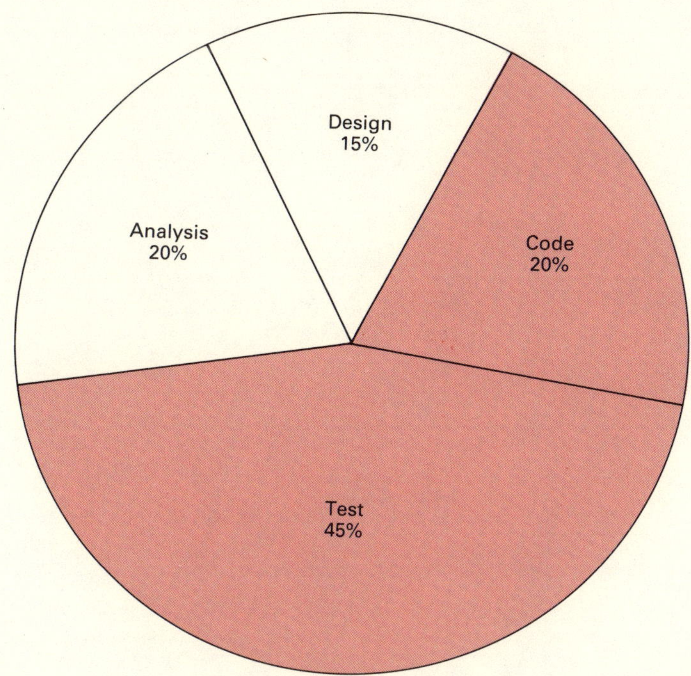

Figure 8.3 The traditional software life cycle emphasized the later phases of software development, with 65 percent of the effort spent in the coding and testing phases [1].

cycle were emphasized over the later phases [3]. As shown in Figure 8.4, this ''front-end loading'' of the software life cycle redistributed effort across the life cycle such that over 60 percent of the development effort was spent during the analysis and design phases. A fundamental part of the structured techniques strategy is to take the time needed to define requirements carefully and to investigate design approaches thoroughly before rushing into implementation details.

CASE SOFTWARE LIFE CYCLE

As shown in Figure 8.5, there is an even greater emphasis on the early life cycle phases with the introduction of the CASE technology. Automation of many analysis and design tasks along with automatic design specification checking results in higher productivity and fewer errors. Automatic checking enables errors arising from incomplete and ambiguous specifications to be identified and corrected sooner in the development process. Automatic code generation virtually eliminates the coding phase from the life cycle.

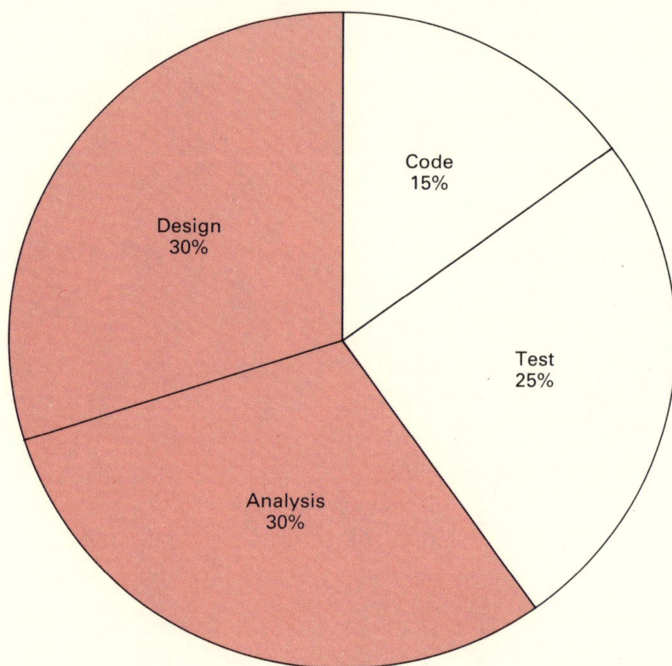

Figure 8.4 The introduction of structured techniques emphasized the early software life cycle phase, with 60 percent of the development effort spent in the analysis and design phases [3].

Also, the CASE technology streamlines the life cycle by cutting the length of the development process by 50 percent, according to several CASE technology users.

CASE Life Cycle Changes

The CASE technology changes and improves the software development and maintenance process in several ways. Box 8.1 outlines the differences between traditional software development and CASE software development through software automation.

First, with CASE, system developers can spend more of their effort on analysis and design and less on coding and testing. Manual program coding can be replaced by CASE code generators that automatically produce 80 to 100 percent of the system code from design specifications. Design specifications take the form of structured diagrams representing program data structures, data entities, and procedural functions. Design specifications can be created interactively at workstations by systems analysts. As they are entered into automated CASE libraries, the specifications can be checked for correctness and cross-referenced with existing system information.

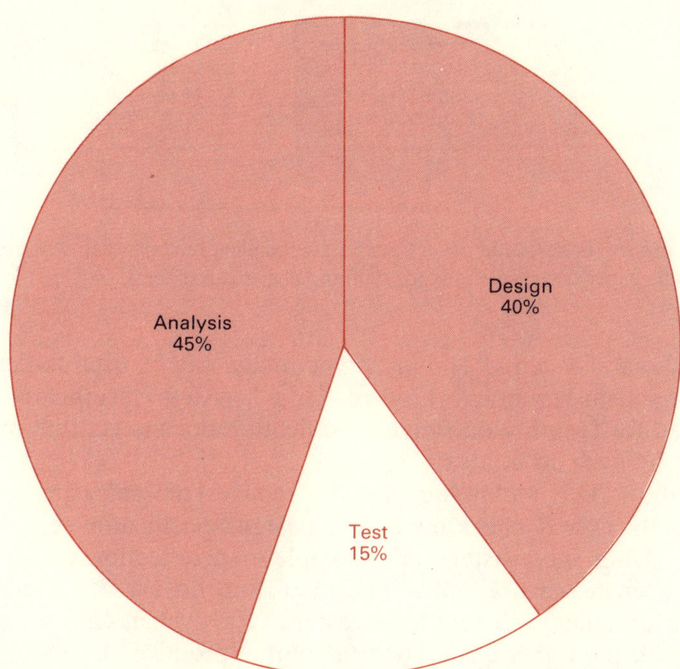

Figure 8.5 In the CASE software life cycle, more time is spent on analysis and design, and the coding phase is virtually eliminated.

Second, the CASE technology changes traditional system analysis methods. Rapid iterative prototyping replaces paper-based methods for defining user requirements (see Figure 8.6). CASE tools such as screen and report painters and executable specification languages can be used to build quickly prototype

BOX 8.1 CASE changes software development

Traditional Development	Software Automation
• Emphasis on coding and testing	• Emphasis on analysis and design
• Paper-based specifications	• Rapid iterative prototyping
• Manual coding	• Automatic code generation
• Manual documenting	• Automatic documentation generation
• Software testing	• Automated design checking
• Maintain code	• Maintain design specifications

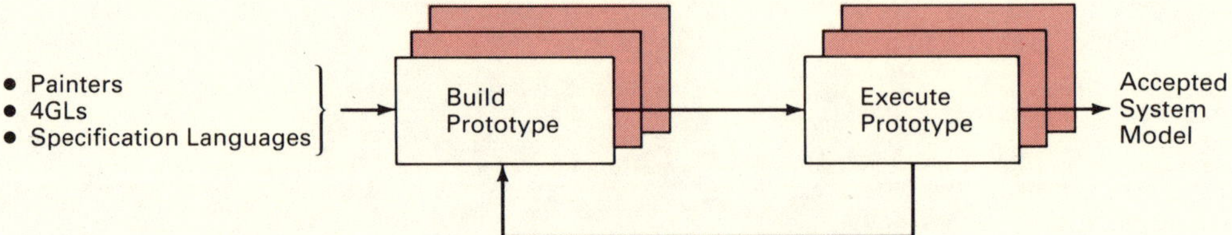

Figure 8.6 Prototyping is a CASE specification method that will replace manual, paper-based methods for defining user requirements.

models of software systems. The prototype model can be used to determine user requirements and to serve as a kind of ''live'' system specification that eliminates the need for lengthly narrative specification documents that must be manually written by systems analysts.

Third, the CASE technology greatly reduces the software testing effort. Automatic analysis and checking of the design specification eliminates many errors arising from inconsistent or incomplete specifications. Automatic code generation eliminates errors that might arise from misuse of programming languages. What remains is system level testing. The system can be executed with carefully chosen input test data. Then the output produced by these tests can be checked to assure that the system as a whole has performed correctly. CASE tools will help in the generation of input test data and analysis of output results.

Next, software maintenance is simplified. The CASE design libraries and code generators eliminate the need to maintain program code. Instead, maintenance can be performed at the design level. When a program change is needed, the design specification will be changed and the code regenerated from the modified specification.

Finally, the whole software development approach can be based on the concept of reusability. Reusing software components is the key to dramatic software productivity increases. The CASE technology makes software reusability practical. Instead of building each new software system or enhancement from scratch, software developers can reuse software components stored in CASE workbench libraries. Not only will the software developers reuse source code modules, but they will also reuse project plans, prototype models, data models, and design specifications. Reusability is discussed further in Chapter 13.

Problems with the CASE Software Life Cycle Model

Figure 8.7 shows a simple model of the CASE software development life cycle. Notice that a prototyping phase has replaced the traditional systems analysis phase. Also notice that although all phases are supported by automated CASE tools, the design checking and code generation phases are the most highly automated phases in the life cycle.

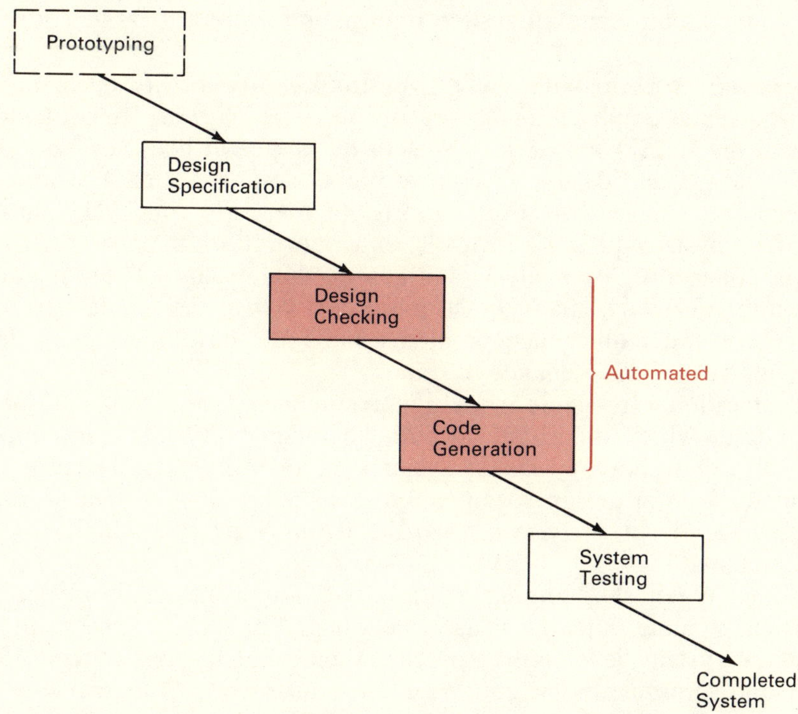

Figure 8.7 A simple view of the CASE software life cycle shows the use of prototyping and automated design checking and code generation phases.

However, there are some problems and limitations with this model of the life cycle. Like the traditional software life cycle model shown in Figure 8.2, the CASE life cycle model shown in Figure 8.7 misrepresents the software development process in practice. They both describe software development as a one-pass, sequential process in which the phases follow one after another. But in practice, software development is seldom a simple sequential process. More often it is an iterative process in which phases are repeated and the whole process is cycled through again during the life of the system. In smaller projects, the phases are treated informally and allowed to merge into one another. In larger projects, in the interest of time, they are performed in parallel. Frequently, because of errors and oversights, phases must be repeated. At each phase of the life cycle, new information and insights become available, making previous decisions inappropriate and causing developers to backtrack, rethink their designs, and redo steps.

Fortunately, the CASE technology really does recognize that software development is an iterative process in which steps are repeated and the whole process is cycled through repeatedly. CASE tools that automatically track, change, control, and relate all system information support iterative software development methods.

A second problem with these two simple software life cycle models is perhaps too much emphasis on the early life cycle phases. The structured approach and the CASE approach to system development both advocate doing a thorough analysis and design to achieve higher software quality at lower cost. Experience has shown that what happens in the early life cycle phases can greatly affect system quality. However, experience has also shown that it is not enough to concentrate on analysis and design. Maintenance is the major phase of the entire life cycle, many times more costly than the whole development effort. To control maintenance problems and costs developers must design a system with ease of maintenance in mind.

The traditional life cycle model ignores maintenance issues until the maintenance phase, which is too late to build maintainability into a system. However, the CASE technology makes systems easier to maintain because systems can be maintained at design specification level rather than at code level. Also, CASE change impact analysis tools make it much easier and safer to change existing systems.

Another major shortcoming of these two simple life cycle models is that they do not separate out logical data modeling. For most business application systems, the system development process should begin with strategic information planning across the organization and the construction of logical data models at least at the business function level, as espoused in information engineering (see Chapter 3).

Thus, a full CASE life cycle for business application systems includes a strategic information planning phase followed by a logical data modeling phase, both of which precede the prototyping phase shown in Figure 8.7. Note, however, that strategic information planning is done once for all business systems to be built.

ONE AND ONLY ONE MODEL

Management standards associated with the software life cycle have acquired the force of law in many organizations. One and only one life cycle model is permitted, yet obviously, many variations are needed to support the development of different types of software systems.

A NEW LIFE CYCLE VIEW

What is needed is a new view of the software life cycle that allows a variety of approaches to building software systems. The traditional software life cycle model automated with the support of CASE tools is appropriate for large complex or scientific systems whose requirements can be completely defined early in development. For real-time system development, a simulation step may be added as the first life cycle phase and a prototyping step included before the system is implemented in its physical environment.

For most business applications, the software life cycle should begin with strategic information planning and data modeling phases that precede system specification. Then, either a prototyping life cycle in which the system is evolved through the building of multiple prototype models or a CASE life cycle can be followed. For small reporting programs, a fourth-generation life cycle, in which the program is built using an application generator, may be appropriate.

In the past, we were restricted to one software life cycle model because of a lack of software development experience and software tools. Because of CASE tools and the CASE technology, we are no longer restricted. To lock developers into one model that does not maximize the use of software automation is backward and very expensive.

REFERENCES

1. Marvin Zelkowitz, Alan Shaw, and John Gannon, *Principles of Software Engineering and Design*. Englewood Cliffs, N.J.: Prentice-Hall, 1979.

2. William Suydam, "CASE Makes Strides toward Automated Software Development," *Computer Design,* January 1, 1987, pp. 49–70.

3. G. Boehm, R. McClearn, and D. Unfrig, "Some Experiences with Automated Aids to the Design of Large-Scale Reliable Software," *IEEE Transactions on Software Engineering,* Vol. SE-1, No. 1, March 1975.

9 RELATIONSHIP TO OTHER SOFTWARE TECHNOLOGIES

COMBINATION TECHNOLOGY

What generation technology is CASE? Figure 9.1 shows the five generations of software technologies that currently exist. Box 9.1 lists examples of third-, fourth-, and fifth-generation software tools. The CASE technology is not really

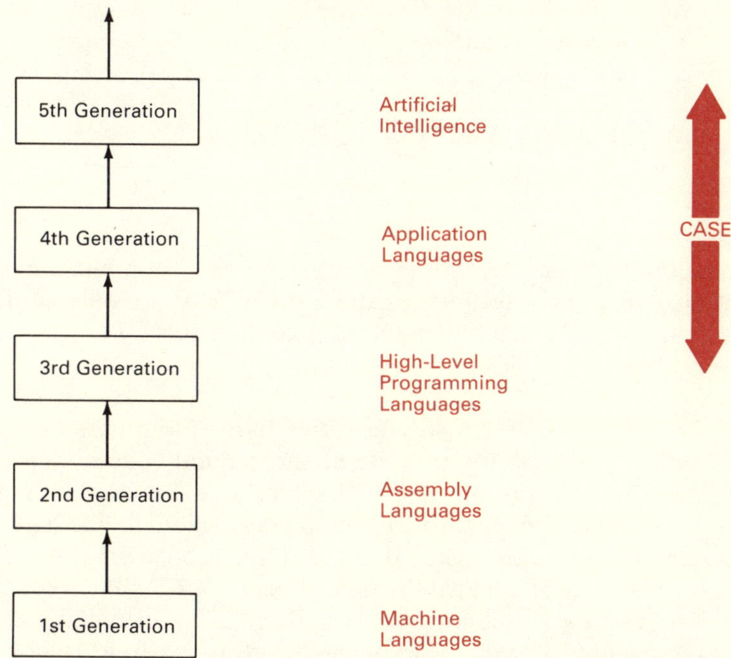

Figure 9.1 There are currently five generations of software technologies. The CASE technology is a combination of third-, fourth-, and fifth-generation technologies.

BOX 9.1 Tool comparison

Third-Generation Tools

- Compilers
- Program editors and libraries
- Test data generators and comparators
- Performance monitors and optimizers

Fourth-Generation Tools

- Fourth-generation languages
- DBMS
- Application generators and code generators

Fifth-Generation Tools

- Natural-language interrupters
- Speech recognizer
- Voice synthesizer
- Parallel processor

a new-generation software technology; rather, it is a combination of third-, fourth-, and fifth-generation techniques and tools. CASE not only combines, but also integrates the various technique and tool components.

FOURTH-GENERATION TECHNOLOGY

When we hear the term "fourth generation," the ability to write nonprocedural code to generate report programs usually comes to mind. Although fourth-generation technologies began in the late 1970s as report generation tools, fourth-generation capabilities broadened throughout the 1980s to include both simple capabilities such as query facilities for data bases and very high level programming languages. Box 9.2 lists several categories for fourth-generation tools. According to James Martin, the fourth generation can best be described as a capability level rather than on a list of categories of fourth-generation tools [1]. A fourth-generation tool must meet a capability level that provides:

1. A 10-to-1 productivity increase in the software implementation phase over the use of traditional second- and third-generation tools
2. Two-day learning rule (i.e., a user can learn a *useful* subset of the fourth-generation tool within two days)

BOX 9.2 Fourth-generation categories

	End Users	DP Professionals
Simple query facilities		
Complex query and update languages		
Report generators		
Graphics languages		
Decision support tools		
Application generators		
Very high level programming languages		

Categories of Fourth-Generation Tools

Box 9.2 also suggests that fourth-generation tools can be categorized as end-user tools or professional-programmer tools. Examples of end-user fourth-generation tools include FOCUS, NOMAD, RAMIS-II, QMF, and QBE. Examples of professional-programmer fourth-generation tools include SQL, IDEAL, ADS/ONLINE, and NATURAL.

Many fourth-generation tools, especially those suitable for end users, are information center tools. They provide to the user report writing and query capabilities through nonprocedural code. On the other hand, fourth-generation tools suitable for professional programmers offer both procedural and nonprocedural coding facilities and full-function replacement for COBOL. They are development center tools. Also, many fourth-generation tools are tied to use with a particular data base management system (e.g., IDEAL with DATACOM, ADS/ONLINE with IDMS, NATURAL with ADABAS).

In general, fourth-generation tools are used to create small-to-medium-sized business application systems. They increase productivity through the use of nonprocedural coding facilities (e.g., screen and report painters, data definition, editing, and validation) and preprogrammed functions that are common to business application systems. They make data entry and editing and report production very easy for the user who is willing to accept a generic rather than a customized format for screens, reports, and error messages. User productivity and system performance efficiency are at their highest when the use of fourth-generation procedural capabilities is minimized and the use of fourth-generation nonprocedural capabilities is maximized.

Fourth-Generation Pluses and Minuses

The benefits of using fourth-generation tools include the following:

- Application development is faster.
- Testing is easier because generated code is highly reliable.
- Fourth-generation languages are user friendly.
- Fourth-generation programs are easy to understand because ill-structured constructs are not allowed.
- Many fourth-generation languages are linked to data base management systems with built-in dictionaries to help avoid data-related errors.
- Many fourth-generation languages are self-documenting.
- End users can write and maintain entire fourth-generation application systems.

On the other hand, several serious limitations of fourth-generation tools have been cited:

- Many fourth-generation tools are DBMS specific and operating-system specific, limiting their portability.
- Many fourth-generation tools do not provide a concurrent data update capability.
- Many fourth-generation tools do not have an automatic recovery/restart capability.
- Most fourth-generation applications are unable efficiently to handle high-volume transaction processing.
- Many fourth-generation programs are incompatible with existing systems written in second- and third-generation languages.
- Fourth-generation languages are not standardized.
- Fourth-generation tools produce less efficient code than that of earlier generation languages.
- Fourth-generation programs use an excessive amount of computer resources.

Another important limitation is that fourth-generation tools support only the implementation phases of the life cycle and do not support the very critical analysis and design phases where most software errors begin. Also, fourth-generation programs are difficult to maintain if they contain a large amount of procedural code.

Fourth Generation vs. CASE

Box 9.3 compares the major differences between fourth-generation tools and CASE tools. First, while the primary user of fourth-generation tools is the end user, the primary user of CASE tools is the professional software developer. Also, fourth-generation and CASE tools also differ in their target application systems. Fourth-generation tools are used primarily to develop small-to-medium-sized MIS applications such as query programs, report production, and transaction processing. CASE tools, however, are more general-purpose tools that are to be used in the development of all types and all sizes of systems. Furthermore, while the use of fourth-generation tools usually results in a generic solution, the use of CASE tools results in a customized solution to the user's problem.

BOX 9.3 Fourth generation vs. CASE

4GL	CASE
• End user	• Professional software developer
• Mainframe-based	• PC-based
• Tied to DBMS	• Tied to structured methodologies
• Special-purpose/MIS —Query —Report production —Transaction processing —Small to medium-sized	• General-purpose —All software —Small to very large
• Menu-assisted application development process	• Graphic-assisted application development process
• Productivity through streamlining development process (preprogrammed building blocks)	• Productivity through automating development process
• Generic systems	• Customized systems
• Target implementation	• Target whole life cycle

Both fourth-generation tools and CASE tools are high-productivity tools. However, fourth-generation tools achieve productivity increases through streamlining the development process with preprogrammed, common functions; while CASE tools achieve productivity increases through automating many software development tasks.

Finally, fourth-generation tools and CASE tools differ in that fourth-generation tools are used primarily during the implementation phases of the software life cycle, while various CASE tools are used throughout the entire life cycle, including maintenance and project management.

FIFTH-GENERATION TECHNOLOGY

When we think of fifth-generation technologies, we think of intelligent systems, that is, software systems that are capable of performing tasks normally associated with human intelligence. Examples of fifth-generation technologies include robotics, natural language processing, automatic theorem proving, knowledge engineering, and expert systems.

Expert Systems

According to Feigenbaum, an *expert system* is ''an intelligent computer program that uses knowledge and inference procedures to solve problems that require significant human expertise for their solution'' [2]. The characteristics of an expert system are listed in Box 9.4. Notice that one predominant characteristic is that an expert system captures expertise in a specific, narrow domain. It is not a general-purpose problem-solving tool.

BOX 9.4 Characteristics of an expert system

- Solves problem in specialized area by mimicking human expert
- Explains results and reasoning used
- Works with incomplete, inaccurate, qualitative data
- Has the ability to reason, that is, to make logical deductions and inferences using formal logic and/or production rules
- Has the ability to add new rules easily and to modify reasoning
- Employs heuristic search methods (pruning) to focus on problem solutions rather than algorithms
- Knows when to break a rule
- Can consider a number of competing hypotheses simultaneously

As shown in Figure 9.2, an expert system has three components:

1. A natural-language-like user interface
2. A knowledge base of formalized facts and heuristics (informal ''rules of thumb'') in a specific problem-solving domain that cap-

ture reasoning used by human experts to solve a problem or perform a task

3. An inference engine that uses this knowledge to solve problems or perform tasks by controlling the firing of rules from the knowledge base and the creation of new rules

Some expert systems replace experts; others help experts solve problems more effectively by extending their base of knowledge and experience.

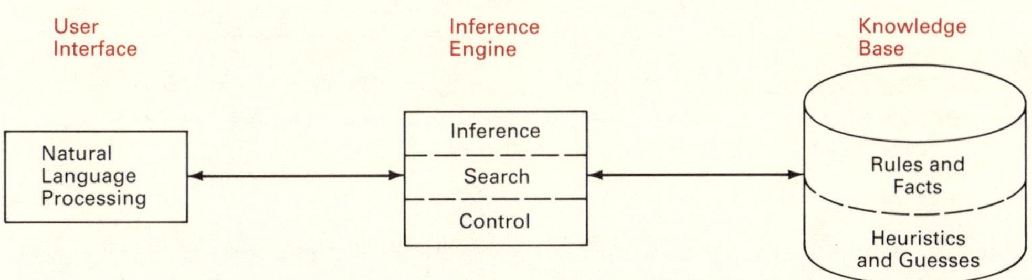

Figure 9.2 An expert system has three components: a natural-language user interface, an inference engine, and a knowledge base.

Fifth Generation and CASE

Expert-system-based CASE tools belong to fifth-generation technologies and for the most part, belong to the future, not the present. One type of expert-system-based CASE tool that will be used in the future to develop software systems is the methodology driver. The methodology driver possesses methodology-specific knowledge and experience in developing and maintaining software systems. It has enough intelligence to make decisions about how to carry out the software life cycle process. The methodology driver is discussed further in Chapter 12.

LIFE CYCLE COVERAGE

Figure 9.3 shows which phases of the life cycle are supported by the various types of software tools. For example, fourth-generation tools support some design tasks, prototyping, and mainly the implementation phases. While some CASE toolkits support primarily the early phases of the life cycle, others support the later phases and project management. On the other hand, CASE code generators support mainly program design, prototyping, and implementation, but are being extended to support the design phase more fully. The way in which many CASE analysis/design toolkits and CASE code generators are being extended to pro-

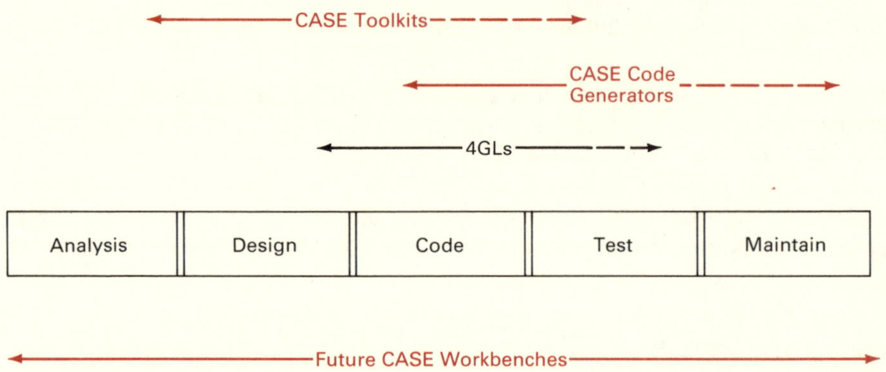

Figure 9.3 Because CASE tools offer more complete coverage of the software life cycle, they are replacing the fourth-generation tools as the software developer's top high-productivity tool choice.

vide full software life cycle support is by combining these two types of CASE tools into one integrated CASE workbench. Another way to bridge these two types of CASE tools is through various kinds of interfaces.

Figure 9.3 also shows how different types of software tools overlap, covering the same life cycle phases. When this happens, the tools become competitive and the user must choose the most appropriate tool for the job. As CASE toolkits and CASE code generators are integrated into a workbench of compatible tools that have been designed to work with one another, CASE tools become very competitive with fourth-generation tools in vying for the title of leading high-productivity tool.

CASE ADVANTAGES OVER FOURTH GENERATION

One major advantage of CASE over fourth generation is that the level of integration uniting CASE tools will make CASE tools easier to use and to learn to use than are fourth-generation tools. Also, the graphic–user interface employed by most CASE tools is more user friendly than are menu-driven fourth-generation tools.

Another advantage of CASE over fourth generation is the CASE repository, in which all system information is stored and managed throughout the life cycle, from the analysis phase through maintenance. The CASE repository promotes information sharing, reduces the need to reenter information, and protects information integrity.

Yet another advantage is that CASE code generators produce source or object code that is often more efficient, more portable, and more compatible with existing systems than is code generated by fourth-generation tools.

Finally, CASE tools excel over fourth-generation tools because they are more general purpose in form than are fourth-generation tools. CASE tools can be used to develop small, medium-sized, large, and very large systems, whereas fourth-generation tools are most useful for developing small-to-medium-sized MIS systems.

All of these advantages offered by CASE tools make them not only competitive with, but also very threatening to, the future of fourth-generation tools. Capabilities that made fourth-generation tools superior to third-generation tools, such as screen and report painting, prototyping, and report and data base generation, have already been incorporated into CASE workbenches. Also, many third-generation tool capabilities have been incorporated into CASE tools. Unless fourth-generation tools are enhanced to include analysis and design support capabilities, they will be replaced in favor of more powerful, more friendly, better integrated CASE tools. The exception may be end-user fourth-generation tools used primarily by and through information centers.

SUMMARY

The CASE technology is a combination of capabilities and techniques from third-, fourth-, and fifth-generation technologies. Box 9.5 predicts what will happen to third-, fourth-, and fifth-generation technologies as the use of CASE becomes more widespread in the future.

BOX 9.5 What will happen to third-, fourth-, and fifth-generation technologies?

What Will Happen to Third-Generation Technology?

Systems written in third-generation languages (especially COBOL) will not go away in the near term. However, the maintenance burden for these systems will be eased with the aid of CASE technologies. Also, their migration to newer technologies and other operating environments will be aided by CASE technologies.

Third-generation systems will be reengineered and maintained with the aid of CASE maintenance toolkits. Code analysis, documentation, restructuring, reengineering, and conversion tools will be added to CASE systems.

BOX 9.5 *(Continued)*

What Will Happen to Fourth-Generation Technology?

By 1990, the CASE technology will replace fourth-generation technologies as the most advanced application development methodology. CASE will produce more efficient, more portable code and provide greater reusability of the applications produced.

Fourth-generation functions such as screen painting, report generations, and DBMS technology will be absorbed into CASE systems to promote maximum information and system sharing. A centralized CASE repository will be the mechanism for sharing, control, and management of computing.

End users will continue to access data bases, generate reports, do analysis and modeling, and produce spreadsheets with the aid of end-user fourth-generation tools. However, end-user computing will be controlled and tied to corporate computing by sharing data models, data definitions, process models, and programs stored in the CASE repository.

What Will Happen to Fifth-Generation Technology?

By 1990, fifth-generation technologies will be added to the CASE technology. Natural language processing, speech recognition, and voice synthesizers will be added to the CASE system user interface. Expert systems, such as tutoring systems, diagnostic systems, and intelligent software designers, will be embedded in CASE systems.

REFERENCES

1. James Martin, *Fourth-Generation Languages,* Vol. I. Englewood Cliffs, N.J.: Prentice-Hall, 1985.

2. I. Zualkerman, W. T. Tsai, and D. Volovik, ''Expert Systems and Software Engineering: Ready for Marriage?'' *IEEE Expert,* Vol. 1, No. 4, Winter 1986, pp. 24–31.

PART IV SOFTWARE DEVELOPMENT IN THE 1990s

10 THE CHARACTERISTICS OF SOFTWARE AUTOMATION

MORE SOFTWARE AUTOMATION

How will software development change in the 1990s? Certainly, automation will play a greater role than in the past. The availability of cheap computing power will accentuate the need for more software. The only realistic way to meet this need is by simplifying and automating the software development process.

It is common knowledge that we cannot keep up with the backlog of software systems waiting to be developed. One solution to reducing the software backlog is to increase the number of people who are developing systems. By teaching more people to develop software, by making computer systems easier to use, and by involving users in the software development process, we can build more systems. This is the strategy behind end-user computing. Although it is a solution with merit, it has not worked very well. End-user computing and fourth-generation tools were introduced in the early 1980s but still have not had a significant impact on reducing the software backlog because they cannot significantly increase software productivity and because they work for only a narrow class of system types.

Another solution to the backlog problem is to teach the computer to build software systems, that is, to automate software development. Many software development tasks that are too laborious or too detailed for human beings would be good candidates for automation. Examples are: remembering the syntax rules of a particular programming language or the command structure of an operating system for a particular kind of computer, and debugging system errors. Also, software tasks that require the knowledge and experience of experts would be good candidates for automation.

Most probably, in the 1990s the computer will not work exclusively on its own to develop software; rather, a mixed-member team approach will be used. Some members of the team will be human developers, and other members will be intelligent software tools whose job it is to assist the developer. Rather than replace the human developers, the intelligent tools will, instead, extend their capability to develop systems. It will be as though each developer is joined by a group of experts—software engineering experts, project management experts, and even application area experts—who give advice, make decisions, carry out complicated tasks, and guide developers through the process of building and maintaining systems.

AGAIN IMAGINE . . .

Again imagine developing software at your own dedicated workstation (see Figure 10.1). But this time, let's move into the future—into the 1990s and beyond. Now you can let your imagination really run wild and imagine the ideal software support environment that is dedicated to meeting all your software development and maintenance needs, whims, and desires as you slip into the driver's seat of a powerful, intelligent, "thinking machine."

Your software support environment resides on a powerful personal computer. It is connected to a mainframe computer where knowledge bases link you

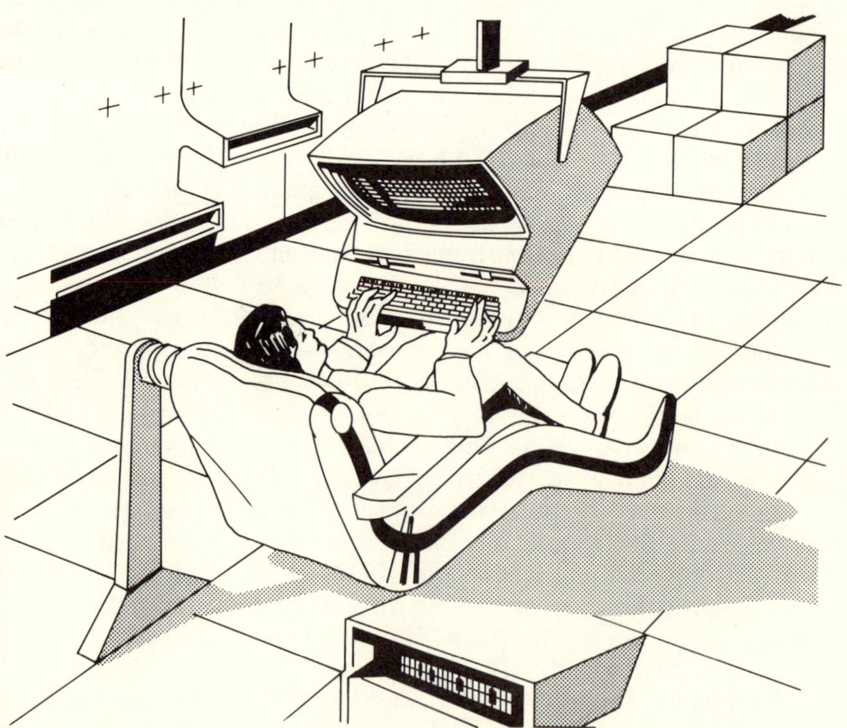

Figure 10.1 The software development environment of the 1990s will be a powerful, intelligent personal computer.

to the rest of your organization and the outside world. You communicate with your workstation by pointing to objects on the screen or simply by speaking to it. You use natural language, and your workstation responds to you in natural language, sometimes with its synthesized voice.

So in the 1990s, the human developer and artificially intelligent software tools will team up to produce software systems in a way that far surpasses productivity and quality accomplishments of the 1980s. Each step of software production will be computer assisted, with a great variety of powerful software tools available on individual workstations. These tools will assist software developers with all aspects of their work, and for some tasks, will take over completely. They will advise what to do next, remind if something has been left out, discover what is wrong, explain why, and perform many routine tasks automatically without bothering the human developer.

CHANGES TO THE SOFTWARE PROCESS

The workstation of the future will be equipped with some very powerful, sophisticated tools that are technically far beyond the capabilities of today's software tools. With these advancements will come a great change in the software development process. Software development will become a highly automated process. The characteristics of software automation are (see Box 10.1):

- A highly interactive and responsive environment dedicated to the individual software developer
- A "specification-heavy" development process featuring rapid prototyping to replace paper-based specifications
- Continual, automatic system consistency, completeness, and correctness checking that is performed as the system is being developed

BOX 10.1 Characteristics of software automation

- Highly interactive and responsive environment
- Specification heavy process with rapid prototyping
- Continual, automated checking
- Building from reusable chips
- Automated code generation and documentation from design specs
- Automated experts to guide software process

- Automatic code and documentation generation from graphic diagrams representing the system design
- Automated libraries of reusable software chips that speed up the software building process by using reusable software components
- Intelligent tools that use knowledge bases and natural language interfaces
- Automated experts embedded in the software development environment to guide the software process

CHANGES TO SOFTWARE TOOLS

Many of the tools used today, such as specification languages, diagramming tools, prototyping tools, generators, dictionaries and data base management systems, will form the core of the 1990s software support environment. However, these tools will be improved in two important ways:

1. Integration
2. Intelligence

First, the tools in the 1900s software support environment will not be simply a collection of tools, but rather, an assembly of *highly integrated* tools (see Figure 10.2). They will be united by one common user interface with one common language—probably a subset of natural languages—to simplify their use. They will be designed not only to coexist, but also to know about one another and to call and feed one another automatically to accomplish the tasks we put before them.

Figure 10.2 The software support environment of the 1990s will be a collection of powerful, highly integrated tools designed to call and feed one another automatically.

Second, around these tools will be added an intelligent shell insulating the user from concerns about individual tool differences and technical details (see Figure 10.3). The intelligent shell will provide:

- Natural-language communication
- Knowledge bases containing general software engineering knowledge and application-domain-specific information
- A set of automated software development experts (e.g., application area expert, software design expert, software debugging expert)

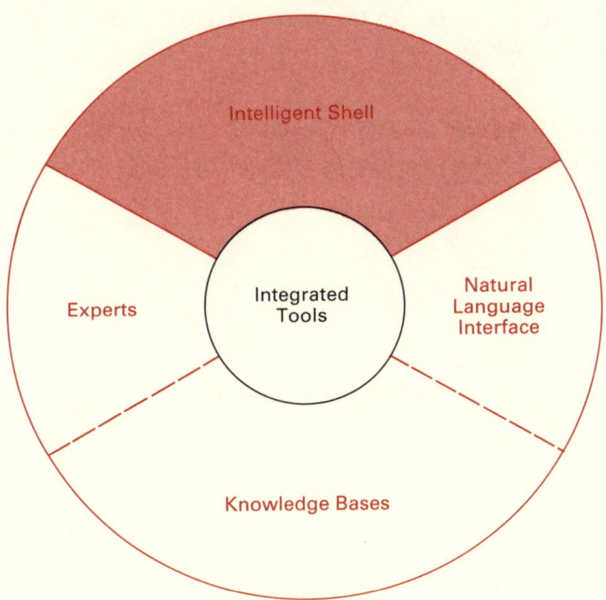

Figure 10.3 The software tools of the 1990s will be surrounded by an intelligent shell freeing the user from technical concerns.

Today's software tools are powerful, but dumb. The tools of the 1990s will be powerful and intelligent. This intelligence will come from applying such advanced technologies as natural language processing, speech recognition, voice synthesis, knowledge engineering, parallel processing, and program animation.

For example, program animation will be one advanced program analysis technique. Besides providing a static view of program and data structures (as from data structure diagrams or structure charts), program analysis tools will also be able to provide a dynamic view of an executing program to improve our understanding of the behavior of software. Program animators will be used to track changes in data values during program execution and to show control flow by displaying the current program execution stack.

INTELLIGENT SHELL

As shown in Figure 10.4, the intelligent shell consists of three components:

1. *Habitable environment,* which is an intelligent user interface [1]
2. *Methodology driver,* which is an expert system that provides methodology guidance through the software life cycle
3. Reusable parts library and an intelligent library management system, which elevate *reusability* to the status of the dominant software development strategy

In the chapters that follow we explore each of these components in more detail.

In the 1990s a new wave of technological advancements will arrive, bring-

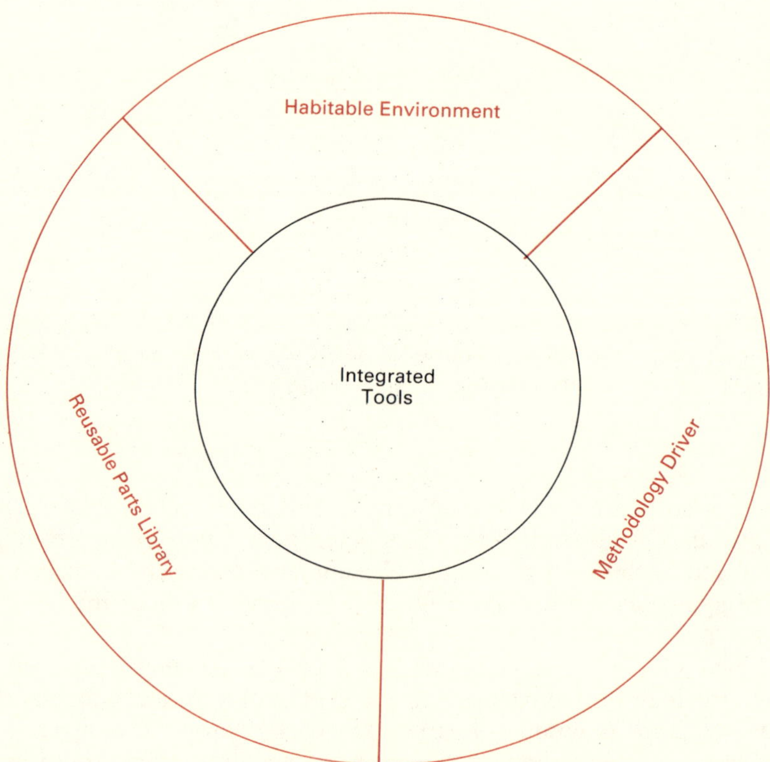

Figure 10.4 The intelligent shell surrounding software tools consists of three parts: (1) habitable environment, (2) methodology driver, and (3) reusable parts library.

ing with them new tools and techniques as well as substantial improvements to existing techniques and repackaging of existing tools.

REFERENCES

1. D. Gleeman and J. S. Brown, editors, *Intelligent Tutoring Systems*. London: Academic Press, 1982.

11 HABITABLE ENVIRONMENTS

USER INTERFACE

Figure 11.1 divides a CASE workbench into three basic components. The front-end component emphasizes graphics and rapid prototyping tools to automate analysis and design. The information repository, together with its information management system, captures all software product and software project information. Finally, the back-end component provides program code and data base generation and testing capabilities. All three components must be present and well integrated into the CASE workbench to hope to achieve increased productivity promises.

In addition, however, there is a fourth component that is at least as important as any of the other three in increasing the productivity of the software developer. The fourth component is the *user interface,* which links the developer to the workbench tools. Although this component is often neglected, its impact on productivity should not be underestimated since ultimately it determines whether or not a tool is used in practice. According to Smith [1, pp. 297–313]:

> The most important factors affecting how prevalent computer usage becomes will be reduced cost, increased functionality, improved availability and servicing, and perhaps most importantly of all, progress in user interface design. The first three are necessary but not sufficient for widespread use. Reduced cost will allow people to buy computers, but improved user interfaces will allow people to *use* computers.

Habitable environments recognize the importance of the user interface in software tools by emphasizing characteristics important to aiding human understanding, ease of use, and ease of learning.

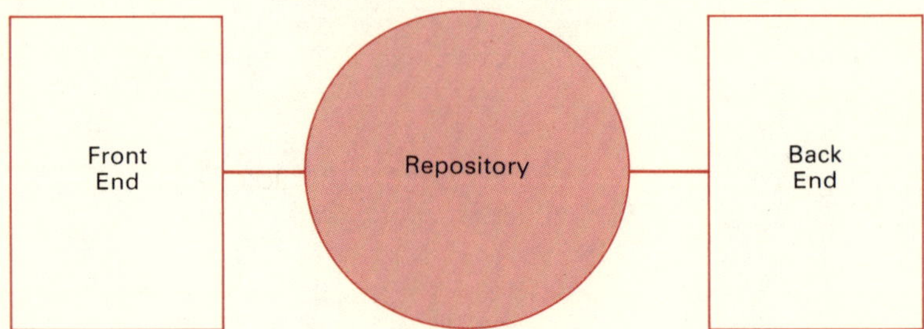

Figure 11.1 The software development workbench consists of three basic components: (1) a front end, to support analysis and design; (2) a repository, to store all system information; and (3) a back end, to support program implementation.

BEYOND CASE ENVIRONMENTS

Habitable environments have capabilities far beyond those offered by CASE workbench environments of the late 1980s. They can perform many software tasks on their own without bothering the user. They can teach as well as learn from the user. They can improve their ability to build systems by growing and changing with each system building experience. They can explain their behavior in terms of fundamental software concepts. Finally, they can give software methodology advice.

CASE environments can be characterized as user friendly, responsive, diagnostic, helpful, and supportive. Habitable environment go beyond these qualities by adding the characteristics of user centered, reactionary, corrective, teaching, and directive (see Figure 11.2). Habitable environments transform the user interface into a friendly, intelligent companion with which (whom) the user can share the software development and maintenance experience.

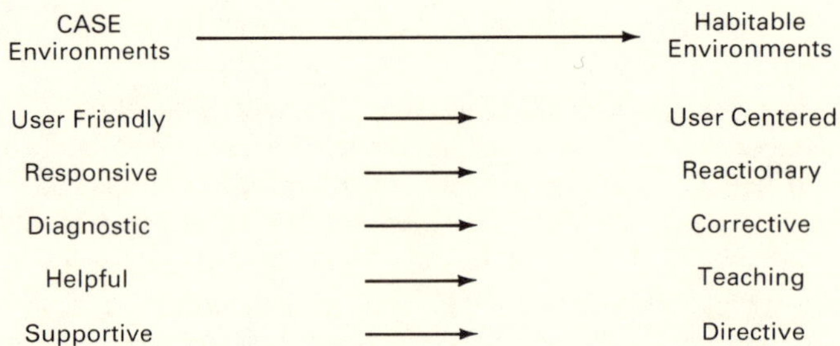

Figure 11.2 Habitable environment goes beyond user friendly to transform the user interface into an intelligent environment with characteristics such as user centered, reactionary, corrective, teaching, and directive.

USER FRIENDLY

User friendly, of course, is at the top of the list of characteristics for a well human-engineered user interface. It is pointed to as the key advancement of fourth-generation over third-generation software tools.

A "user-friendly" style has the following characteristics:

- Easy to use
- Robust
- Helpful
- Error detecting and error avoiding
- Extendable
- Easy to learn
- Tailorable

Whether or not a system is user friendly in a sense is a matter of its style, and style is normally considered a matter of personal preference and a mark of individuality. Different software systems (products) exhibit different styles. For example, Lotus 123 has a particular style; Unix has a different style; and Interlisp has yet another style. But whatever the particulars may be, there are some elements common to any good style. A good style is simple, consistent, and complies with standard conventions. Its rules are not so complicated that we become bogged down attempting to understand the form and never reach the content. Above all it clarifies, not obscures, what is being communicated. If the style is good, much of the difficulty of understanding the content disappears.

Easy to Use

A system that is *easy to use* is *obvious* and at the same time *transparent*. It is obvious because its users can rely on intuition of how they expect the system to work to find their way through the system. As Stahl explains: "Intuitive software feels good to the user, who can just slide into the driver's seat, make a few intelligent guesses and be off" [2].

Obvious systems have meaningful command names, self-explanatory prompts, descriptive error messages, and help routines to provide more detailed information. *Direct manipulation* systems are a good example of an obvious system [3]. Everything is depicted visually on the screen.

Transparent systems do not get in the way of performing the task at hand [4]. In a transparent system, the underlying aspects of the computer are invisible to the user, there is an easy log-on procedure, and the human–computer dialogue is conducted with minimum delays and maximum flexibility.

Robust

A *robust* system is "user-proofed," meaning that for all practical purposes it is impossible for the user to break the system. There is virtually nothing the user can do to cause the system to terminate abnormally or to lock-up, refusing to accept any further commands, including QUIT or EXIT [5]. A robust system responds to every user input, regardless of whether it is correct or incorrect. This requires extensive checking of user input and logic to handle both correct and incorrect input.

Easy to Learn

Zloof cites Query-By-Example, a data base query language, as an example of a system that is *easy to learn* to use [6]. Query-By-Example allows the user to access a data base with very little knowledge about the records or fields. The user is presented on the computer screen with the skeleton of a table (see Figure 11.3). To format a query, the user simply fills in the table name and field names as headings in the table. The system then responds to the query by filling in the columns of the table with the information the user has requested. With less than three hours of instruction, any user should be able to create a fairly complicated query.

Query-By-Example is easy to learn to use because only a few symbols, a few syntax rules, and a few basic concepts need to be learned before the user can begin forming queries.

Tailorable

A *tailorable* system is designed to handle different types of users. Figure 11.4 shows five classes of users distinguished by their level of experience [7, pp. 130–138]. The first class, the novice, has the least experience; the fifth class, the master, has the greatest experience. It should be obvious that different classes of users interact very differently with a system. The novice needs constant guidance and feedback, probably makes many mistakes, and attempts only simple tasks using a small subset of the available commands. The expert, on

Employee #	Name	Salary	Department

Figure 11.3 Query-By-Example is an easy-to-use query language in which queries are formatted by filling in a table name and fields as headings in the table.

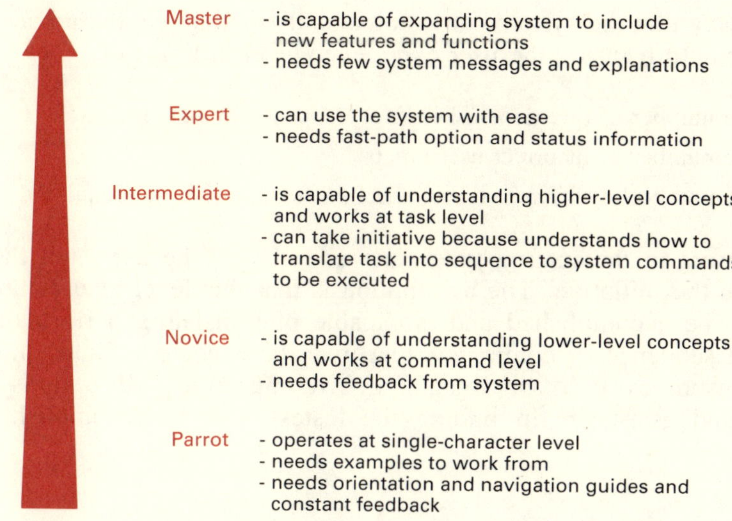

Figure 11.4 Different classes of user interact differently with the system and require different types of support and information from the system.

the other hand, needs little prompting and few explanations from the system, looks for the shortest, most efficient way to perform a task, and occasionally needs to change or expand the system functions.

Also, it should be obvious that the system needs to interact very differently with different classes of users. For users in the first two classes, the system must take the initiative and be explicit with the user. The user should be given orientation and navigation guidance to answer questions such as:

- Where am I?
- Where did I come from?
- Where can I go from here?
- What can I do at this point?
- How can I get help?
- How can I get out or quit?

The best type of assistance often is an example that the user can follow. The user should be notified of the successful completion of each command (e.g., EMPLOYEE FILE HAS BEEN SAVED). When an error is made, the system should respond with an explanation of what is wrong and how to correct it (e.g., FILE NAME CAN ONLY INCLUDE LETTERS AND DIGITS).

One way that the system can automatically distinguish the novice from the expert user is to measure the user experience level in terms of:

- The number of questions asked (i.e., requests for HELP)
- The number of incorrect user inputs
- The number of different types of commands the user has requested

For users in the intermediate class and above, the user, not the system, should take the initiative. The assumption is that this level of user understands the task to be accomplished and is capable of translating performance of the task into a sequence of commands that must be executed. Status information, such as resources used or remaining, waiting time, all options currently available and assistance in finding the fastest path to accomplish the task, are useful.

BOX 11.1 Characteristics of user friendly

- Easy to use
  —Minimum number of concepts to understand in order to get started
  —Minimum number of syntax rules
  —Unified language used throughout system
  —Underlying aspects of computer hidden from user
- Robust
  —Virtually impossible for user to cause the system to terminate abnormally
- Helpful
  —At any point in using the system command level HELP and orientation information are available to the user
- Error detecting and error avoiding
  —Meaningful error messages explaining what is wrong and how to correct it are given when an error is made
  —System is designed to avoid commonly made user errors
- Extendable
  —System is easy to change, and new functions can easily be added
- Easy to learn
  —Fundamental features of the system can be learned in a few hours
- Tailorable
  —System engages the knowledgeable user in a way that is fundamentally different from the way it engages the novice

USER CENTERED

In a habitable environment, the concept of *user centered* replaces the concept *user friendly* to upgrade the user interface. ''End'' is dropped from the term ''end user'' to emphasize the importance of the user [1, pp. 297–313]. Think user first, not last. The user-centered concept is best realized in the software development workstation that acts as a personal assistant dedicated to its user's needs. This means that the user interface is viewed as the central issue when designing a software development workstation. Rather than being tacked on at the end of the design, the user interface is designed first.

Thus a user-centered interface is user friendly and more. Box 11.1 summarizes the characteristics of a user-friendly interface. In addition to possessing all the traits of user friendly, a user-centered interface is also:

- Simple
- Consistent
- Flexible
- User controlled
- Natural-language like

Box 11.2 summarizes the characteristics of a user-centered interface.

BOX 11.2 Characteristics of user centered

- Simple
  —Minimum number of syntax symbols and rules
  —Minimum number of exceptions to the rules
  —Each symbol has one meaning and one purpose throughout the system
  —Minimum number of overlapping commands
- Consistent
  —One model of how system works adhered to throughout entire system
  —Unified language used throughout system
- Flexible
  —System allows some latitude in user input, permitting abbreviations, spelling errors, and semantically meaningful but syntactically incorrect requests
- User controlled
  —It always appears that the user, not the system, is in control
- Natural language
  —User can communicate with system using a restricted natural language vocabulary and a restricted set of syntactic construction rules

Simple

In a well-human-engineered system interface, simplicity is truly elegance. Simplicity is the opposite of complex. Whereas a complex system complicates the user's job, a simple system attempts to make each task as straightforward as possible.

A *simple* system uses the minimum number of syntax symbols, the minimum number of syntax rules, and the minimum number of exception rules, according to Zloof [6]. Each symbol has one meaning and one purpose throughout the system.

A good example of a simple system is the Xerox Star, whose user interface design introduced the ideas of icons, windows, and the desktop. The Star design strongly influenced the design of many later systems, such as Lisa and Macintosh. When designing the Star, Xerox identified certain concepts as difficult and others as easy for users to understand (see Figure 11.5). They kept Star simple by incorporating only those concepts that were easy for users to understand.

Hard	Easy
Abstract	Concrete
Invisible	Visible
Creating from Scratch	Copying and Modifying
Filling in Blank	Choosing from List
Generating	Recognizing
Programming	Editing
Batch	Interactive

Figure 11.5 Some concepts are difficult for the human mind to understand; others are much easier. When designing an interface, we should implement concepts that are easy, not hard, to understand [1].

Unfortunately, there are many more examples of complex systems than simple ones. A common example is the use of modes in systems. *Modes* allow a symbol, command, or key to do double duty or more. A mode identifies a certain system state and the meaning of the symbol when the system is in that particular state. The interpretation of how the system behaves depends on the mode. Modes violate the principle of simplicity because a symbol has more than one meaning or purpose. Xerox cites an amusing but painful example of the trouble that modes can cause when a user does not pay close attention to the system mode.

Bravo is a text editing system developed by Xerox [1, pp. 297–313]. It has two modes: Insert and Command. In the Xerox story, a user lost his entire document because he mistakenly thought he was in Insert mode when the system was actually in Command mode. The fatal mistake was to type the word "edit" into the document. In command mode, Bravo interpreted "edit" as the following sequence of commands [1, pp. 297–313]:

E select everything in the document

D delete it

I enter Insert Mode

T type a "t"

The result was that the entire document was lost and all that remained was the letter "t."

Another example of violating the principle of simplicity is shown in the FOCUS code in Figure 11.6. In the second line of the code the slash "/" represents the arithmetic operator division and means divide AMOUNT by UNITS. However, in the third line of code, the "/" has a different meaning. It is used to separate the name of a data item from the format description of the field. In this example, the data item ADJUSTED is defined as a decimal number eight digits long, including two places to the right of the decimal number.

This is an example of allowing one symbol to have multiple meanings. To determine what the symbol means, the user must first understand the context in which it is used. Obviously, this complicates system understanding.

A system is also more difficult to understand when several different command names have a similar meaning or when several different commands perform the same function. The first case is the more confusing for the user. For example, in IBM/VM the synonymous words DELETE, PURGE, ERASE, and DISCARD represent commands that perform different functions. It is not realistic to expect the typical user to remember, for example, that DELETE means get rid of lines from a file being edited, while ERASE means get rid of files from a disk [8]. Incidentally, in the DEC System 10, ERASE and DELETE have just the opposite meaning as in IBM/VM.

Consistent

Design integrity manifests itself in the characteristic of *consistency*. There is one underlying model of how things work and how things appear that has been adhered to faithfully across the entire system. Integrity has not been compromised over time as new features were added or by the various designers that have tinkered with the model. It is as though the system were the uninterrupted creation of one system architect. One common language is used throughout the system. The syntax rules are the same throughout. The meaning of symbols and rules is the same throughout. The user menus and input/output screens have the same format throughout.

Figure 11.6 In this piece of FOCUS code, the symbol "/" has two meanings. In the second line, it is the arithmetic operator division, but in the third line, it is a separator symbol separating the field name from the field format description.

```
DEFINE FILE PROD
PRICE = AMOUNT/UNITS;
ADJUST/D8.2 =
  IF FACTOR EQ 0 THEN PRICE
  ELSE FACTOR *.5* PRICE
```

Consistency translates into a predictable uniformity that enables the user to apply what has been learned in one part of the system to other parts. This shortens the time needed to learn the system, reduces the number of mistakes the user is likely to make, and in general, increases the user's productivity.

Consistency is best explained by examples. In a consistent system, the process of executing a command, issuing the next command, and canceling a command is always the same. The command arguments in a keyword system are always arranged in the same order. Orientation information and system status information are always located in the same place on the screen. For example, the leftmost mouse button is always used to select an object and then to select an operation to be performed on that object. The rightmost button is always used to jump to the system-level menu. The EXIT command is always used to leave the system, and the user is always asked if the current work is to be saved before the EXIT command is executed.

Because consistency, like simplicity, is a difficult characteristic to achieve, there are many examples of inconsistency in systems. For example, consider IBM VM/CMS operating systems. As many systems, IBM VM/CMS tries to accommodate the user by allowing command names to be abbreviated. To disconnect a virtual machine, the user may issue the command CP DISC. But if the user tries to ask for HELP to learn about the disconnect command by issuing the command HELP DISC, the command fails because the operating system does not allow the command to be abbreviated when asking for HELP. This type of inconsistency is extremely frustrating and results in discouraging rather than encouraging the user to ask for HELP from the system [8].

User Illusion

Simplicity and consistency take the system a long way toward being user centered. Systems that are simple and consistent are said to adhere to the *principle of least astonishment* [9]. Such systems never behave in a way that surprises the user (see Figure 11.7).

As a user interacts with a system, he or she creates a conceptual model that explains the system's behavior. This conceptual model is called the *user illusion* [9]. A system that is inconsistent and complex shatters the user illusion and violates the principle of least astonishment because the user cannot rely on intuition, and fears that expectations will be disappointed. When the user does not have an accurate model of the system limits, he or she will continually be asking for capabilities that the system does not have and never uses other capabilities that the system can provide.

Flexible

A *flexible* system offers the user at least some latitude when entering system input. User input can run from short, abbreviated commands to full sentences. To make certain that the user command has been interpreted correctly, the sys-

Figure 11.7 Systems that are simple and consistent adhere to the principle of least astonishment. They never surprise the user with unexpected behavior.

tem should rephrase the user input in its syntactic format and then ask the user to approve its interpretation before executing the command.

Many user errors are caused by the system's inability to accept variations in the user input. As shown in Figure 11.8, Hebditch notes an example where the user must enter a date three times because the system allows only one strict syntactic format (DD/MM/YY) for entering a date [4]. Hebditch claims that 50 percent of error messages are caused by unreasonably inflexible systems. In a study by Senay and Stabler of the HELP queries on the IBM 4341 VM/CMS operating system, it was discovered that one out of five queries failed because of the system's inability to understand the users' requests [8].

A flexible system accepts abbreviations, user declarations of synonyms, missing words, run-together words, incorrect word orderings, spelling errors, and semantically meaningful but syntactically incorrect user requests.

```
PLEASE ENTER DATE: 20.8.80
ERROR-DATE MUST BE DD/MM/YY. TRY AGAIN
PLEASE ENTER DATE: 20/8/80
ERROR-DATE MUST BE DD/MM/YY. TRY AGAIN
PLEASE ENTER DATE: 20/08/80
```

Figure 11.8 Fifty percent of error messages are caused by inflexible systems that do not permit any variations when entering system input [4].

User Controlled

Whereas novice users may prefer to have the system in control, more experienced users tend to resent the appearance that the computer system is in charge and that they are subject to its decree. When the system appears to be in control, there is a risk of turning the user into a passive, uninterested observer of the system operations. Even the illusion of control can increase user motivation to perform a task and lead to increased productivity [10].

In a user-centered system, the user always has control of the system, or at least it appears to the user that he or she is in control. This sense of control is established in several ways:

1. System always responds immediately to the user.
2. System always informs the user of the correct system status.
3. Error messages are polite and meaningful, explaining what is wrong and how to correct it.
4. User is notified and asked for confirmation for special situations such as deleting a file or retrieving a very large number of records to answer a request.

Natural-Language-Like

Although people prefer communicating in natural language, computer systems do not. Computers always have had a very difficult time parsing natural language because of its inherent ambiguities and lack of structure. On the other hand, people often introduce errors when translating natural language into the required computer-language format. In a habitable environment, the users' preference is acknowledged. The user is able to communicate in natural language, but probably using only a subset of natural language that has a vocabulary of 300 to 1500 words and a restricted set of syntactic constructs [7, pp. 72–82]. When the vocabulary is restricted in this manner, natural-language processing can be performed efficiently by the computer.

This level of restriction is not really an impediment to someone using software tools for specific tasks or in the development of certain classes of application systems. When the context for interpretation is clearly defined, many possible ambiguities disappear because certain meanings make no sense in this particular context.

In an experiment by Shneiderman, it was shown that restricting the users' vocabulary did not necessarily hamper the user. In this experiment, one of two groups was told to limit the number of words used in problem solving. The result of the experiment was that the group with the restriction solved the problem in less time and used one-fifth the number of words as the unrestricted group [7, pp. 72–82]. In another experiment, users were asked to write down as many forms as possible for asking a particular question. They easily wrote down one form but had difficulty coming up with even one additional form [11, pp. 240–244]. It appears that limiting the syntactic constructs may not be much of a restriction, especially when the user is working in a specific application domain.

One problem with natural-language interfaces is that the user may not have an accurate understanding of the scope of the system's understanding. For example, the user may think the system understands more than it actually does. This problem is called *semantic overshoot* [7, pp. 130–138]. It is difficult for the system to detect and report semantic overshoot errors other than by stating that it does not understand a word(s) or by limiting the user to expressing one concept per statement [11, pp. 240–244].

BEYOND RESPONSIVE TO REACTIONARY

A user-friendly environment is expected to be responsive, but a habitable environment goes beyond responsive to reactionary (see Figure 11.9). A *responsive* system responds to every user input since a lack of system response can be detrimental to the user's basic understanding of the system. According to Skinner's theory of reinforcement, immediate feedback strengthens behavior, whereas no feedback weakens it [12, pp. 10–32]. If the user input is incorrect, a responsive system informs the user, explains what is wrong, and states how to correct it. If the user input is a request that can cause major consequences such as deleting a file or retrieving a large number of records, a responsive system informs the user and asks for confirmation before processing the request.

A *reactionary* system is responsive and *adaptive*. It not only responds to user requests, but also studies and learns from the user how the system is being used. It captures information about which system functions are most frequently used, which system functions are infrequently or never used, what user errors are most commonly made, and any user input the system does not understand. Based on this information, a reactionary system can easily be changed to better fit its user needs.

The position taken by a reactionary system is one of helping the user avoid errors in the first place because errors can lead to motivation and productivity problems. System constructs and functions that are frequently used incorrectly

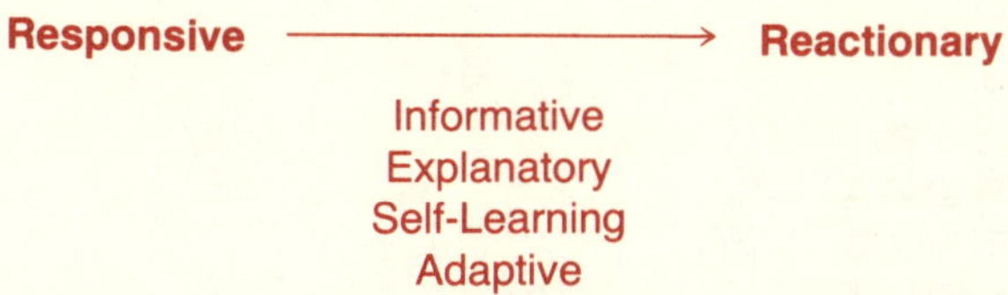

Figure 11.9 A reactionary system not only responds immediately to every user request in a meaningful way, but also learns from the user how the system is being used.

are identified and changed. Help in learning new system functions is offered to the user before he or she has an opportunity to learn it incorrectly. According to Skinner, a user learns most efficiently by being correct, not by being told that he or she is wrong after making an error and then having to relearn the correct way [12, pp. 10–32].

DIAGNOSTIC

How should a habitable environment respond when a user makes an error? There are several possibilities. First, the system may respond with an error message. Second, the system not only issues an error message but may also prevent the user from continuing until the error has been corrected. Third, the system itself may attempt to correct the error. Finally, the system may do nothing, completely ignoring the user input that was in error.

The last possibility, doing nothing, is unacceptable because the lack of a system response does not provide the user with any assistance to correct the error. In this situation, the user often tries to reenter the same incorrect input, and eventually becomes more and more frustrated, but no closer to correcting the problem.

At the very least, when an error is made, the system should inform the user with an error message. Although this is common practice for most user-friendly systems, most error messages are not very informative. For example, it has been said that for the CDC 6600 COBOL compiler, 80 percent of the errors were inaccurately diagnosed [13]. Some amusing but equally frustrating examples of error messages for actual systems are listed in Figure 11.10. Messages such as these give no real clue about what is wrong, nor about how to correct it. They only serve to frustrate, antagonize, and demoralize the user.

In some systems, error messages are accompanied by a ringing bell that embarrasses the user further. A user who is trying to get a real job done will see no real humor here.

A habitable system gives the user who made an error constructive advice and sometimes actually corrects the errors for the user (see Figure 11.11). It is both *courteous and insensitive*. A system that is courteous never assigns blame to the user, never is critical, never implies that the user is stupid, and never makes demands of the user. There is no proof that threat, anxiety, or punish-

?
NO SUCH FILE
INVALID DATA
ERROR 7036D
JOB ABANDONED
CATASTROPHIC ERROR
AWK BAILING OUT NEAR LINE 100
FATAL ERROR IN PASS ZERO

Figure 11.10 Error messages from most systems are not very informative and offer the user no real clue about how to correct the errors.

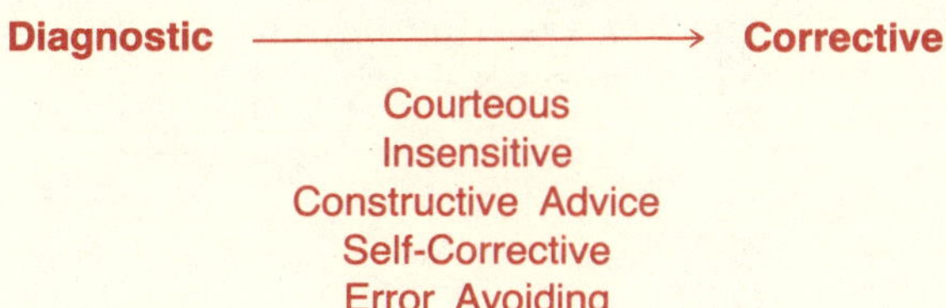

Figure 11.11 A habitable environment not only diagnoses user errors but helps the user correct the errors with courteous, meaningful error messages and sometimes self-corrects the error for the user.

ments are effective motivators [12, pp. 25–30]. Instead, a habitable system is politely informative, telling the user very specifically what is wrong and how to correct it.

Not this	But this
INVALID DATA	SALARY MUST BE IN RANGE OF $10,000 TO $100,000

Nasty and vague error messages lead to poor productivity and unsatisfied users. In an experiment by Shneiderman, an almost 50 percent improvement in user productivity occurred when the system error messages were improved. According to Badre and Shneiderman [7, p. 55]:

> Normal prompts, advisory messages and system responses to commands may influence user perceptions, but phrasing of error messages or diagnostic warnings is critical. Since errors occur because of lack of knowledge, incorrect understanding or inadvertent slips, the user is likely to be confused, feeling inadequate and anxious.

CORRECTIVE A system that is sensitive can self-correct many types of "slip of the pencil" and syntactic errors. Self-correcting systems are also called *do-what-I-mean (DWIM) systems* [13, pp. 411–432]. By analyzing the user input, the system guesses what the user actually meant and changes the input accordingly. Of course, sometimes the system's guess is wrong and therefore the change is also incorrect. To protect the user from an incorrect system change, a self-correcting system should always inform the user of its correction. In addition, a self-correcting system should include an UNDO command, enabling the user easily to "undo" any change made by the system.

HELPFUL

HELP is available on most on-line systems. It is provided in several ways:

1. Command level
2. System prompts
3. Error messages
4. On-line documentation
5. Off-line reference manuals
6. On-line tutor

Command-Level HELP

Command-level HELP is the most commonly provided form of HELP. The user types HELP followed by the command name. The system responds with an explanation of how the command works. Sometimes an example is included. To use this form of HELP, the user must know the command name or an acceptable abbreviation. Some systems provide an INDEX command, which lists all system commands to aid the user in finding the command that is of interest. Of course, when command names are meaningful, users have less need for HELP and tend to remember commands longer.

More sophisticated systems offer *context-sensitive* HELP. In this case, the system must know what the user is doing at the time HELP was requested. Using the input data of the user, the system helps the user correctly construct the command that he or she is attempting to use. This is a form of learning by doing—a form of *active* HELP. It is much more effective than simply reading about a command. According to Skinner, passive reading without manipulation of underlying concepts results in little learning [12, p. 14].

In addition to command-level HELP, most on-line systems provide a form of introductory or orientation HELP to explain in general how to use the system. A first-time user needs to know what the system does, how the commands and menus are structured, how to get started, how to quit, and how to get help.

System Prompts

System prompts can also be used to help a user. When the system prompts the user for input, it can describe what input is needed from the user. For example, the system might prompt: ENTER 4 DIGIT CUSTOMER STATUS CODE. If the user needs further assistance, he or she can request HELP. The system then responds with a list of legal codes and their definitions. This is a form of *leveled or layered* HELP in which more information is given to the user in stages. The idea is not to overload the user with unnecessary information.

Meaningful, constructive error messages offer another form of HELP. However, system prompts can be used instead of error messages. When the system detects an incomplete or incorrect user input, it responds by prompting the user with input format information. In this case, the system, not the user, has recognized the need for HELP and has initiated the HELP process.

On-Line Documentation

Many on-line systems have put the entire system reference manual on-line. This is not very useful unless the user is also given a mechanism for conveniently finding concepts and commands in the manual. This form of HELP can inundate the user with too much information to wade through to get to the pertinent place. Most users who are presented with pages of documentation about a particular command will prefer experimenting with the command or asking another user rather than reading documentation. There is evidence that neither experienced nor novice users read manuals, regardless of whether the manuals are off-line or on-line, because manuals do not provide information that is specific enough or complete enough to be helpful [13, pp. 399–410]. Furthermore, on-line HELP is more useful to experienced users because novices are too confused and lack the confidence needed to ask for HELP [14].

Thus the trend is away from developing more complete, more friendly manuals toward embedding HELP indirectly into the system. Systems that are designed as habitable environments lessen the need for the user to ask for HELP. Box 11.3 summarizes methods for both direct and indirect introduction of HELP into the system.

BOX 11.3 HELP story: methods for embedding HELP in a system

- Minimize need for HELP
  —Self-explanatory menus
  —Meaningful command names
  —Meaningful error messages
  —Orientation information
  —Automatic error correction and undo command
  —Index of commands
  —Glossary of terms
- Remember that on-line HELP is more useful to experienced users
- Level HELP information to avoid drowning user in unnecessary detail
- Provide leveled and context-sensitive HELP as powerful combination
- Concentrate on troubleshooting HELP, examples, advice

Sometimes, users need a description of how a particular system command works, but more often they need more than command-level help, even more than context-sensitive command-level help. For example, they need to know what sequence of commands is necessary to perform a task, what the difference is between two commands that appear to implement the same function, a better way to use the system, or why (at a conceptual level) something is wrong.

Types of HELP

Since the users may not know the right HELP questions to ask, they need to be able to carry on a dialogue with the system. Since users may not know when they need help or lack the confidence to ask for it, the system must be able to recognize a user in trouble and to initiate the HELP process. Box 11.4 shows a table of two fundamental types of HELP that a system can provide. The right side of the table shows the type of HELP frequently offered by user-friendly systems. This type of HELP is at a command level, is initiated by the user, and describes how a command works. This is a *passive* form of HELP that may include *active reading* when context-sensitive HELP is also included.

BOX 11.4 Types of HELP

Habitable	User Friendly
Task procedural	Command
System initiated	User initiated
Advise explanatory	Descriptive

The left side of the table shows another type of HELP that should also be offered. It is at a task level, can be initiated by the system, and offers advice and explanations to the user. This is a higher level of HELP. It is a form of *interactive* HELP and in some cases, *intelligent* HELP. The examples by Rich shown in Figures 11.12 and 11.13 illustrate the differences between these two types of HELP [15].

The first request for HELP show in Figure 11.12, HELP FTP, requires that the user know the command about which information is sought and also know the proper abbreviation for the command name. The second request, HELP FILE COPY, does not require that the user know the specific command name nor that the user form the HELP request in a particular way. Using natural-language words, the user simply asks for HELP in understanding how to copy a file. The

```
HELP FTP
————————————————————————————————————————
HELP FILE COPY
————————————————————————————————————————
HOW CAN I COPY A FILE FROM ONE MACHINE TO ANOTHER ON
  THE NETWORK?
————————————————————————————————————————
USER:  I NEED TO DELETE 2 FILES
SYSTEM:  USE DELETE COMMAND
USER:  I TRIED THAT
SYSTEM:  HAVE YOU CHECKED THE PROTECTION ON THE FILES
```

Figure 11.12 User-friendly systems offer command-level HELP as illustrated in the first two HELP requests in this figure. Habitable systems go beyond command-level HELP to offer advice and explanations to the user, as shown in the last two HELP requests in the figure [15] (Copyright ©1984 IEEE).

third request for HELP is a complete natural-language question that asks how a specific task can be accomplished. The fourth request is in the form of a dialogue between the system and the user. It is a request for the system to explain why the DELETE did not work and what will work.

The first two requests are command-level HELP that a user-friendly system should be able to provide. However, the last two requests require an intelligent system that understands natural language and has some knowledge of common user errors associated with deleting a file. A habitable environment is expected to provide intelligent HELP by which the system can give advice and offer explanations.

In the example shown in Figure 11.13, the user is attempting to format paper with the command SCRIBE PAPER.MSS when the system runs out of space and responds with the message QUOTA EXCEEDED AT 676647. An experienced user probably knows that the message is relaying the fact that more space is needed, while an inexperienced user would find it quite mysterious. In this ex-

```
@ SCRIBE PAPER.MSS
QUOTA EXCEEDED AT 676647
————————————————————————————————————————
@ DELETE *.TMP
@ CONTINUE
————————————————————————————————————————
ADVICE:
DELETE MARKS FILES FOR DELETION. EXPUNGE REMOVES FILES
FROM DIRECTORY
```

Figure 11.13 A system with intelligent HELP capabilities can anticipate when the user is in trouble and can offer explanatory HELP without being asked by the user [15] (Copyright ©1984 IEEE).

ample the user responds with a command DELETE *.TMP and CONTINUE. However, this is not a complete, correct response because the EXPUNGE command must also be used to free up the temporary file space. Most systems would respond with the same message, QUOTA EXCEEDED AT 676647, giving the user no clue about what to do or even worse, giving the user the impression that other files must be deleted to obtain sufficient space to continue. A system with intelligent HELP overcomes this barrier by anticipating the need for HELP. Without the user asking, the system observes that the user needs more information and the system offers advice explaining that to free space, both the DELETE and EXPUNGE commands must be executed. Now the user has the information needed to continue.

Figure 11.14 shows four levels of HELP, ranging from low-level passive HELP to high-level intelligent HELP. Command-level HELP and context-sensitive HELP are examples of passive and active HELP, respectively. At the interactive level, the system crosses the boundary from helping the user to training the user. At this level, the system can teach the user underlying concepts as well as help the user correct an error or decide what command to execute next. At the top level, the system has intelligent capabilities. It is user sensitive, context sensitive, error predicting, and has explanatory and natural-language-processing capabilities.

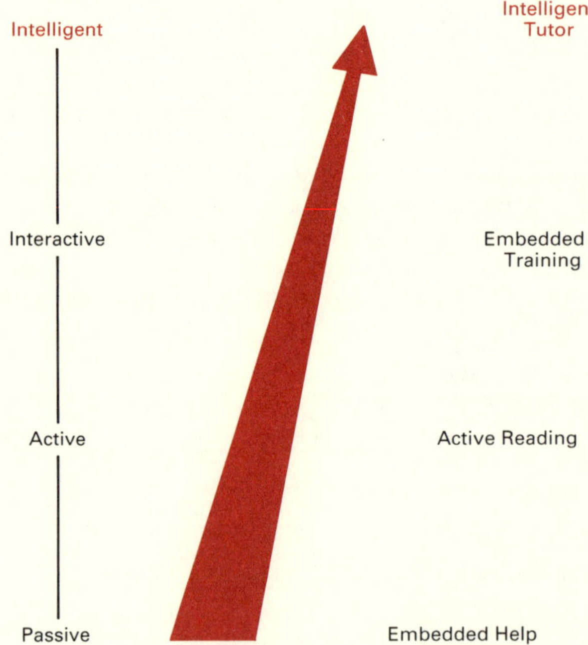

Figure 11.14 A habitable environment provides the highest level of help—intelligent HELP—which not only helps the user but also teaches the user.

INTELLIGENT TUTOR

A major obstacle to the use of new software tools, regardless of how powerful they may be, is the amount of user training needed. For many organizations, training has become a major issue, slowing technological advancement and a major expense item. According to T. Capers Jones [16]:

> The number of staff instructors and educational personnel in the set of Fortune 500 companies in the U.S. approximates the total faculty size of all U.S. universities. In terms of student-days, it is possible that the private in-house training programs of major corporations approach the combined computer science departments in U.S. academic institutions. For a number of corporations, technical training is a major commitment and targets such as 10–20 days of training per staff member year are not uncommon.

Intelligent tutors help solve the training problem by embedding training into the tool itself. Intelligent tutors can provide a superior learning environment to the traditional classroom environment with a human instructor. Box 11.5 summarizes the characteristics of a good tutor (human or artificial) according to Skinner [12, p. 12]. Box 11.6 summarizes the capabilities of an intelligent tutor.

With the intelligent tutor, we return to a one-to-one learning environment tailored to the needs of an individual user (a student). Because the tutor has only one student with whom to deal, all its attention can be focused on that student. The tutor can engage the student in continuous activity, which provides the optimum learning environment. There is constant interchange between the tutor and the student, which keeps the student more alert and able to absorb more information in a shorter time. The student can learn at his or her own pace, ask questions, and review material whenever appropriate, which gives the student a sense of control over the learning experience. The tutor gives the student immediate feedback and can detect mistakes as soon as they occur, which prevents the student from getting too far off track with misconceptions

BOX 11.5 Characteristics of a good tutor

- Constant interchange between tutor and student
- Engages student in continuous activity
- Insists that each point be thoroughly understood before moving on
- Presents just that material for which the student is ready
- Helps student come up with the right way
- Reinforces every correct response

BOX 11.6 Intelligent tutor

- Transmits own problem-solving heuristics to user
- Chooses appropriate examples for user to work
- Handles user-posed problems
- Handles and adapts to different user backgrounds
- Compares abilities of user with tutor
- Learns superior problem-solving heuristics from user

that will be hard to overcome later. The tutor uses an incremental learning method in which the student learns just that material for which he or she is ready. Working in an exploratory learning environment, the student constructs new knowledge by building on existing knowledge. New knowledge evolves through examples, generalization, refinement, and modification. However, the tutor does not allow the student to move on to more complex concepts until the basic concepts are fully understood. Teaching the underlying concepts is stressed because real and lasting learning does not take place until the basic concepts are understood.

Intelligent tutors are also superior to simpler, nonintelligent computer-based instruction (CAI) methods because they are less rigid. In nonintelligent CAI, the training method is predefined and cannot be adjusted to each person's requirements. With intelligent tutors, the student can explore the system in his or her own fashion, communicate in natural language, and expect the tutor to explain its advice.

To provide this superior learning environment, an intelligent tutor needs four types of knowledge [17].

1. Subject area
2. Student information
3. How to teach
4. How to communicate

The tutor must be an expert teacher and an expert tool user. It has expert-level knowledge of the subject area for which the tool is used (e.g., software design, programming debugging). The tutor is an expert system that can identify for the student the next step of the task to be performed, can explain why something is correct or incorrect in terms of the underlying concepts, and can suggest approaches that the student did not consider. The tutor uses natural language to communicate.

If the tutor is not more knowledgeable than the student, it will be of little help to the student. Therefore, an important capability of an intelligent tutor is that it can learn as well as teach. An intelligent tutor should employ a self-improvement strategy in which it studies how the student uses the tool to perform tasks. If the student's method is superior to the tutor's (e.g., can perform the task in fewer steps), the tutor should replace its approach with the student's approach. Or if the student performs a task that the tutor has not seen before, the task should be added to the tutor's knowledge base about how to use the tool.

An intelligent tutor can handle and adapt to different student backgrounds. It alters the tutorial strategy, depending on the student's prior background, past performance, and past errors. The intelligent tutor stores student information in a model of the student. The subject area expertise of the intelligent tutor consists of a set of facts and rules. Heuristics are added to the rules to give the tutor more flexibility in interpreting student questions and explaining the tutor's own reasoning. The student's knowledge is modeled as a subset, and simple variations of, the tutor's knowledge. Thus tutoring is an attempt to increase this subset by expanding the student's facts and rules about the subject area [11, p. 51]. To accomplish its teaching job, the tutor requires not only knowledge about the student, but also knowledge about mistakes the student is likely to make, manifestations of these mistakes, and methods for constructing them. Commonly made mistakes include missing substeps, extra substeps, or correctly following an incorrect (inefficient) procedure to accomplish a task.

Examples of Intelligent Tutors

Figures 11.15 and 11.16 are examples of dialogues between user and tutor from two intelligent tutoring systems. Figure 11.15 is a calculus tutor, developed at Stanford in Lisp, and is used to teach integration techniques in calculus [11, pp. 293–304]. Figure 11.16 is a tutor called SPADE-O, developed at the MIT artificial intelligence labs, and is used to teach program design methods [11, pp. 123–140].

In both examples, the tutor and the user communicate in natural language. The user often responds with a single word, but the tutor uses full sentences to make certain that it is clearly and easily understood. In both examples, the tutor is an expert that is able to solve calculus problems on its own (in the case of the calculus tutor) or able to design programs on its own (in the case of SPADE-O).

Notice that the tutor knows the user and what system commands the user has tried thus far. At each step in either the integration or the program design process the tutor is capable of choosing the next best step, but will defer to the user's preferences.

(INTEGRATE)
HELLO! WHAT IS YOUR NAME?
RUTH
HAVE YOU EVER STUDIED PARTIAL FRACTIONAL EXPANSION?
NO
OK, DO YOU HAVE A PROBLEM?
NO
ALL RIGHT, I'LL SELECT ONE FOR YOU. THINKING FOR A MOMENT.
OK, RUTH
OUR INTEGRAL IS $\int \times \log(x)\, dx$
WHAT SHALL WE DO TO SOLVE IT?
SUB
CAN YOU THINK OF A SUBSTITUTION?
(YES, HELP, OR EXIT)
YES. LET U = log(X)
OK, RUTH. WE WILL LET U = log (X)
OUR NEW INTEGRAL IS $\int Ue^{2}dU$
PLEASE TYPE GOOD, BAD, OR GIVE UP
BAD
CAN YOU THINK OF A SUBSTITUTION?
(YES, HELP, OR EXIT)
HELP
I CAN'T FIND A SUITABLE SUBSTITUTION!
WE'LL EXIT . . .
OK, RUTH
OUR INTEGRAL IS $\int \times \log(x)\, dx$
WHAT SHALL WE DO TO SOLVE IT?
HELP
I SUGGEST YOU TRY INTEGRATION BY PARTS
WHAT SHALL WE DO TO SOLVE IT?
PARTS
WE WILL USE THE NOTATION
$\int UdV = UV - \int dU$
CAN YOU THINK OF A CHOICE FOR U?
(YES, HELP, OR EXIT)
HELP
HOW ABOUT LETTING U = log(X)
THUS dV = XdX
HMMMM . . . .
AN INTRIGUING CHOICE!
THUS $V = X_2/2$ and $dU = 1/X$

.

.

.

YOU DID THAT PROBLEM IN 3 STEPS COMPARED TO 2 FOR ME!

MY SOLUTION	YOUR SOLUTION
1. INTEGRATION BY PARTS	1. SUBSTITUTION
2. KNOWN INTEGRAL ROUTINE	2. INTEGRATION BY PARTS
	3. KNOWN INTEGRAL ROUTINE

Figure 11.15 Calculus Tutor [11].

WHAT IS YOUR NAME?
> **JOHN SMITH**
HELLO JOHN. GOOD TO SEE YOU AGAIN.
DO YOU WANT ME TO GET YOUR WORK FROM THE FILE (JS WORK 35)?
> **NO**
OK. WHAT NAME FOR PROCEDURE YOU WISH TO PLAN TODAY?
> **WW**
WHAT TYPE OF PLAN WOULD YOU LIKE TO USE?
A. IDENTIFY AS PREVIOUSLY SOLVED PROBLEM
B. DECOMPOSE INTO SUBPROBLEMS
C. REFORMULATE INTO ALTERNATIVE PROBLEM
> **SEQUENTIAL**
OK. I AM ASSUMING
  PLAN → DECOMPOSE → SEQUENTIAL
> **WELL POLE ROOF**
DO YOU WANT TO INCLUDE A SETUP STEP?
> **LATER**
OK. JOHN. I AM POSITIONING THE [SETUP] OF WW UNTIL LATER.
WHAT NOW?
> **GO TO A SECOND [INTERFACE] OF SEQUENTIAL PLAN.**
WHAT NOW?
> **RUN WW**
{RUNNING WW . . . DONE} WHAT NOW?
> **DEBUG**
DEBUGGING WW. THE TOP LEVEL OF WW CONTAINS 7 DESIGN DECISIONS WHICH COULD BE FAULTY. THERE ARE WARNINGS ATTACHED TO SEVERAL NODES IN THE PLAN FOR WW.

DO YOU WANT TO TRY TO DIAGNOSE BUGS IN WW?
> **YES**
WHAT NOW?
> **WARNINGS**
I AM ASSUMING DIAGNOSE → PLAN → WARNINGS
THE WW PLAN CONTAINS THE FOLLOWING WARNINGS
  THE [SETUP] GOAL OF THE SEQUENTIAL PLAN
  HAS NOT BEEN COMPLETED.
  THE FIRST [INTERFACE] HAS NOT BEEN COMPLETED.
WHAT NOW?
> **REPAIR THE [INTERFACE] BETWEEN POLE AND WELL.**
I SEE JOHN. YOU HAVE CONCLUDED THAT THE [INTERFACE] BETWEEN POLE AND WELL HAS A SEMANTIC BUG; SPECIFICALLY, THE MISSING STEP, WHICH IS SYNTACTICALLY OPTIONAL, IS NEEDED FOR THIS PROBLEM. COMPLETING . . . THE RULE IS DEBUG → [DIAGNOSE] + [REPAIR].

Figure 11.16 SPADE-O [11].

(Continued)

> **YES**
DIAGNOSING MEANS FIGURING OUT WHICH NODE IN THE PLAN REPRESENTS AN INCORRECT CHOICE. THERE ARE FOUR SOURCES OF EVIDENCE

.
.
.

OK, THE WW PROBLEM IS WELL-DEFINED. WHAT NOW?
ROOF POLE AND WELL.
THESE ARE PARTS IN PROBLEM SPECIFICATION ARE YOU PURSUING A SEQUENTIAL DECOMPOSITION PLAN?
> **YES**
OK. WHAT NOW?
> **ADVICE**
WELL IS DESCRIBED AS A SQUARE IN THE WW SPECIFICATION. THE ANSWER LIBRARY CONTAINS A PROCEDURE, RECT, WHICH DRAWS RECTANGLES. A SQUARE IS A KIND OF RECTANGLE. HENCE, I SUGGEST TRYING AN IDENTIFICATION INVOLVING RECT AS THE PLAN FOR WELL.

Figure 11.16 (Continued)

For example, the calculus tutor allows its user, Ruth, to choose substitution as her method for solving the integral $\int x \log(x)\, dx$, but does not harshly criticize Ruth when it becomes obvious to Ruth that substitution will not help her solve the integral. At this point, Ruth asks the tutor to show her how to solve the integral, which the tutor successfully does. At the end of the session, the tutor compares its solution to Ruth's solution. The tutor's solution is better. However, if Ruth's solution had been the better of the two, the tutor would have replaced its own solution with Ruth's. During the first six weeks of experimentation with the calculus tutor, 25 percent of its solutions were replaced by the users' problem solutions because they used fewer steps.

In the SPADE-O example, the user, John Smith, is designing a program whose purpose is to draw a wishing well consisting of three parts: (1) well, (2) pole, and (3) roof. The tutor refers to John's program design as a "plan." When the session begins, the tutor suggests to John that there are three kinds of plans that he can follow when designing a program:

A. Identify as previously solved problem
B. Decompose into subproblems
C. Reformulate into alternative problem

However, John does not select any of these choices, but instead, prefers to use a sequential approach. The tutor is flexible enough to allow a method not included in its repertoire. John continues by stating that this program plan will consist of three components, corresponding to the three parts of the wishing well. John not only designs his program, but when the design is complete, he asks the tutor to generate the code, execute it, and help John debug it. Since the tutor recognizes that John has never used the debug feature, it offers to explain it to John to prevent him from using it incorrectly. Finally, when John asks for advice, the tutor explains that one design approach for the wishing well program is to reuse the RECT procedure that already exists in the system library, rather than building from scratch.

SUMMARY

Habitable environments provide an intelligent user interface that is easy to use, easy to learn to use, and

BOX 11.7 Characteristics of a habitable environment

User friendly: System is easy to use, easy to learn how to use, helpful, and tailorable to different types of users.

Responsive: System responds quickly and meaningfully to every user request.

Diagnostic: When an error occurs, the system informs the user what is wrong, why, and how to correct it.

Helpful: A helpful system provides a high-level description of what the system does and a command-level description of how each system command works.

Supportive: System assists the user in performing tasks, but the user, not the system, must always take the initiative and direct the system by selecting what commands are to be performed.

User centered: User is seen as the center of the system and is considered first and foremost in the design of the system.

Reactionary: System studies how it is being used and frequently made errors and suggests how it should be modified to better meet user needs.

Corrective: System has the ability to self-correct many types of user errors automatically.

Teaching: The system can teach as well as help the user to use the system by providing intelligent tutoring capabilities.

Directive: The system can take the initiative by selecting which commands are to be executed, and in what order, to accomplish a specific task.

promotes human understanding. Habitable environments have capabilities far beyond those provided by user-friendly CASE environments of the late 1980s. The characteristics of a habitable environment are summarized in Box 11.7.

REFERENCES

1. David C. Smith, Charles Irby, Ralph Kimball, Bill Verplank, and Eric Harslem, ''Designing the Star User Interface,'' in *Integrated Interactive Computing Systems*. Amsterdam: North-Holland, 1983.
2. Bob Stahl, ''Friendly Mainframe Software Guides Users toward Productivity,'' *Computerworld,* February 3, 1986, pp. 53–66.
3. Ben Shneiderman, ''Direct Manipulation: A Step beyond Programming Languages,'' *Computer,* Vol. 16, No. 8, August 1983, pp. 57–69.
4. D. Hebditch, ''Dialogue Design for User-Friendly Systems,'' User Friendly Systems Report, *Infotech State of the Art Report,* Vol. 9, No. 4, 1981, pp. 289–294.
5. Anthony Wasserman, ''User Software Engineering and the Design of Interactive Systems,'' *Infotech State of the Art Report,* Vol. 9, No. 4, 1981, pp. 375–387.
6. Moshe Zloof, ''Query-By-Example,'' *AFIPS Conference Proceedings,* Vol. 44, 1975.
7. A. Badre and B. Shneiderman, editors, *Directions in Human/Computer Interaction,* Norwood, N.J.: ABLEX Publishing, 1982.
8. Hikmet Senay and Edward Stabler, ''Diambiguating HELP Queries for a User Friendly Interface,'' *COMPSAC Proceedings,* 1985, pp. 399–405.
9. R. E. Sweet, ''The Mesa Programming Project,'' *SIGPLAN Notices,* Vol. 20, No. 7, July 1985, pp. 216–239.
10. J. M. Carroll, ''The Adventure of Getting to Know a Computer,'' *IBM Computer,* Vol. 15, No. 11, November 1982, pp. 49–58.
11. D. Sleeman and J. S. Brown, editors, *Intelligent Tutoring Systems*. London: Academic Press, 1982.
12. W. A. Deterline, *An Introduction to Programmed Instruction*. Englewood Cliffs, N.J.: Prentice-Hall, 1962.
13. Donald Norman and Stephen Draper, editors, *User-Centered System Design*. Hillsdale, N.J.: Lawrence Erlbaum, 1986.

14. Raymond C. Houghton, Jr. "Online Help Systems: A Conspectus," *CACM,* Vol. 27, No. 2, February 1984, pp. 126–132.

15. Elaine Rich, "The Gradual Expansion of Artificial Intelligence," *Computer,* Vol. 17, May 1984, No. 5, pp. 4–12.

16. T. Capers Jones, "How Not to Measure Productivity," *ComputerWorld,* January 13, 1986, pp. 65–76.

17. B. Woolf and D. McDonald, "Building a Computer Tutor: Design Issues," *Computer,* Vol. 17, No. 9, September 1984, pp. 61–73.

12 THE METHODOLOGY DRIVER

AUTOMATING SOFTWARE METHODOLOGY KNOWLEDGE AND EXPERIENCE

The second component of the intelligent shell is the *methodology driver.* Its purpose is to internalize knowledge about software development methodologies in software tools. Experienced software developers are usually many times more productive than novices because they use their experience from previous, similar development efforts to guide them through the complicated software development process. Capturing this knowledge in software tools makes the expertise of the best system builders available to every developer. It frees developers to concentrate on strategic rather than process-level concerns.

There are three levels of knowledge that can be supported by software automation:

1. Documentation
2. Guidance
3. Process

Documentation-Level Knowledge

Software tools that automate the production of the documentation deliverables required by a software development methodology reside at the first level. Examples include CASE diagramming and documentation tools that support the graphic symbols and notation conventions required by particular structured methodologies. (e.g., DeMarco data flow diagram used to represent a system specification in the structured analysis methodology).

Guidance-Level Knowledge

At the *guidance level,* software tools guide the software developer in the use of a particular software development methodology (see Box 12.1). Techniques such as help panels, checklists, context-dependent menus, checking mechanisms, and forcing functions are used to "prompt" the user in the proper use of the methodology (see Figure 12.1). These tools give context-dependent advice about how to get started, what to do next, what input and output are required by each step of the methodology, and how to check the quality of the system being developed.

Process-Level Knowledge

Automating software methodologies is the most fundamental component of software automation because it is the software methodology that drives the process of developing software systems. Experience has shown that the key to a successful software project is choosing the right software methodology—one whose application can lead the developer to a good software system. Choosing the right methodology is more important than using the best, most powerful tools.

Tools that automate the deliverables required by a software methodology are but the first small step toward software automation. They automate only the production of the deliverables required by the methodology, not the process of producing those deliverables. Tools that automate the process steps of the methodology are the basis for true software automation.

BOX 12.1 Automated guidance system

- Developer must progress through stages of methodology in an orderly and ordered fashion.
- Guidance is implemented via menus that limit valid menu choices based on rules of the methodology and quality assurance checks (i.e., developer cannot proceed to next step in the methodology until the current task has been completed and the outputs from this task have been certified complete, correct, and in compliance with current standards).
- Through the use of help screens and menus, developer is told the next step to be done, the input needed to perform this step, and the output that is to be produced.
- When a change is made, developer is notified as to which previous steps may be affected, which output may be affected (and has been automatically changed), and which steps must be revisited before the developer is allowed to continue.

Main Menu

CHOICE:
→

1. DATA DESCRIPTION
2. GENERATE APPLICATION
3. PROGRAM DESCRIPTION
4. REVIEW SPECIFICATION
5. NEXT FUNCTION
6. USER SIGN-IN
7. STATUS
8. SET MENU OFF
9. HELP
10. EXIT

Figure 12.1 Context-dependent menus guide users in the correct use of the methodology by choosing the next step in the process for the user.

Tools that provide the first level of methodology knowledge, the documentation level, can be generic, supporting the documentation requirements of many different software methodologies. However, by their very nature, tools possessing guidance-level and process-level knowledge must be methodology specific. Because these tools actively encourage or enforce the use of specific software methodologies, the developer must be committed to a specific methodology.

To automate the higher levels of methodology knowledge, a model of the software methodology process must be embedded into the tools. This presupposes (1) an understanding of how the process is carried out in practice; (2) what models are likely to guarantee a high degree of productivity, management control, and success culminating in a high-quality software system; and (3) a way to encode the model into the tools [1].

Guidance-level tools fall short of providing full software automation because they do not incorporate real understanding of the methodology whose use they encourage or enforce. They cannot carry out the methodology's process on their own independent of the guidance of the human developer. However, at the third level, the *process level,* the methodology driver has this understanding and this capability. It is a bonafide expert system. It can advise how to get started, suggest what to do next, notify when finished, state what is wrong and explain why, document what has been left out, suggest a better approach, and in some cases, carry out the methodology's process on its own. In other words, it can mimic the behavior of a human software methodology expert.

COMPONENTS OF THE METHODOLOGY DRIVER

Figure 12.2 shows the methodology driver as a pyramid composed of four components. At the top of the pyramid is a set of powerful, integrated software development tools such as diagramming tools, specification languages, prototyping tools, and code gener-

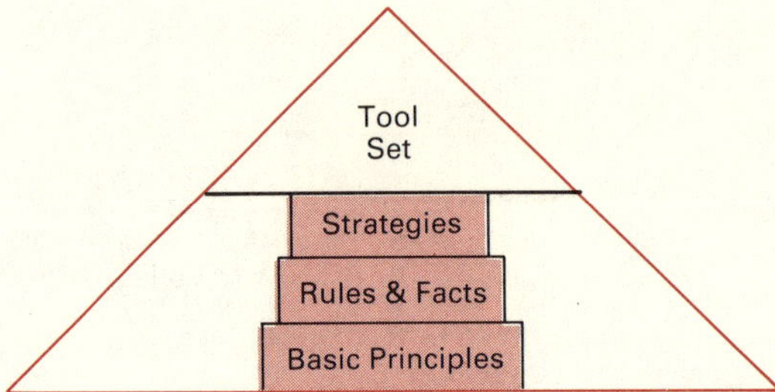

Figure 12.2 The methodology driver is an expert system that understands and can carry out the process steps of a software methodology. It consists of four basic components. Software strategies, rules, and facts, and basic principles form the knowledge base that guides the use of a powerful, integrated tool set.

ators. Use of these tools during the system building process is directed by an intelligent base consisting of the bottom three layers in the pyramid:

1. Software development strategies and heuristics
2. Software technology rules and facts
3. Software technology basic principles

Basic Principles

At the very bottom of the pyramid's base sit the *basic principles.* This is the foundation of reasoning for any expert system. These are the basic principles of software technologies that have been discovered over the history of programming [2]. Boxes 12.2 and 12.3 list some of these basic principles that belong to the disciplines of software engineering and information engineering and are the foundation of the structured philosophy. They began in the world of programming and then extended into design, analysis, and information planning. Although the techniques for creating software will certainly change, these basic principles will remain constant over time. They are principles relevant to managing complexity. They are concerned with the introduction of standardization and discipline to the software product and process.

Divide and conquer is one basic principle. It is the principle of solving difficult problems by dividing a problem into a set of smaller, independent problems that are easier to understand and solve. It is a powerful and essential technique for dealing with complexity. It allows the software developer to work confidently on one piece of a large system without worrying about the enormous number of details covering the entire system. When applied to a software system, it means partitioning a program into independent pieces that are manageably small and separately testable. When applied to the software development process, it means partitioning the process into steps that are manageably small.

The principle of *hierarchical ordering* is another basic principle. It is closely related to divide and conquer. In addition to finding that it is easier to understand a problem (and a software program) if it is divided into pieces, the arrangement of the pieces is equally important to understandability. Always or-

BOX 12.2 Basic principles of software engineering

Principle of Abstraction

To solve a problem, separate out those aspects that are tied to a particular reality in order to represent the problem in a simplified, general form.

Principle of Formality

Follow a rigorous, methodical approach to solve a problem.

Divide and Conquer

Solve a difficult problem by dividing the problem into a set of smaller independent problems that are easier to understand and to solve.

Hierarchical Ordering

Organize the components of a solution into a tree-like hierarchical structure.

Principle of Hiding

Hide inessential information, allowing a module to know only the information it needs.

Principle of Localization

Place logically related items close together in physical proximity to one another.

Principle of Conceptual Integrity

Follow a consistent design philosophy and architecture.

Principle of Completeness

Check to make certain that nothing is left out.

Principle of Logical Independence

In analysis and design, concentrate on logical functions to be accomplished independently of the physical implementation.

BOX 12.3 Principles of information engineering

Principle of Data Analysis

Data analysis to formally identify the inherent structure of data should be done *before* process logic is designed.

Principle of Data Independence

Data models representing the inherent logical structure of data should be formally designed independently of how the data are used and independently of the physical structure and distribution of data.

Principle of Strategic Data Planning

Data requires planning, defining, and structuring across an enterprise so that data can be exchanged among processes and management can obtain information most valuable in running the enterprise.

Principle of End-User Access

End users should be given the tools for accessing data bases which they can use directly without programming.

ganizing the pieces into a tree-like hierarchical structure enhances understandability. The program can be understood and built level by level, where each new level adds more detail.

Rules and Facts

On top of the basic principles sit the *rules and facts* for implementing these principles. For example, program modularization is an application of the principle of divide and conquer. The rules for a program module are given in Box 12.4. Object-oriented design is another application of the principle of divide and conquer.

The hierarchical program control structure, which is the required architectural structure for all structured programs, is an application of the principle of hierarchical ordering (see Box 12.5). One of the essential differences between structured and unstructured programs is that structured programs are ordered hierarchically, whereas unstructured programs are ordered only sequentially. A hierarchical structure allows us to remove upper layers and still have usable lower-level layers, which can become the building blocks for a variation of the system or the base of a new system. This can be a powerful mechanism for

BOX 12.4 Rules for a program module

- Each module represents one logical, self-contained task.
- Modules are simple.
- Modules are closed.
- Modules are discrete and visible.
- Modules are separately testable.
- Each module is implemented as a single, independent program function.
- Each module has a single entry point and a single exit point.
- Each module exits to a standard return point in the module from which it was executed.
- Modules may be combined into larger modules without the knowledge of the internal construction of the modules.
- Modules have well-defined interfaces. Modules have control connections via their entry points and exit points; modules have data connections via passed parameters and shared data; modules have functional connections via the services they perform for each other.

creating programs that are easy to change and introducing reusability as a development technique. The inheritance feature of object-oriented programming languages is another application of the hierarchical ordering principle.

When applied to the software process, rules implementing the principle of divide and conquer take the form of a methodology stating a sequence of steps

BOX 12.5 Properties of a structured program

- The program is divided into a set of modules arranged in a hierarchy defining their logical and execution-time relationships.
- The execution flow from module to module is restricted to one simple scheme in which control is always passed back to the invoking module.
- Module form is standardized and legal control constructs are restricted to sequence, selection, and iteration.
- Documentation is required to explain what the program does but not how it works.

to follow when performing a task. For example, Figure 12.3 shows the traditional "waterfall" version of the software life cycle as a sequence of five phases. There are several widely used structured methodologies that divide each of these phases into a sequence of steps. At each step, the function to be performed is described and the input needed by the step and the output produced by the step are specified. The purpose is to standardize the software development process and to ensure the quality of the software system that is produced.

Many methodologies focus on one phase of the life cycle, such as analysis or design. Some methodologies have been designed to fit together and feed one another. For example, the DeMarco structured analysis methodology (see Figure 12.4) produces the input needed for the Yourdon structured design methodology (see Figure 12.5) [3, 4]. The Martin information engineering methodology is divided into a set of integrated stages that cover the entire software development process, beginning with strategic data planning (see Figure 12.6) [5].

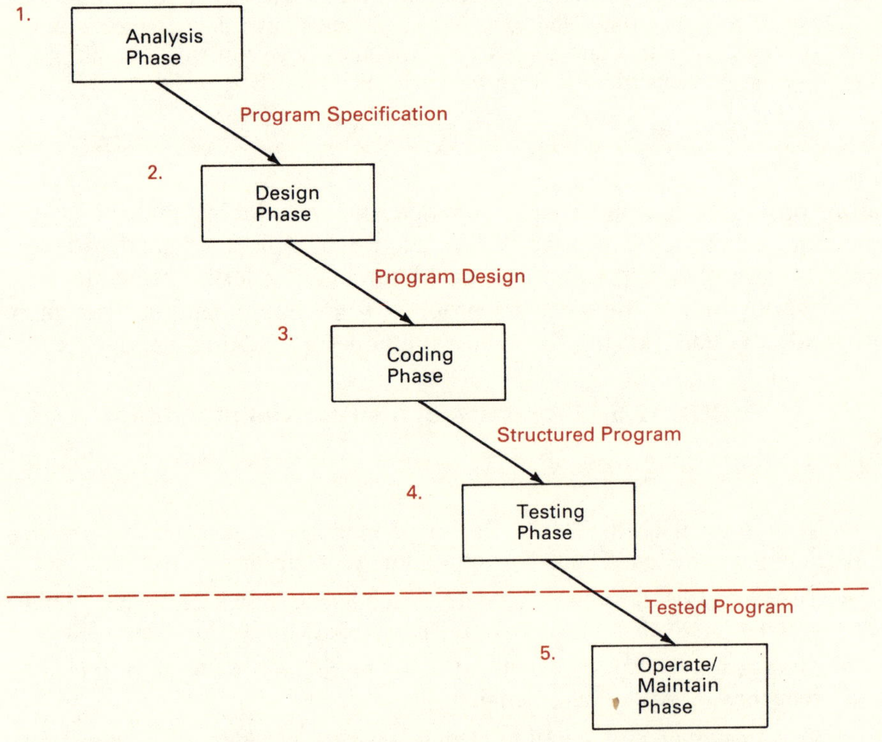

Figure 12.3 The software life cycle is a multistep process consisting of five basic sequential phases: analysis, design, code, test, and maintain.

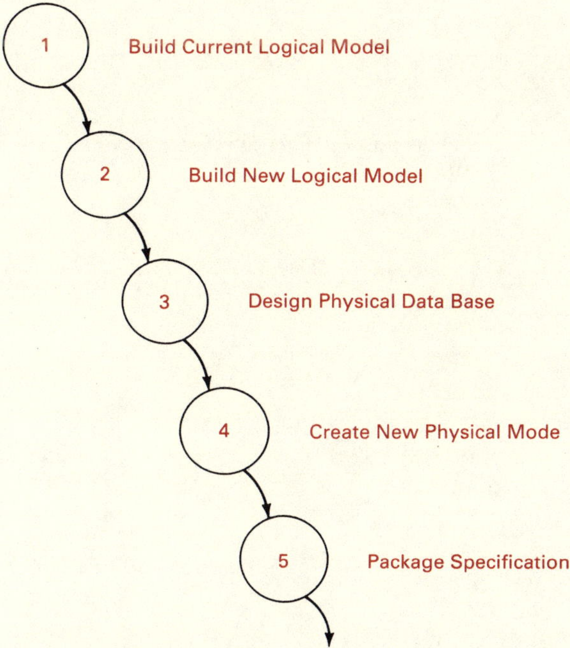

Figure 12.4 The Gane–Sanson version of structured analysis consists of five steps.

Strategies and Heuristics

The *strategies* for developing software are on the level above rules and facts. They include strategies such as:

- Top-down development featuring functional decomposition (see Box 12.6)
- Bottom-up development featuring reusability of software components developed previously
- Combination top-down/bottom-up approaches
- Object-oriented design featuring object decomposition and class inheritance

The methodology driver helps the developer correctly apply these strategies by:

- Enforcing the rules and basic principles of software technologies
- Checking for incompleteness and special cases
- Giving advice on how to apply the strategy practically
- Choosing the task to be done next

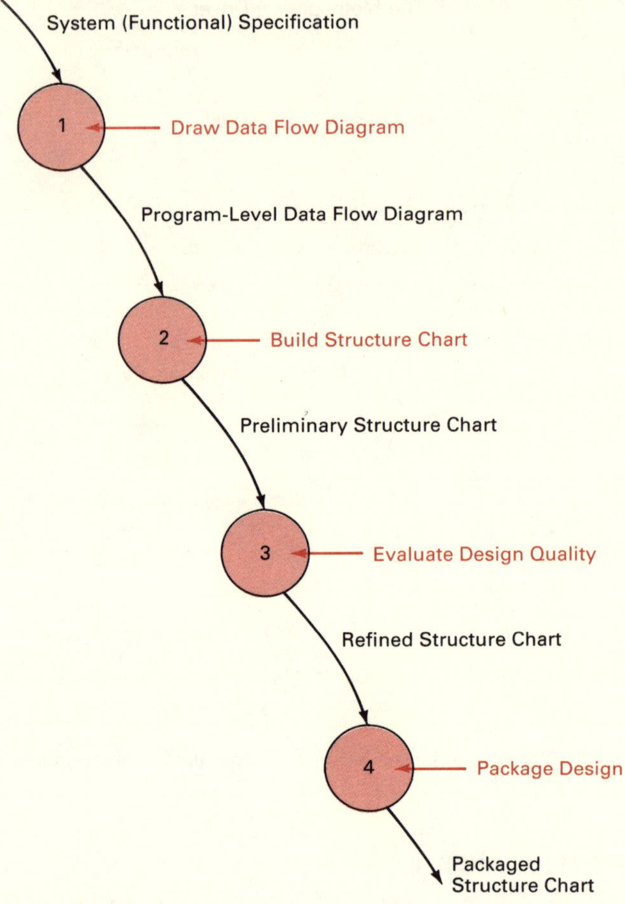

Figure 12.5 The Yourdon–Constantine structured design process consists of four sequential steps.

BOX 12.6 Strategies to guide functional decomposition

- Decompose into independent pieces.
- Defer decisions about implementation details.
- Keep interface between modules simple.
- Hide inessential information from modules.
- Keep data use as local as possible.
- Make the easiest design decisions first.

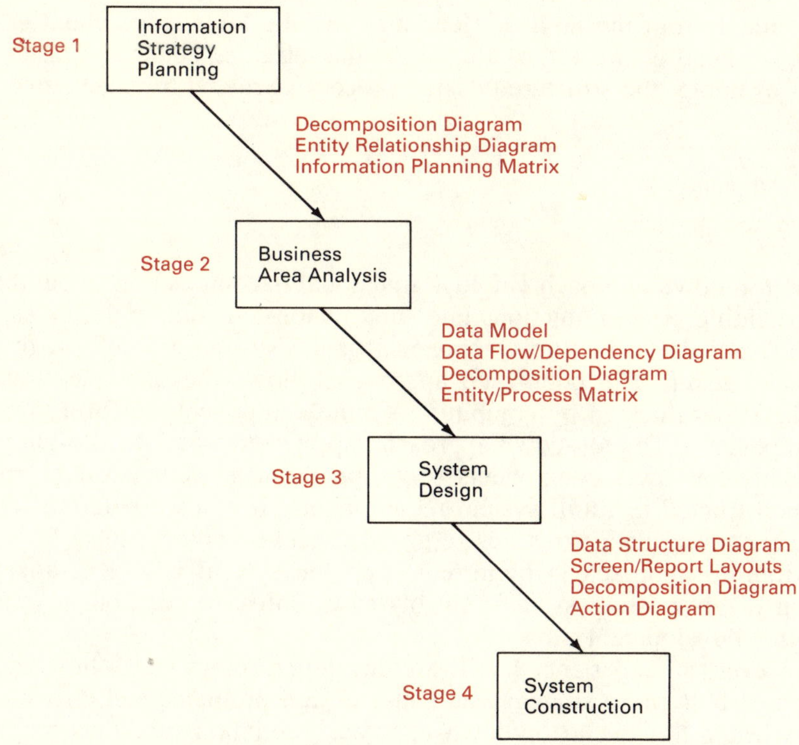

Figure 12.6 Information engineering is a top-down, data-driven process for system development. It begins with strategic information planning.

For example, the methodology driver may guide the software design process by using the functional decomposition method and answering such questions as:

- When do I stop decomposing a component?
- Which modularization scheme is best, or is this modularization scheme at least acceptable?
- Where do I put decisions in the program structure; that is, have I placed each decision in the best place to minimize its impact on the system when I need to change it?
- What should the next step be?
- Do some components exist that I can use?

Heuristics

Heuristics are an important part of strategies. *Heuristics* are unwritten "rules of thumb" that comprise much of the practical experience that separates the expert system builder from the novice. Heuristics include knowledge about shortcuts and when to bend or break the rules to get the job done better and faster.

For example, the structured design process is guided by one of two design strategies:

1. Top-down approach
2. Bottom-up approach

The top-down approach employs functional decomposition to build the design by dividing system functions into subfunctions. In simple design steps, the procedural and data structure components of the system are defined in greater and greater detail. The bottom-up approach follows the opposite strategy. It builds the system design by combining simple components to form more complex components. The top-down approach is preferred when the designer is sure that feasible low-level components (e.g., operating system interface routines) can be constructed to fulfill system requirements. It is also preferred when decisions concerning data structures (e.g., file access methods) must be delayed. The bottom-up approach is preferred when the system is a generalization or extension of an existing system. In this case, software component reusability can shorten development time.

However, an experienced software developer knows that following a strict top-down or bottom-up strategy can cause design problems and errors. For example, when following a top-down approach, common functions may not be recognized, or a top-down design may require too much time when developing a large system. On the other hand, following a pure bottom-up approach can result in poorly designed module interfaces, making thorough integration testing impossible. In practice, the design process is usually a combination top-down/bottom-up process.

NEW SOFTWARE DEVELOPMENT PROCESS

Use of an intelligent methodology driver changes the software development process and the division of labor between the human developers and their automated assistants. From the human developers' perspective the process becomes less formal and more specification-heavy. Most of the system development work to be done by the human developers concerns specifying the problem to be solved (i.e., the requirements of the system to be built).

The form of this specification changes from a narrative description to a graphic representation, and in many cases, to an executable prototype model. Earlier structured development methodologies required that a complete, correct specification document be produced before the system could be developed. This meant that developers expended a great deal of effort creating, reviewing, and correcting specification documents until they were judged complete and correct. However, this was an almost impossible task because requirements change frequently. It is hard to hit a moving target.

The intelligent methodology driver uses artificial intelligence techniques, such as fuzzy logic, redundancy, plausible reasoning, and belief revision, that can work with incomplete, incorrect, and changing requirements data. The methodology driver's role in the software development process is to take a partial, informal specification described by the human developers and to transform it into the complete system.

Suppose, for example, that the developers begin by describing a subscription system they wish to build. The purpose of the subscription system is to process three types of transactions (new subscriptions, renewals, and cancellations) against a master subscription file to produce subscriber bills and refunds. This description could be expressed as a high-level data flow diagram shown in Figure 12.7. It describes the basic inputs, outputs, relationships, and assumptions for the system processes in application-specific terms.

The developer begins the system development process by drawing the data flow diagram on the software development workstation screen. From this point on, the methodology driver can assist the developer in building the subscription system. The first step towards a formal description of the subscription system is

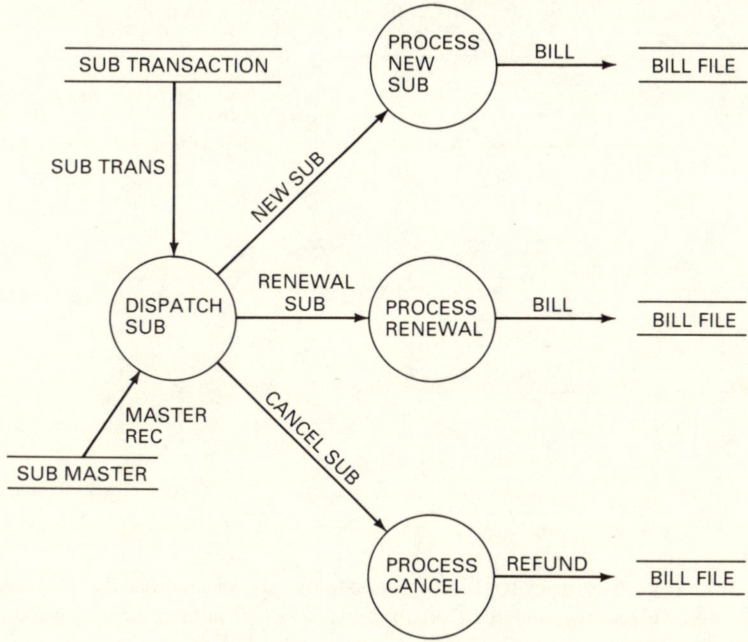

Figure 12.7 High-level data flow diagram describing the subscription system.

to refine the data flow diagram to show more detail, such as conditional input and error processing. The methodology driver assists here by suggesting that this system be modeled after existing system specifications stored in its knowledge base. It presents the developer with one or several candidate specifications after searching and matching it with the contents of its knowledge base. It also expands the specification to include standard processing components to handle functions such as data validation, data base access, file updating, and error processing.

Building the specification is an interactive process where the developer and methodology driver exchange information and ask questions of each other. The methodology driver will prompt the developer for missing information. It will suggest a possible next step but defer to the developer if another is chosen. It will keep track of what remains to be done and remind the developer of steps

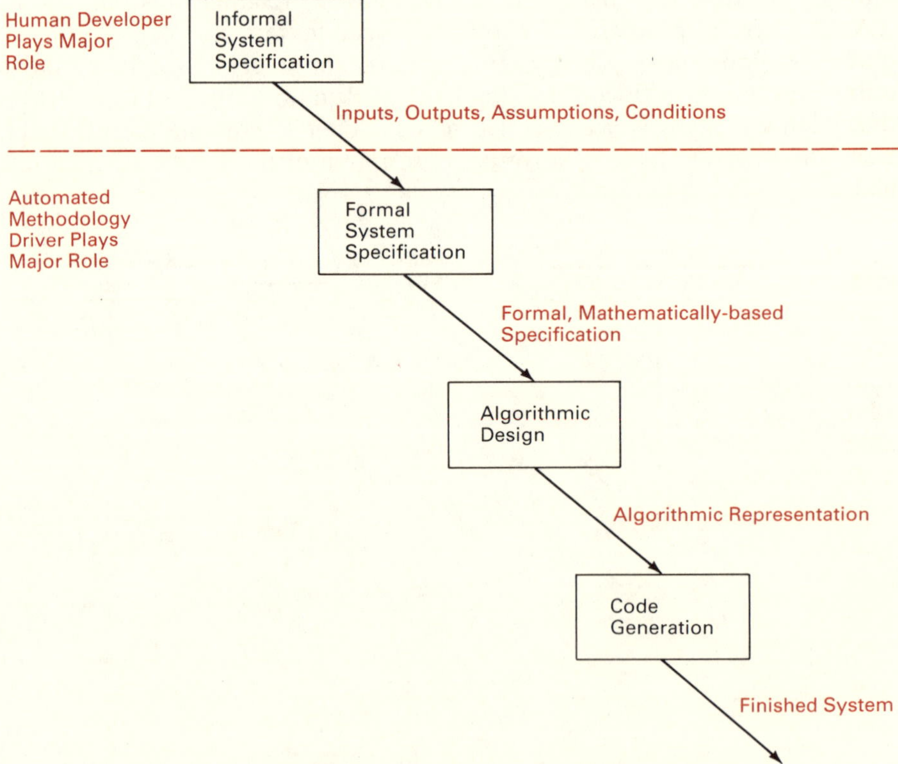

Figure 12.8 Use of an intelligent methodology driver changes the software development process and division of labor between human developers and their automated assistants. The developer's role is to define the system requirements. The methodology driver's role is to transform an informal specification into the completed system.

that have been skipped. It will identify what it has added to the specification and any inconsistencies that must be resolved.

Although it appears to the developer that an informal method such as data flow diagramming is used to define the system specification, an underlying, formal, mathematically based specification language is actually used by the methodology driver. Each specification object that is defined has a formal meaning associated with it. A set of formal rules govern how it can relate to other objects and what operations can be performed on it. As the informal specification is transformed by the methodology driver to a formal specification, its correctness can be checked.

Once the formal specification is complete, the system can be designed, and then the design can be transformed into executable code. As shown in Figure 12.8, the methodology driver plays the major role in these remaining development steps, which are a series of transformations culminating in the finished system [6].

Again, the methodology driver uses its knowledge base containing designs for similar application systems to find possible design algorithms for the subscription system. With the help of the developers, the algorithms are adjusted to fit this system by refining data types, data flow, and control flows. The last transformation of the design into code is quite straightforward and is accomplished with the use of a code generator.

SUMMARY

The methodology driver is an expert system that embeds knowledge about software development methodologies into software tools. Its purpose is to guide and direct the user in the correct use of a software development methodology. The methodology driver understands the process steps of a particular methodology and is the basis for true software automation. Box 12.7 summarizes the characteristics of a methodology driver.

BOX 12.7 Methodology driver

- Includes tools that actively encourage or enforce use of software methodologies
- Provides context-dependent checklists for specific tasks
- Automates knowledge about best practices and plans
- Gives suggestions, advice, and explanations
- Employs an expert system that models the software development process—mimics the behavior of a software engineering expert

REFERENCES

1. William E. Riddle and Lloyd G. Williams, ''Software Environments Workshop Report,'' *ACM Software Engineering Notes,* Vol. 11, No. 1, January 1986, pp. 73–102.

2. James Martin and Carma McClure, *Structured Techniques*: The Basis for CASE, Revised Edition. Englewood Cliffs, N.J.: Prentice Hall, 1988.

3. C. Gane and T. Sarson, *Structured Systems Analysis: Tools and Techniques*. New York: IST Databooks, 1977.

4. M. Page-Jones, *The Practical Guide to Structured Systems Design*. Englewood Cliffs, N.J.: Yourdon Press, 1980.

5. James Martin, *Information Engineering*. Englewood Cliffs, N.J.: Prentice Hall, 1989.

6. David R. Barstow, ''A Perspective on Automatic Programming,'' *Schlumberger–Doll Research Notes,* November 14, 1983.

13 SOFTWARE REUSABILITY

REUSABILITY WITH CAD/CAM SYSTEMS

An analogy often is drawn between CASE systems for developing software and CAD/CAM systems that are widely used in the manufacturing world today. CAD/CAM systems have brought a high degree of automation to the design process for many types of manufactured products, ranging from airplanes to eyeglasses.

When creating a new product design, the designer sits down at a CAD/CAM workstation and begins by accessing an automated library to look for a similar kind of product on which to base the design for this new product. Once the designer finds an appropriate product design, he or she then looks at the component parts, subassemblies, and the current inventory of available materials, and then modifies the design to meet the specifications for the new product. This approach can substantially reduce the risks, the cost, and the time for designing and manufacturing products. The designer is not building from scratch, but building from parts that already exist. The design process is based on reusability and is made practical by CAD/CAM systems.

REVOLUTIONARY CHANGE FOR SOFTWARE DEVELOPMENT

The analogy between CAD/CAM systems and CASE systems is not really appropriate until reusability becomes the central development approach for building software. When this happens, we will see a truly revolutionary change in the way we build software. When we use reusability as the development methodology, we will no longer build software systems from scratch. Instead, we will go to the automated library of reusable software parts, take the parts, modify them, and put them together to form the new system.

Reusing software components is the key to dramatic software productivity increases. Reusability can cut development schedules by months or even years. The CASE repository, in which reusable software components can be stored, makes reusability practical. Not only does CASE enable the reuse and sharing of source code, but better yet, the reuse of project plans, prototype models, data models, and design specifications.

By reusing software components and software development experience to the greatest extent possible, reusability can significantly:

1. Streamline and simplify software development
2. Improve software reliability
3. Reduce software costs

But a word of caution is needed here. ''Revolution'' is an overused term in the software field. For that matter, most software managers and developers are anything but excited at the suggestion of another promised software revolution because no software revolution thus far has significantly changed or speeded up the software development process.

Basically, there are two ways in which to speed up software development:

1. Use of automated techniques generating desired program code
2. Use of reusable software components and software experience to reduce the total development effort

Automated techniques reduce mainly implementation time while reusability can also reduce design time. It seems obvious that both are necessary to increase software productivity substantially. The CASE technology, which was discussed earlier in this book, speeds up the software development process by automating many tasks that previously were done manually.

Reusability of software development experience is the primary means of reusing software today. In the future, this experience will be captured in knowledge-based systems called methodology drivers. (The methodology driver was discussed in Chapter 12.) The methodology driver is an expert system that captures the expertise of experienced software developers and enables all developers to have access to this knowledge. In this chapter we look at how the concept of reusability combined with the CASE technology changes and improves software development.

SOFTWARE LIBRARIES

The concept of software reusability certainly is not new. Software libraries have existed for years in most organizations. They are filled with routines that are commonly found in many kinds of software systems (e.g., data conversion routines, mathematical routines, statistic libraries, linear programming packages, I/O processing routines). Subroutines were the first laborsaving technique invented by programmers. A subroutine for sin x was written in 1944 for the Mark I calculator [1, pp. 182–188].

Many experienced programmers have their own personal library of reusable software components. It has been observed that some of the most productive software developers have productivity rates five times as great as the average. Much of their productivity can be attributed to an extensive use of reusable software components, standard program forms, and standard implementation methods.

The benefits of software reusability are clear. As shown in Box 13.1, reusability can reduce the risk of project failure, shorter development time, and greatly increase the productivity of the individual software developer. According to T. Capers Jones [2]:

> Depending on the quantity of reused code, productivity rates of more than 25,000 lines of code per person-year are not uncommon, with peaks of more than 100,000 lines of code. It is now technically possible to develop some new applications that consist entirely of reused code, with no unique hand-coded modules being developed at all.

BOX 13.1 Benefits of reusability

- Reduces development time and cost
- Improves software quality
- Increases productivity
- Shares knowledge about system and how to build systems
- Facilitates learning about system architecture and how to build good systems
- Shares system specification, design, code, and other project documents produced by other teams

MANY FORMS OF SOFTWARE REUSABILITY

The application of the concept of software reuse can take on many different forms, such as:

- Reusable prototypes (software reuse can make rapid protyping truly rapid)
- Reusable data
- Reusable system and program architectures

- Reusable program and data structure designs
- Reusable data models
- Reusable program code
- Reusable software packages

REUSABILITY STUDIES AND PROJECTS

Studies of existing software programs reveal that most of the functions performed by a program are common to many different programs. For example, in a study of commercial COBOL application programs at the Raytheon Company, many functions common at the company, plant, and application levels were found to be reusable [3]. Based on an examination of 5000 production COBOL programs, Raytheon developed a library containing 3200 reusable modules that cover the following program categories:

- File descriptions
- Record descriptions
- Edit routines
- Data base I/O areas
- Data base interface modules
- Data base search arguments
- Data base calls
- Application function routines

In addition, the library contains six basic types of program logic structures:

- Sequential file update program structure
- Report program structure
- Edit file program structure
- Extract programs
- Bridge programs
- Data fix programs

These basic logic structures cover the six major functions performed by commercial application programs: sorting data, editing data, manipulating data, combining data, exploding data, updating data, and reporting on data.

By using the Raytheon library, software developers have been producing programs that on average contain 60 percent reusable code and a range of 15 to 85 percent reusable code. Raytheon believes that reusability can mean a 50 percent increase in software development productivity. In addition, Raytheon software developers feel that reusability introduces a new level of program standardization that makes programs easier to understand and to maintain. This can mean a 60 percent reduction in maintenance effort.

The Programming Environment Project at the University of California–Irvine reported that a 62 percent software reuse level in building prototypes helped increase productivity by 20 percent [4]. In Japanese software factories, an 85 percent software reuse level helped increase software productivity eight times [4].

The Department of Defense (DOD) spent $10 billion annually on mission critical computer software in the mid-1980s. The introduction of more complex defense systems promises to increase this expenditure. Since DOD believes that software reuse is a critical part of controlling rising software costs, DOD launched the STARS (Software Technology for Adaptable, Reliable Systems) project, a $300 million initiative to investigate software reuse [5]. CAMP (Common Ada Missile Packages) is the STARS program that is developing a library of reusable missile software parts and a parts composition system. CAMP has defined three types of software parts:

1. Simple parts: atomic parts that cannot be modified
2. Generic parts: templates for building specific parts
3. Schematic parts: blueprints for a family of parts and the construction rules for assembling the parts

PROBLEMS WITH SOFTWARE REUSABILITY

Although recognized as a great productivity idea, software reusability has had only limited success in practice. Why? The first reason is that reusability requires planning for reusability when a component is originally defined and implemented. The second reason is that it is difficult to represent a software component in a way that it can easily be classified, described, understood, and reused without causing unforeseen side effects. Box 13.2 lists the major obstacles to software reusability.

The solution to the software reusability practicality problem is threefold:

1. Choose an appropriate formalism for representing a reusable software component.
2. Provide tools to support a reusable development approach.
3. Provide a library of reusable parts.

BOX 13.2 Problems of implementing in practice what sounds like a good idea

- Question of what is a reusable part
- Lack of standardization in programs
- Programming language dependence
- Deciding what goes into parts library
- Understanding the interface requirements as well as internals of a software component
- Lack of plug compatibility
- Understanding side effects from change

BOX 13.3 What is a reusable software component?

- Program code
  - —Source
  - —Object
  - —Whole program
  - —Subroutine/macro
  - —Module/procedure
  - —Data structure
- Program design
  - —Specificating documents
  - —Diagrams
  - —Report layouts/screen designs
  - —Templates/program schemas
- Project management forms
  - —Spreadsheets
  - —Schedules
  - —Assignments
  - —Report formats
  - —Project plans

REPRESENTING A REUSABLE SOFTWARE COMPONENT

What types of software components are candidates for reusability? Box 13.3 suggests some possibilities.

PACKAGES

Most often when we think of software reusability we think of reusing program code, either a complete program or some of its parts. Software packages are one example of program-level reuse. In this case of packages, the user takes the complete program in an as-is generic form, adjusts the program through parameters, or more extensively changes some of the program code to customize the program. Packages are particularly popular in application areas such as payroll, banking, insurance, accounting, networking, inventory control, and systems software. Box 13.4 lists typical examples of available application packages.

Perhaps, the biggest unforeseen danger with application packages is the difficulty of maintenance. Most business applications change substantially with time and the package has to be modified. If the modifications have to be made in a language such as COBOL, PL/1, or FORTRAN, this requires much work. To facilitate maintenance, excellent documentation and clean design of the package are needed. These characteristics need to be examined when the package is bought. Box 13.5 lists the major pitfalls of packages.

BOX 13.4 Typical examples of available application packages

Accounting
- General
- Banking
- Tax
- Trust

Accounts payable
Accounts receivable
Airline reservation
Application development aids
Architecture

Banking systems
Bill-of-material processing
Bond and stock management

Job accounting
Job casting
Job performance measurement systems

Letter writing/mailing systems
Liability insurance
Library systems
Life and health insurance
Loans
- Commercial
- Installment
- International
- Mortgage

(Continued)

BOX 13.4 *(Continued)*

Check processing
Commercial loans
Computer-aided design
Computer-aided instruction
Computer management aids
Construction accounting
Construction/job costing
Conversion aids
Correspondence control systems
Customer information file (CIF)

Data base management systems
Data management systems
Demand deposits
Distribution systems
Document/text processing

Education
Engineering
  Electrical
  Mechanical
  Space

Financial
  General
  Control/planning
  Management
Forecasting and modeling

General ledger
Graphics
Government
  Local
  Federal
  State

Health care
Health insurance

Mailing/correspondence lists
Management sciences
Manufacturing
Mathematical/statistical
Medical and health care
Modeling
Mortgage and loans

Order entry

Payroll, general
Performance measurement
Personnel systems
Petroleum industry
Preprocessors, computer language
Process control
Production control
Project control and planning
Property and liability insurance

Query languages

Real estate management
Remote job entry
Report generators
Resource management
Route scheduling

Sales and distribution
Savings systems
Scientific
Securities management
Statistical and modeling
Stock portfolio management

Tax accounting

BOX 13.4 *(Continued)*

Hospital accounting
Hospital administration
Hotel accounting
Hotel reservations

Information storage and retrieval
Installment loans
Insurance
- General
- Accounting and billing
- Life and health
- Property and liability

Inventory management
Inventory manufacturing

Teleprocessing systems
Text/document editors
Time deposit accounting
Trust accounting

Utilities accounting

Word processing systems
Work in progress

BOX 13.5 Pitfalls of application packages

- The package is insufficiently parameterized and does not fully adapt to changes in requirements.
- DP modifies the package when it is installed and subsequent maintenance becomes almost as expensive as with in-house application programs.
- Expensive maintenance becomes necessary later when the hardware, operating system, terminals, or network are changed or when the user requirements change.
- The package is difficult to maintain due to poor documentation, lack of hooks for user-created code, ill-structured design, absence of source code, excessive complexity, low-level languages, or poor-quality coding.
- The package has been made difficult to maintain because it has been tinkered with and modifications that are ill-documented and difficult to understand made to the package.
- The package does not fit with corporate data base implementation and strategy.
- The software house that owns the package ceases operations.

To avoid these pitfalls, a careful analysis is required by the application under consideration before a decision is made as to whether to develop the application programs or buy a package:

- Consider the functional characteristics of the application itself. How complex is it? What is the priority of implementation? What is the time scale for development?
- A long development backlog may be a good enough reason to consider a package. In-house projects may take several years to develop and may go seriously over budget at the end of it. An application software package should be implemented in a month or two at a fixed price.
- Often some aspects of the in-house development never reach a programmer's coding pad for a variety of reasons, whereas the content of software packages is well known and defined.
- Do the application data have close links to other applications, for example, in a database environment? Can the database administrator accommodate the package with some form of bridge between it and the database systems?
- Sometimes senior management resists the whole idea of purchasing applications from outside sources. One way around this problem is to represent the clear economic advantages and point out that the programming staff will be free to concentrate on more important areas of application development.
- Documentation, which is so often neglected with in-house development, can be a necessary prerequisite for the purchase of a software package. It is also a good indication of the quality of the product itself.

Selecting an application package should be approached systematically using a formal, logical procedure. Box 13.6 lists suggested steps in acquiring a package.

PARTS

Reusing parts of a program (i.e., code reuse) involves taking code from one program and reusing it in another program. Usually, the parts to be reused are taken from a program that performs a similar application function, and reuse is at the discretion of the individual programmer. Most programmers tend to reuse code from programs that they or their teammates have previously written because they know of its existence and intimately understand the inner workings of the code.

Another form of parts reuse is shared libraries of reusable code modules. These library modules perform application-specific functions and common program functions such as HELP, I/O, sorting and invoking, controlling, and terminating program calls.

A higher degree of reusability is more likely to be achievable when the parts are originally designed with reusability in mind. For example, in a reus-

BOX 13.6 Steps in the acquisition of an application package

- List the present and future requirements of the application in detail.
- Survey all available packages for that application.
- Examine their documentation.
- Check whether they are sufficiently parameterized.
- Check whether they have adequate aids to maintenance.
- Draw up a short list of suitable packages.
- Examine the vendor. Will it provide adequate service?
- Talk to users of these packages.
- Can the package link into the corporate database plans?
- Conduct benchmarks if performance is critical.
- Allow end users to use packages on a temporary basis if the end-user interface is critical.
- Write an appropriate contract.

able procedural component, all data descriptions, literals, constants, and input/output control should be external to the component. Box 13.7 lists the properties for the ideal reusable components.

LIMITATIONS OF CODE REUSE

At the code level, software reuse is very limited. Code reuse is language dependent, operating-system dependent, application dependent, and at the discretion of the individual programmer. Also, there are the problems of (1) finding code to be reused, and (2) that most code was not written with reuse in mind (i.e., is not well documented, does not use explicit parameter passing, does not have a simple, easy-to-understand interface, does not perform one logical function). Finally, no development methodology provides for code-level reuse between dissimilar application systems nor for classifying and selecting modules to be reused.

However, the major problem with code reuse is that the code often must be changed before it can be reused. With change comes the risk of introducing errors and other unforeseen side effects. The difficulty of changing code has been a major deterrent to considering software reusability as a feasible development technique.

BOX 13.7 Properties of a reusable component

- Expressiveness: capable of expressing many different kinds of components
- Additivity: able to combine components with minimal side effects and without destructive interaction
- Formal mathematical basis: allows correctness conditions to be stated and combination process to preserve key properties of components
- Machine representable form: machine manipulable and computable
- Self-contained: each component embodies only a single idea
- Easily describable: easy to understand
- Programming language independent: not unnecessarily specific about superficial language details
- Able to represent data components and fragmentary procedural components: offers fine granularity
- Verifable: easy to test
- Simple interface: minimal number of parameters passed and parameters passed explicitly
- Easily changed: easy to modify with minimal side effects

CASE AND CODE REUSE

The CASE technology can help solve many of the problems associated with code reuse. First, code reuse is not really practical without a library of reusable components and a powerful library management system. Components stored in the library should have a standard format and should be well documented and well structured. Procedural modules should be modularized, table-driven, and parameterized to keep the interfaces simple. They should be of high quality (i.e., low complexity, low coupling, and high cohesion). They should separate I/O processing from algorithmic processes, should not limit data volumes and values, and should avoid nonstandard, machine-dependent operations. Data components should have a standard data interchange format.

A library management system is needed to effectively and efficiently organize index, describe, cross-reference and maintain reusable software components. A scheme for classifying and selecting components must be devised. One possibility is a hierarchical organizational scheme in which components are organized by application type and by function within application type. Functions could be divided into application-specific types and common-function types (such as data base access, error processing, or date conversion). Probably most reusable code libraries will be application or industry specific (e.g., an insurance business reusable software components library). A high degree of reusability can be achieved when building applications such as banking, insurance, order entry, inventory control, and reservations. For these types of applications, customized versions of the system can be built mainly from a library of reusable parts.

CASE Repository

Box 13.8 lists the properties of a reusable components library. The CASE repository is the mechanism for providing the reusable parts library and the library management system. The CASE repository provides techniques for describing and specifying parts so that they can easily be identified and retrieved for reuse. The CASE repository contains the shared knowledge between the software developer and the CASE tools that automate various software development tasks.

BOX 13.8 Properties of a reusable components library

- Comprehensive DBMS for storing and retrieving components to facilitate access, search, version control, and security
- Operations that allow user to create, edit, view, and combine
- Organization scheme to act as navigational aid through library
- Support component standardization
- Easy to grow

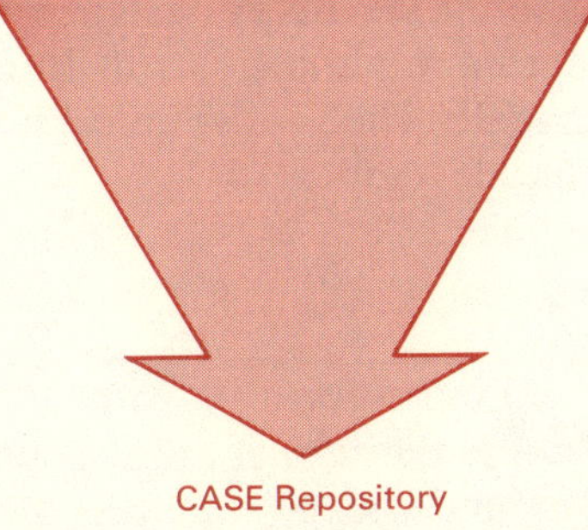

CASE Change Impact Analysis Tools

Second, code reuse is not practical unless the code can be modified easily and safely. Tools for automatic analysis of the impact of change and for implementing change are needed. Only in rare instances can code be reused without modifying it. When reusing a part, it must be spliced into the new program and modified to fit the new requirements (e.g., data type, boundary conditions, error conditions).

CASE analysis tools that give where-used and how-used information help determine the impact from change. With CASE analysis tools, a system developer can automatically find the answers to such questions as:

- Where are all the places in the code in which a particular variable is modified or referenced?
- What modules call this module?
- What parameters are passed to a module?
- Is there any unreachable code?
- What test cases will give the greatest coverage of changed code?

While other CASE analysis tools provide static views of the program procedural and data structures, CASE animators provide dynamic views of the program execution to give the developers an accurate understanding of the program execution-time behavior to evaluate its run-time efficiency. Animators help developers detect efficiency problems related to reusable code.

Finally, code reuse is not practical without tools to support the assembly of reusable software components. CASE tools such as syntax-directed program editors, generators, verification systems, timer, and portability checkers guide the system developer to combine the components efficiently and correctly to create the new system. For example, the intelligent editor in the Programmer Apprentice System has knowledge about the programming language syntax and a side-effects checker. It has a special set of commands (e.g., DEFINE, FILL, SHARE, REPLACE, REMOVE, and COMMENT) designed to facilitate software components reusability and program modification [6]. Before executing a command, the program editor automatically checks the side effects of change on the program and reports them to the developer.

HIGHER LEVEL SOFTWARE REUSE

A higher form of software reuse is needed to overcome the limitation of code reuse. The closer we get to code level, the less feasible software reuse becomes. Therefore, we should think in terms of reusing program specifications instead of program code. At the specification level, the problems arising from programming language dependencies, operating system dependencies, and inefficiencies of reusable code disappear. The CASE technology and in particular the CASE repository make program specification reuse practical.

SPECIFICATION REUSE

Specification reuse with the support of CASE works as follows. The system developer selects from the CASE repository the program specification design that is similar to the program to be built. He or she locates candidate designs by searching the CASE repository directory for systems that perform the same or similar function as the system that he or she is currently designing. The specification design is in the form of a family of related structured diagrams that represent the program architectural structure, procedural components, data structures, data entities, and attributes. The CASE repository automatically links together all related system diagrams. CASE code generator tools are used for automatic generation of the program code and database definitions from this high-level specification.

Probably, however, the design cannot be used as is. It may be too general, or on the other hand, address only a subset of the functions. Therefore, the existing design must be modified to meet all the requirements for this new program. It is important to note that the changes will be made at the design specification level, not at the code level. Since the CASE repository stores all system information and the relationship between system components and automatically tracks and controls all changes, reuse of program design specifications is practical. With the use of CASE analysis tools, the developer can adjust the design to meet the requirements of the new system.

Adjusting an existing design, rather than designing from scratch, should substantially reduce analysis and design effort. Generating code from the adjusted design rather than manually coding the system should substantially reduce implementation time.

Formal Specifications

Reuse at the program design specification level requires more formality. Each object in the specification should be formally defined. In a formal specification system, composition of design specification objects is controlled by a strict set of formal rules. Relationships between objects are also formally defined and restricted by a set of rules. This level of formality is mathematically based. Formal specifications can be in predicate calculus, algebraic, relational, or declaration form. This enables syntactic correctness checking, some semantic correctness checking, and redundancy control needed for automatic transformation into an efficient, executable program in which computational equivalence to the specification form is guaranteed.

To be practical to use, formal specifications must be sufficiently concise and easy to understand, requiring less effort to create than at the program code level. Also, formal specifications must be sufficient and easy to debug at specification level, not requiring the developer to drop down to the code level for final implementation and maintenance work.

PROGRAM BUILDING WITH REUSABLE COMPONENTS

As shown in Figure 13.1, there are two basic approaches for building software programs from reusable software components:

1. Parts approach
2. Whole approach

The *parts approach* is a *composition method* that starts with atomic parts and assembles them to create the new program. Either a top-down or bottom-up stepwise refinement strategy is followed to construct the program. This is problem solving by abstraction (i.e., using a simplified view of the problem to guide the problem-solving process). Construction methods for the parts ap-

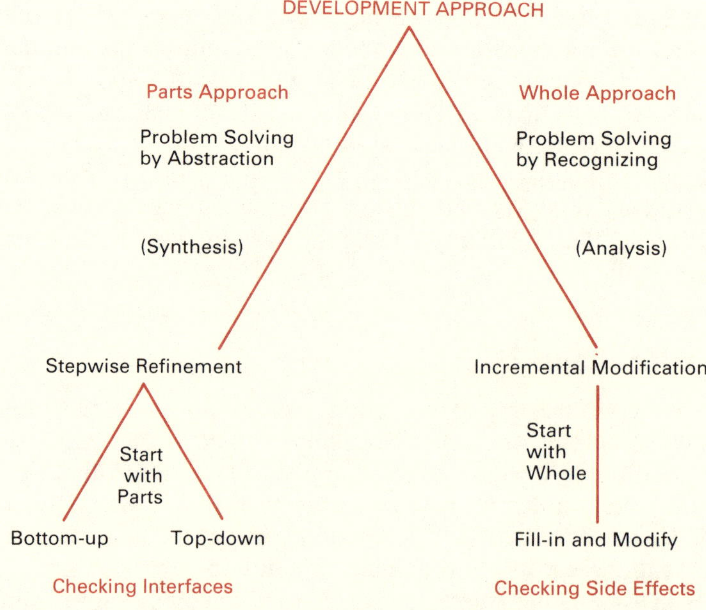

Figure 13.1 There are two basic approaches for building software programs from reusable software components: the parts approach and the whole approach.

proach are concerned mainly with organizing and combining parts to form new programs according to well-defined composition rules. One example of composition rules is the Unix pipeline, which is a method of constructing programs from simpler programs by connecting one program's output to another program's input [7].

The parts are designed to be self-contained and represent one simple data or procedural component. The correctness of each part is checked before it is used as a building block. The program grows one part at a time. Much of the development effort focuses on integration of parts. Checking the interfaces between parts is critical because this is where most system complexity lies and this is where development errors are mostly likely to occur.

On the other hand, the *whole approach* is an *analysis method* that starts with a whole program architecture and modifies it in steps to meet the requirements of the new program. An incremental modification strategy is followed in which an existing program is adjusted to evolve into the new program [6]. Some possible adjustments include:

- Filling in parameters or stubs in templates
- Joining together two components along a common interface (e.g., Unix pipeline, Smalltalk objects)
- Enhancing an existing component with new features
- Slicing an existing component to eliminate unwanted functionality
- Changing data types

The program evolves one adjustment at a time. This is problem solving by recognizing and editing (i.e., find an almost satisfactory solution and then incrementally modify it until it becomes a satisfactory solution). Each time the program is modified, unwanted side effects from change may occur. Therefore, much of the development effort focuses on checking for possible side effects from change.

Box 13.9 summarizes the different development concepts associated with the parts approach versus the whole approach. They represent two different theories in engineering problem solving. Of the two, the whole approach is simpler. It is easier for the human mind to recognize than to create from scratch, to edit than to assemble, and to paste than to refine—provided that there are powerful support tools.

CASE tools help the developer find an appropriate reusable program design; analyze the impact of design changes; perform program design consistency, correctness, and completeness checks; and generate computably equivalent program code from the program design.

Of the two, the whole approach has the greater potential for increasing productivity. We can get higher leverage from reusing larger, higher-level reusable components. The whole approach enables the developer to reuse whole

BOX 13.9 Parts approach vs. whole approach concepts

Parts Approach Concepts	Reusable Whole Approach Concepts
Abstraction	Generalization
Synthesis	Analysis
Creating	Recognizing
Assembling	Editing
Refining	Pasting
Building block	Template

programs and program design specifications, whereas the parts approach focuses on the reuse of software components such as functional modules and macros.

REUSABILITY INCREASES PRODUCTIVITY

The whole approach not only dramatically changes software development but also reaches into maintenance phase of the life cycle. When the whole approach is used, techniques needed for developing a program become much more similar to techniques needed for maintaining a program (i.e., techniques for making changes and controlling the impact from change). The line that has always existed between software development and software maintenance disappears. This is the reason why reusability has the potential to substantially improve overall software productivity. It is also the reason why reusability revolutionizes the software development process.

SUMMARY

Software reusability is one important answer to software productivity problems. Software reusability is much broader than simply reusable code. Possibilities for software reusability include reusable code, designs, formal specifications, software packages, prototypes and application generators, and transformation systems. Higher levels of reusability (i.e., above the code level) offer greater promise since they avoid problems of language dependence and the subtleties of side effects from modifying existing code. However, even at higher levels (i.e., reusable designs) reusable components will for the most part be domain or application specific. It is likely that libraries of reusable components will be created for different domains (applications). Industries such as insurance and banking and systems such as defense and communications will lend themselves particularly well to reusability.

With reusability, we must reconsider the fundamental ways in which software is developed. When reusability is the central development approach, incremental modification replaces stepwise refinement as the program construction strategy. The program is created by modifying an existing program that performs a similar function to fit the requirements of the new program.

CASE tools play an important role in making software reusability a practical system building strategy. The CASE repository (and its information management system) forms the cornerstone of the CASE tools needed for reusability. Other CASE tools needed include CASE analysis tools, syntax-directed editors, generators, verification systems, and portability checkers.

REFERENCES

1. Donald Knuth, *The Art of Computer Programming,* Vol. I. Reading, Mass.: Addison-Wesley, 1973.
2. T. Capers Jones, "Reusability in Programming," *IEEE Transactions on Software Engineering,* Vol. SE-10, No. 5, September 1984, pp. 488–493.
3. R. G. Lanergan and C. A. Grasso, "Software Engineering with Reusable Design and Code," *IEEE Transactions on Software Engineering,* Vol. SE-10, No. 5, September 1984, pp. 498–501.
4. T. A. Standish, "An Essay on Software Reuse," *IEEE Transactions on Software Engineering,* Vol. SE-10, No. 5, September 1984, pp. 494–497.
5. Christine M. Anderson, "Reusable Software—A Mission Critical CASE Study," *IEEE Compsac 85 Proceeding,* Chicago, October 9–11, 1985, p. 205.
6. R. C. Waters, "Programmer Apprentice: A Session with KBEmacs," *IEEE Transactions on Software Engineering,* Vol. SE-11, No. 11, November 1985, pp. 1296–1320.
7. T. J. Biggerstaff and A. J. Perlis, "Foreword: Special Issue on Software Reusability," *IEEE Transactions on Software Engineering,* Vol. SE-11, No. 11, p. 474.

PART V EPILOGUE

14 CASE CLOSED

CLOSING THOUGHTS

At the time of writing, there are 600,000 to 700,000 system analysts and programmers who can make good use of the CASE technology to improve their productivity significantly and to prepare the way for higher levels of software automation that will surely follow.

Already almost 100 vendors are offering CASE tools worldwide. Moreover, CASE is one of the most rapidly growing areas in the computer industry. In 1985, only a few thousand copies of CASE tools had been sold in the United States and there was virtually no market outside the United States. In 1985 the CASE market was dominated by only a handful of vendors.

In 1986, the number of copies of CASE tools sold topped 10,000, the market size rose to $50 million in sales, and the market extended worldwide. Many new vendors entered the market, and some of the newcomers captured a substantial portion of the market share.

In 1987 the total market size was $100 million for CASE front-end tools and another $50 million for generator sales. Companies bought several copies of CASE tools for their software staffs. For example, Nastec had an average of 18 copies of DESIGNAID installed per client site in 1987, and Index Technology had over 20 customers with 100 copies per site in 1987. Many companies made a commitment to the CASE technology and have adopted it as the basis of their software productivity strategy. Future growth rates in the CASE tools market are predicted to be at least 100 percent per year.

Although the CASE technology is likely to evolve into a much more powerful, comprehensive technology in the future, it does have powerful capabilities that are here today. Three capabilities that are particularly powerful and present today in CASE tools are:

1. Automatic checking
2. CASE repository
3. Automatic code generation

If you are an organization that can be characterized by any one of the following, you are an organization that can benefit from the CASE technology now.

- Organization with large backlogs of software systems waiting to be developed
- Organization that spends the majority of its software personnel effort maintaining existing software systems
- Organization that needs better discipline and control over the software development process
- Organization that wants to increase software productivity substantially
- Organization that wants to use state-of-the-art software technologies

By the 1990s, CASE tools and software development workstations will be as common to software development as programming languages and compilers have been for the last three decades. Computer-aided software engineering will take a central position among software technologies.

INDEX

D

E

F

G

H

I

U

W

X,Y

TEAR OUT THIS PAGE TO ORDER OTHER TITLES BY CARMA McCLURE/JAMES MARTIN

QUANTITY	TITLE	TITLE CODE	PRICE	TOTAL
______	STRUCTURED TECHNIQUES The Basis for CASE, Revised Edition	85493-5	$54.00	______
______	ACTION DIAGRAMS Clearly Structured Program Design	00330-1	44.00	______
______	DIAGRAMMING TECHNIQUES FOR ANALYSTS AND PROGRAMMERS	20879-3	56.00	______
______	SOFTWARE MAINTENANCE The Problem and Its Solutions	82236-1	55.00	______
			Subtotal	______
			less discount (if appropriate)	______
			Total	______

AND TAKE ADVANTAGE OF THESE SPECIAL OFFERS!
When ordering 3 or 4 copies of the same or different titles, take 10% off the total list price.

When ordering 5 to 20 of the same or different titles, take 15% off the total list price.

To receive a greater discount when ordering more than 20 copies, call or write:
Special Sales Department
College Marketing
Prentice Hall
Englewood Cliffs, NJ 07632
(201) 592-2046

SAVE! If payment accompanies order, plus your state's sales tax where appropriate, Prentice Hall pays postage and handling charges. Same return privilege refund guarantee. Please do not mail cash.

☐ PAYMENT ENCLOSED—shipping and handling to be paid by publisher (please include your state's tax where applicable).

☐ SEND BOOKS ON 15-DAY TRIAL BASIS and bill me (with small charge for shipping and handling).

Name ______________________________

Address ______________________________

City ____________________ State ____________ Zip ____________
I prefer to charge my ☐ Visa ☐ MasterCard

Card Number ______________________ Expiration Date ____/____

Signature ______________________________

All prices listed are subject to change without notice. This offer not valid outside U.S.

Mail your order to: **Prentice Hall Book Distribution Center**
Route 59 at Brook Hill Drive
West Nyack, NY 10994

Dept. 1: D-JMAR-NK(4)